The People are Represented

THE PEOPLE ARE REPRESENTED

A Discourse Analysis
of Contemporary Programs
in the Television Crime Genre

Maria Siano

<teneo> // press

YOUNGSTOWN, NEW YORK

Copyright 2008 Maria Siano

All rights reserved
Printed in the United States of America

ISBN: 978-1-934844-05-2

No part of this publication may be reproduced, stored in or introduced into a retrieval system, or transmitted, in any form, or by any means (electronic, mechanical, photocopying, recording, or otherwise), without the prior permission of the publisher.

Requests for permission should be directed to:
permissions@teneopress.com, or mailed to:
Teneo Press
PO Box 349
Youngstown, New York 14174

Table of Contents

Acknowledgments ix

Introduction: The Crime Genre 1

Chapter 1: Media Effects and Cultural Studies: Previous Studies 15

Chapter 2: American Society: 1998–2004 37

Chapter 3: Methodology 65

Chapter 4: Legal Authorities: Police Officers, Judges, and Lawyers 97

Chapter 5: Criminals 123

Chapter 6: Society 149

Chapter 7: Reality Series 175

Chapter 8: Four Crime Documentaries 191

Chapter 9: Audience Impact 213

Chapter 10: Progressive Depictions 227

Appendix: Timeline of the Criminal Genre 237

References   **239**

Index   **257**

Acknowledgments

After writing about crime shows on television while working on a paper for a popular culture course in the PhD program at Rutgers University, I realized that there were many aspects that could be—and should be—explored further. Several years later, I began to formally develop the ideas presented in this book.

Linda Steiner, who served as my dissertation director at Rutgers, was supportive and offered encouragement and guidance throughout the entire process. It was an intellectually and personally enriching experience to work with her.

The other members of my dissertation committee, Robert Kubey, Laurie Ouellette, and Jack Bratich, all offered unique perspectives about the topic, and I appreciate the feedback they provided.

Personally, I would like to thank my parents, Alphonse and Lorraine Siano, for all their support. They, along with friends and family members, were always interested in discussing the crime shows they watched on television, and those conversations were not only useful but enjoyable.

The People are Represented

Introduction

The Crime Genre

"In the criminal justice system, The people are represented by two separate yet equally important groups: the police who investigate crime and the district attorneys who prosecute the offenders. These are their stories."

This statement opens each episode of the NBC television crime program *Law & Order*, which has been airing since 1989. With this concise explanation, viewers are told in advance what they are about to watch for the next 60 minutes:

> Someone will commit a crime.
> Police detectives will solve the crime.
> District attorneys will prosecute the offenders.

In comparison to other crime shows in the genre—which has spanned more than 50 years—*Law & Order* presents more perspectives on crime within one program. Unlike previous series in the genre, it includes two aspects of the criminal justice system: the police process of capturing criminals and the state's role in prosecuting them. Most series in the past focused on only one aspect of crime fighting. However, in this research, I reveal how more is presented in *Law & Order* than its opening statement of the program suggests. In addition to watching the work of police and prosecutors, viewers also learn about criminals, some of what leads up to the crimes, and the impact of crime on society. In the process, specific crime policies, particularly punitive ones, are supported. Explicitly, as the opening statement of *Law & Order* suggests, the episodes are about prosecuting criminals, and viewers are asked to focus on a dominant tough-on-crime message. However, embedded in the messages of *Law & Order*—and other series in the genre—are representations of criminals as "Others," and societal norms as well. These serve to create and reinforce a connotation of "the criminal" in society that often makes it difficult for criminals to assimilate back into society after having served their time in prison. In addition, these representations reveal frustration over societal inequities, particularly economic inequities, which provide a motivation for crime.

Even with the added perspective present in *Law & Order*, only a small part of the larger story about crime and criminals is being told in this series. However, newer programs that emerged in the genre between 1998 and 2004 revealed additional aspects of crime stories, beyond those of the law enforcers. During this time, the genre collectively presented the criminal justice system as involving more than just the police and the district attorneys. "The People" were represented as well, and not just by the prosecutors. They were represented by the criminals, who were shown in several series to be *among* "The People" of a society, rather than merely "Outsiders."

It is essential to understand how criminals are represented culturally because representations can influence officials who create laws, judges who determine sentences for convicted criminals, and citizens who are all potential jurors. Through cultural assumptions criminals are defined in society, and that can lead to support for specific crime policies. Culture can also reinforce perceptions about potential motives for crime.

Norms about crime, how to combat it, and how to punish people for it are established, in part, through media messages. Lawyers, judges, jurors, police officers, and journalists are influenced by these norms when they carry out their professional responsibilities. As Carey pointed out, "Culture gives us broad as well as specific contexts of meaning and *scripts*, or plausible statements and courses of action that are accepted by others familiar with situations we share" (1989, as cited in Altheide & De Gruyter, 2002, p. 31). Culture is part of the process of communication, as well as part of our thought processes, as Altheide and DeGruyter (2002) suggested: "Complex rules of communication involve the interaction between minds, seldom seen but always presumed, selves, and social situations. The critical point is that what we think about and talk about is reflexively joined with how we communicate" (p. 31). Within our culture, the media messages we watch, hear, and read shape our opinions about groups of people, societal structures, and our cultural institutions. This process is part of the socialization of individuals in a culture. As Mauer (1999) pointed out, "The mass media and popular culture contribute to the definition of situations in social life. This process informs the generalized other for some actors, as well as demonstrates that the media perspectives inform certain situations and subsequent definitions" (p. 8).

To analyze the discourse about criminals presented in the television criminal genre, and to identify shared media messages used to socially construct "the criminal" in society, using a critical-cultural-studies approach, I examine representations presented in the fictional programs *The Practice*, *The Shield*, *NYPD Blue*, *Cold Case*, and *Law & Order* (which feature legal authorities as the main characters); *Oz* and *The Sopranos* (placing criminals as the stars); and *The Jury* (showing crime from the perspective of jurors); the reality programs *COPS* and *America's Most Wanted*; and the documentaries *Capturing the Friedmans*, *America Undercover: Gladiator Days: Anatomy of a Prison Murder*, *Deadline*, and *In the Jury Room*. The research questions I answer are:

- *What do these texts say about whether criminals are redeemable or able to be rehabilitated?*

- *What do these texts present as a typical cause of crime? Do confining societal structures—specifically based on economic and social class—limit opportunities and provide motivation for crime?* (I originally planned to examine whether the texts also presented race and gender as limiting opportunities and providing motivation for crime, but I narrowed the scope of the research to focus only on economic and social class. I include discussions of race and gender where these issues impact economic and social class, as well as the judicial process overall.)
- *What do these texts present about whether personal relationships with others, specifically with family members, impact criminal behavior?*
- *Do these texts celebrate a punitive or preventive crime policy in dealing with crime? Is the focus on only punishing the criminal, or are policies that are preventive—that include rehabilitation of the criminal—encouraged?*

I will show in this research that a wide range of depictions about crime, criminals, and legal authorities was evident in the television crime genre between 1998 and 2004. These messages contributed to a cultural connotation of "the criminal" that progressed beyond the previous singular connotation of criminals as "Others" in society. In the process, these shows addressed issues of inequality and injustice in the United States.

From pilot studies I conducted, it was clear to me that during this 6-year time period, the focus of the genre changed and expanded, beginning with the HBO series *Oz*, which first aired in 1997 and starred convicted criminals. Main characters no longer included only police officers and lawyers. In this analysis, I explore how the focus of crime stories shifted from the traditional singular "Us versus Them" context—with criminals portrayed as "Others" and police detectives and lawyers portrayed as protecting society from these criminals—to one that showed backgrounds and motivations of criminals. As I will show, at the same time that *Oz* and *The Sopranos* depicted criminals in starring roles, there was a change in how legal authorities were portrayed in the genre as well. Series began to depict corrupt legal authorities alongside the portrayals of the traditional hero/cop.

Turow (1989) suggested that media messages are part of institutions in society, which are established, reinforced, and changed through cultural assumptions presented in media messages. Turow defined institutions as "loosely knit sets of organizations (hospitals, bar association, teacher unions) that hold authority over fundamental aspects of social life" (p. xiv). In his historical analysis of depictions of doctors on television, Turow pointed to how the focus of programs in the medical genre have historically been on the physicians, not the patients. These messages, he suggests, contributed to the institution of medicine in society, reinforcing doctors as authorities in society. As such, Turow explains, the messages that construct institutions require evaluation. He said, "a key task of research on television fiction should be to investigate how portrayals of institutions get established, reinforced and changed" (p. xv).

My goal with this study is to add to the existing research on media representations of criminals in the television crime genre, including depictions of inequitable societal structures as a motivator for crime. I use genre theory, ideological analysis, and discourse analysis for this research. Each is discussed in the next section.

GENRE THEORY

A literary concept used by Aristotle, genre is a way of classifying literature or film into basic types. Aristotle used two primary classifications: tragedy and comedy. Among the subgenres that fall under the genre of tragedy are police shows, detective stories, and soap operas (Quinn, 1999). It is in looking at several programs in the genre—as a system through which ideology, representing values, beliefs, and ideas, are naturalized based on assumptions of a culture—that these messages can reveal the messages of the culture (in this case, what is said about criminals).

Traditionally, three approaches have been used by genre theorists for evaluating genres: aesthetic, ritual, and ideological. The aesthetic approach deals with dramatic development and artistic expression from an individual author (Feuer, 1992). This method views genre for its visual and constructed elements. For example, traditionally in police shows, the cops are shown to possess exceptional strength and skill (Robards, 1985). Further, the element of realism, which can be presented in the form of using actual places and time, is one way of conveying the real nature of the program (Robards, 1985). Each producer develops the drama of a series in a specific way. *NYPD Blue* and *Oz* are presented as intense programs that are gritty and "real." The setting, the characters' clothes, and even their material possessions collectively create this aesthetic. In contrast, programs such as *Law & Order* present a more sanitized upper-middle-class world of melodramatic, soap-opera-style crimes. In the detective genre, there are often trademark elements that are attributed to the hero characters (Norden, 1985). Columbo wore the trademark tan raincoat, and often looked disheveled; Kojak, whose bald head was itself a trademark, was often seen with a lollipop. These elements also served to create an aesthetic of the characters within the genre. There are also references to individual authors, most recently as the criminal genre has continued to expand. New programs are being touted as "from the producers of *Law & Order*" or from other producers of successful programs in the genre.

On the other hand, the ritual approach views genre as an exchange between the industry and the audience to work within an established structure (Feuer, 1992). This approach focuses mostly on plot elements. In his analysis of *The Avengers*, Miller (1997) presented genre as setting a norm for programs to be measured against. In the crime genre, apprehending the criminal is the norm—the ritual—that is played out. This reinforces the idea that society is safe from the danger of the criminal, as is portrayed in *Law & Order* and *NYPD Blue*. A plot element that has been added to the genre in recent years is that of revealing the personal lives of police officers (Robards, 1985), evident in *NYPD Blue*. Often, programs in the crime genre are situated in an urban context, another ritualistic element. Robards (1985) pointed out that the more contemporary cop/detective shows have elements similar to those found in Westerns, but they are presented in an urban setting. Each presents similar themes, including that of outlaws as "Others," and the sheriff or marshal as the leader.

The third approach to genre studies, from an ideological viewpoint, analyzes texts as reinforcing the dominant ideology by looking for the embedded meanings that are presented through genre elements (Feuer, 1992). Through the 1980s, the crime genre represented the police officer as the patriarchal figure (Robards, 1985). Police are shown as symbols of respect and authority (Robards, 1985). Similarly, the detective story, like the Western, presents a hero who is against violence, but often uses it (Barson, 1985). These factors serve to present a view of the world, an ideology, that is seen as normal, or common sense (Casey, Casey, Calvert, French, & Lewis, 2002).

The three approaches to genre can be combined, as Feuer (1992) suggested. I see the aesthetic and ritualistic elements of the crime series as contributing to the ideology of the crime genre as a whole, so in this study I emphasize ideological factors, which are constructed through aesthetic and ritualistic conventions. Stereotypes and cultural assumptions about criminals are presented in media texts, which reflect a discourse about crime in society—in some cases where the criminal is viewed as something that is done to society, and in others where he or she is viewed as part of society. However, contradictory representations are also presented throughout the genre.

Genre can also be viewed as a means through which discourse occurs (Bawarshi, 2000). Recent work in genre theory has sought to expand the theory beyond its traditional literary roots to recognize the importance of the context in which a genre is created, and also the context that the genre helps to create. Genre is seen as playing a part in the production and interpretation of texts and culture, and that process has "linguistic, sociological, and psychological assumptions underlying and shaping these text types" (Bawarshi, 2000, p. 335). As with Foucault's discourse theory, genre theory is approached in this context with the premise that change is possible. Therefore, integrating the two theories, discourse and genre, is also possible as genre theory continues to be expanded, even within literary frameworks. Also acknowledging the ideological framework within which genre works, Bawarshi (2000) stated, "Because genres function on an ideological level, constituting discursive reality, they operate as conceptual schemes that also constitute how we negotiate our way through discursive reality as producers and consumers of texts" (p. 354).

IDEOLOGICAL ANALYSIS

For the purpose of this research, an ideological approach to genre—focusing on the dominant ideology presented in the texts as well as where contradictions are evident—is used to present the range of representations of criminals and the context in society in which they are represented in these texts. Ideological analysis is of particular interest and importance because it is an implicit part of a text. Unlike the physical codes of television, as Fiske (1987) pointed out,

> the codes of class, race, and morality are working less openly and more questionably: their ideological work is to naturalize the correlation of lower-class, non-American with the less attractive, less moral, and therefore villainous. Conversely, the middle-class and the white American is correlated with the more attractive, the more moral and the heroic. (p. 10)

While classification is one element of genre studies, the approach goes beyond simply classifying; it is also used to analyze literature, film, and television. Genre is seen as creating a standard expectation, or norm, by which texts can be evaluated, either by determining that the text meets the expectation of the genre or that it does not (Quinn, 1999). Genre studies use standard genre elements or norms as bases for comparison for all texts within the genre (Quinn). However, when applying literary-genre theories to studies of television and film texts, new approaches are needed to account for the change in medium. Television and film texts, seen as culturally specific, do not fit into the broad terms used by literary-genre theorists, and therefore the literary categories do not explain the differences inherent in the film and television industries' productions (Feuer, 1992). Therefore, Feuer (1992) stressed the importance of television-genre theorists recognizing the differences and developing their own definitions of genre that are more appropriate for the structure of the medium. As culture changes, so do the classifications of genres in television and film. As a result, genre criticism is seen as a form of cultural criticism (Feuer, 1992). Marchetti (1989) noted: "Particular genres tend to be popular at certain points in time because they somehow embody and work through those social contradictions the culture needs to come to grips with and may not be able to deal with except in the realm of fantasy" (p. 187).

Therefore, combining discourse analysis with ideology is a logical fit, since both deal with discursive reflection, as well as the embeddedness of ideology. Hall (1996) explored the concept of discourse in connection with ideology. Hall pointed out the following:

> Ideologies do not operate through single ideas; they operate in discursive chains, in clusters, in semantic fields, in discursive formations...Ideological representations connote—summon—one another. So a variety of different ideological systems or logics are available in any social formation, (creating an) interplay of different ideological discourses and formations in any modern developed society. (p. 24)

White (1992) explained that "ideological practice concerns relations between the individual and the social formation via interpellation, it focuses attention on individuals as social subjects who not only construct but are also constructed by systems of representation" (p. 169). The system can present various ideologies through representation.

White (1992) defined ideological analysis as "based on the assumption that cultural artifacts—literature, film, television, and so forth—are produced in specific historical contexts, by and for specific social groups" (p. 163):

> It aims to understand culture as a form of social expression. Because they are created in socially and historically specific contexts, cultural artifacts are seen as expressing and promoting values, beliefs,

and ideas in relation to the contexts in which they are produced, distributed, and received. Ideological analysis aims to understand how a cultural text specifically embodies and enacts particular ranges of values, beliefs, and ideas. (p. 163)

I found various and conflicting representations about crime and criminals, but there are limitations to the range that was presented. White (1992) pointed out that the most extreme and nontraditional ideas that deviate from the dominant discourse are rarely represented in television programs, so that they appeal to a wide audience, which is necessary for television as a commercial medium. I did find more extreme positions in the cable programs compared to network programs.

DISCOURSE ANALYSIS

Discourse analysis is used in this research, with a focus on locating ideological constructions in discourse about criminals presented in the contemporary fictional, reality, and documentary television programs. The goal is to reveal what is presented in these texts as natural—common sense. Discourse analysis is a method that has been used by cultural-studies scholars in communication, as well as by feminist-theory scholars (Glynn, 2000; Fiske, 1996; Williams, 1993; Mills, 1992). As Barthes (1977) pointed out, discourse is an expression of ideology through language. He said, "In every society various techniques are developed intended to *fix* the floating chain of signifieds in such a way as to counter the terror of uncertain signs; the linguistic message is one of these techniques" (p. 39). "This common domain of the signifieds of connotation is that of *ideology*, which cannot but be single for a given society and history, no matter what signifiers of connotation it may use" (p. 49).

Discourse analysis in practice views "language as socially and historically shaped" (Casey et al., 2002, p. 64). The analysis of discourse seeks to reveal the naturalized ideology that is at work in order to socially construct reality. "Discourses…can be defined as particular sets of beliefs and attitudes which are embedded in specific socio-historical contexts and which embody cultural practices that function to shape the identities and actions of social participants" (Casey et al., 2002, p. 65). Discourse, as Fiske (1996) defined it, is language in context, not separated from its context. The analysis of discourse must include, as Fiske (1996) suggested, what is not said, and how power is negotiated within that context. Fiske (1987) pointed to how ideology is embedded in discourses on television, but that the depictions are naturalized in such a way that they are not seen as being constructed. Discourse analysis looks at structures and patterns that create discourse (Casey et al., 2002). This is important because "discourses exist in hierarchical relations, so that one of the key objectives of discourse analysis is to make explicit which discourse(s) is the prevailing one and in whose interests it can be seen to be operating" (Casey et al., 2002, p. 66).

Discourse theory originated with Michel Foucault, and is applicable to the study of genre, as its premise is that power is manufactured through discursive frameworks. Foucault (1980) explained the following:

> Power must b[e] analyzed as something which circulates, or rather as something which only functions in the form of a chain. It is never localised here or there, never in anybody's hands, never appropriated as a commodity or piece of wealth. Power is employed and exercised through a net-like organisation. And not only do individuals circulate between its threads; they are always in the position of simultaneously undergoing and exercising this power...individuals are the vehicles of power, not its points of application...The individual which power has constituted is at the same time its vehicle. (p. 98)

Foucault (1980) pointed out that within society "there are manifold relations of power which permeate, characterize, and constitute the social body, and these relations of power cannot themselves be established, consolidated nor implemented without the production, accumulation, circulation, and functioning of a discourse" (p. 93). Mills (1992) pointed out that it is through discourse that concepts "are being constructed all of the time and negotiated in each interaction" (p. 221). The concepts are a "collection of disparate statements, some of which can be resisted, some colluded with, according to context" (p. 221). Fiske (1996) discussed how discourse also becomes part of the process of establishing power: "Putting an event into any discourse always involves centering some elements and marginalizing or repressing others: because verbal language obeys no laws other than those that society has produced to organize it, putting an event into verbal discourse is a *purely* social process" (p. 222). Foucault's discourse theory recognizes contradictions within the discourse that both support and resist power, resulting in a struggle and negotiation over power.

My goal in this analysis is to "confront and analyze the mobilization of multiple perspectives and contradictions, through and across the texts that comprise television, in order to develop our understanding of ideological practice in all its complexity" (White, 1992, p. 197). For this research, following White (1992), ideology is defined as a system through which ideas are presented in various forms in the culture, including through television fiction texts that consist of "beliefs that are taken as 'natural' when in fact they perpetuate the status quo and continue the class system of oppression" (p. 165). As a result, "ideological analysis is empowering insofar as it helps lift the blinders of false consciousness and enables people to understand the way the system—even, perhaps, their favorite television shows—help perpetuate their oppression" (White, 1992, p. 165). This definition is appropriate to determine the "system" through which ideas are presented in media texts and, ultimately, contextualized within a genre, as well as other media texts. Ideology is a naturalized presentation of values, beliefs, and ideas that are embedded in the text. These implicit messages about how crime occurs speak to what is upheld—accepted—in society as common sense.

A Crime-Genre Analysis

The scope of this research will include representations of legal authorities and criminals, and specifically will examine how personal relationships and group membership are depicted in the genre as influencing criminals, either to commit crimes or to rehabilitate their lives. Further, I will point to depictions of social structures as a motivator for crime, as well as portrayals of a flawed justice system.

In chapter 1, I review two approaches to communication research: media effects and cultural studies. I describe the approach I followed in this research—critical-cultural studies. I also review existing research that followed each approach.

In chapter 2, I review crime statistics between 1998 and 2004 and opinion polls that indicate the types of crime people fear most, and the types of crime policies they support to combat crime. I also examine research conducted by criminologists and sociologists, specifically the factors that have been determined to motivate and influence criminals. In addition, I discuss the political climate and the types of crime policies supported during this 6-year period.

In chapter 3, I discuss the specific method I used to explore the representations in eight fictional programs, two reality programs, and four documentaries to determine what they reveal about cultural norms in society. I also provide summaries of each fictional program.

In chapter 4, I illustrate how traditional depictions of crime—and specifically legal authorities—remained in the genre, but additional representations emerged about legal authorities as well. Two extremes were identified: a rogue cop in *The Shield* and a compassionate and sympathetic detective in *Cold Case*. Therefore, as criminals were being represented more completely, the representation of legal authorities broadened, and they were not represented by one singular depiction.

In chapter 5, I explore how backgrounds and motivations of criminals are revealed in the genre. In the series starring criminals, specifically *Oz* and *The Sopranos*, criminals are sometimes shown to care about the same things as law-abiding citizens—particularly the safety of their family members. In some depictions, this constructs criminals as able to be rehabilitated, a new representation of criminals in the genre.

In chapter 6, I show how *Oz* blurs the "Us" (law-abiding citizens) versus "Them" (criminals) distinction that exists in society. As a result, the problem of crime in America is presented as a complex one that requires more than the "lock-them-up-and-throw-away-the-key" solution that has previously been encouraged in the genre.

In chapter 7, I analyze reality series in the genre, which also offer a different perspective about the role of police officers in fighting crime than had been seen previously in the genre. Unlike the traditional law-and-order depiction—that crime fighting is a job only for police officers—*America's Most Wanted* encourages individuals to assist police by calling in tips. I show how the series is primarily geared toward suburban, middle-class families who are constructed in the program as victims. Crime is no longer depicted as confined to urban areas—specifically New York City and Los Angeles—as previously depicted in the genre. At the same time, the reality series *COPS* provides a more traditional view of the role of police in crime fighting, but does offer a glimpse into tactics used by police—beyond the use of force so commonly depicted in fictional series.

In chapter 8, I examine four crime documentaries that aired on television between 1998 and 2004 and show that the fictional depictions mirror real life situations. The documentaries particularly addressed inequalities and flaws in the American justice system.

In chapter 9, I address the implications of these new depictions for the cultural connotation of "the criminal" by looking at specific examples of the impact the genre has had on audiences. I examine how prosecutors and defense attorneys have identified a "CSI effect" among jurors. These attorneys apparently believe that the CBS program *CSI*—with storylines that are forensic based—has influenced jurors, who now expect forensic evidence to be presented in virtually every case.

In chapter 10, I conclude that this research identifies a shift in representations of both criminals and legal authorities between 1998 and 2004. I suggest that future studies of the crime genre should seek to identify the representations of victims and should also focus on additional studies of audiences who watch programs in the crime genre in an effort to confirm "the CSI effect" and potentially identify additional effects.

CHAPTER 1

MEDIA EFFECTS AND CULTURAL STUDIES: PREVIOUS STUDIES

Within communication studies, the media effects approach—especially when taken to an extreme—assumes that media representations have a direct impact on viewers' behavior; it views the media as being more powerful than viewers. The cultural-studies approach analyzes implicit and explicit messages in media representations, and also examines whether the texts have an impact on viewers' behavior. In this chapter, I identify existing research that followed each approach.

MEDIA EFFECTS

Scholars who have studied specific effects of violent images on audiences tend nearly always to believe that media have effects. Sociologists, psychologists, and media researchers have studied whether viewing violent images in television and film leads to aggressive behavior by viewers. For example, Linz, Donnerstein, and Penrod (1988) studied the effects of multiple exposures to filmed violence against women and found that subjects became desensitized to violence over time. Centerwall (1989) also found that television had a direct effect on homicide rates, which increased between 1965 and 1975. Through telephone surveys, media scholars Hoffner and Buchanan (2002) asked parents whether they believed that viewing television violence had an effect on their children. They were specifically asked how television violence affected viewing the world as a dangerous place, approving of aggression, and behaving aggressively. The majority of parents said that their own children were not impacted by these images, but other children were. Psychologists Wood, Wong, and Chachere (1991) assessed unconstrained interpersonal aggression by studying the way children and adolescents played together after viewing violent and nonviolent films. They found that spontaneous aggression increased in the children who viewed violent films. Sociologist Felson (1996), studying aggression in adults, found that exposure to violent television images affected violent behavior, but attributed this to the "novel forms of violent behavior they might not otherwise consider" (p. 124).

Agenda Setting and Framing
Agenda setting and framing are two factors commonly studied by communication researchers to examine media effects. Wanta (1988) pointed out that editors serve as gatekeepers, and that they can focus readers' attention to issues that readers will perceive as important based on the size of photographs that accompany an article. Shaw (1999) examined this process in a study of people who viewed events surrounding the 1992 and 1996 presidential campaigns. Shaw found that "favorable television coverage of Democratic events reduced the Republican vote, while favorable television coverage of Republican events boosted it" (p. 192). However, major events, such as the conventions and debates, had little effect on voters. They concluded that media effects may not be

specifically related to favorability, and they attribute the impact to agenda setting and framing by the media.

Johnson (2002) pointed to the impact of media messages that inform people about things with which they have no personal experience. While AIDS had a specific connotation in the United States when it was first discovered, specifically as a "gay plague," the disease spread differently in Africa. She noted that when the Clinton administration identified AIDS in Africa as a threat to the national security of the United States, the media "served an important role either propagating or counteracting the moralistic public sentiment around the disease, resting on sexuality, gender, and geography" (p. 86). She noted the role of journalists in this agenda-setting process:

> In order to explain the epidemic, the media draw on factors as diverse as sexual behavior, gender relations, ritual behavior, health systems, family structure, political systems, and globalization. This information represents most of what Americans learn about Africa, although it may be augmented by personal knowledge or other secondary sources such as nongovernmental organizations. (p. 86)

After an article was published in *The Washington Post* in April 2000 noting that the administration identified AIDS in Africa as a national-security threat to the United States, Johnson pointed to "inter-media agenda-setting" as the reason the idea was disseminated publicly. Joe Lockhart, White House Press Secretary at the time, said that a formal designation or announcement was not made by the administration in the days prior to the publication of the article. That designation had occurred several months prior. The journalists, Johnson noted, chose to bring the issue to the public's attention.

Jasperson, Shah, Watts, Faber, and Fan (1998) found that the framing and frequency of coverage "add to the ability to predict issue importance in the mind of the public" (p. 271). They found that the budget was cited as the most important issue in public-opinion polls in 1995 and 1996 because of "shifts in how the news about budget politics was framed" (p. 271). They further cited the characterization, or framing, of the issue—particularly what journalists emphasized about the issue—as having an impact on audiences. As a result, they cited the quantity, or agenda setting, and quality, or framing, of an issue as significant factors that impact public perception.

Cultivation Theory

Gerbner (1998) said that television viewing has limited effects. His cultivation theory claims that television has the function to "define the world and legitimize the social order" (p. 178). As a result, television helps people socialize. "Transcending historic barriers of literacy and mobility, television has become the primary common source of socialization and everyday information (mostly in the form of entertainment) of otherwise heterogeneous populations" (p. 177).

Gerbner (1998) found that not all viewers will respond to media messages, particularly those depicting violence, in the same way; he cited "differences found in the responses of different groups of viewers, differences that usually are associated with the varied cultural, social, and political characteristics of these groups" (p. 183). He said that these effects "are diminished in the responses of heavy viewers in these same groups" (p. 183). Gerbner found that the impact of these shared messages varies based on the amount of television viewed. Ultimately, Gerbner's findings point to long-term exposure to violence on television as cultivating "the image of a relatively mean and dangerous world" (p. 185).

The television crime genre has been at the peak of its popularity in recent years, and it is in the context of the entire genre, not just a single program, that the impact of its messages can be determined, as Gerbner suggested. "Exposure to the total pattern rather than only to specific genres or programs is what accounts for the historically new and distinct consequences of living with television: the cultivation of shared conceptions of reality among otherwise diverse publics" (Gerbner, 1998, p. 178).

Cultivation, as Gerbner (1998) described it, is "a continual, dynamic, ongoing process of interaction among messages and contexts" (p. 180).

In looking at the direct impact of violent messages on audiences, Gerbner found the following:

> The relationship between amount of viewing and fear of crime is strongest among those who live in high crime urban areas. This is a phenomenon we have called "resonance," in which everyday reality and television provide a "double dose" of messages that "resonate" and amplify cultivation. (p. 182)

While I view audiences to be active, I also recognize that representations of criminals in the media may have more of an effect on audiences than other media representations because few viewers may have real-life experiences with the types of crimes—particularly murder and other violent crimes—depicted in the television genre. Following Saltiel and Woelfel, Watt and van den Berg (1981) noted:

> If relatively little information is known about an object, all messages will have a strong effect. If these messages are discrepant with previous messages, they will change beliefs or attitudes. If they are consistent with already held beliefs, they will reinforce those beliefs by adding consistent information. (p. 43)

Researchers have found that television viewing can have an effect on audiences that mirrors the effect of real-life experiences. In a study of people who either witnessed the World Trade Center attacks in 2001 firsthand or watched images of the attacks on television, Jarolmen and Sisco (2005) found that the degree of post-traumatic stress did not differ significantly between the two groups.

Using cultivation theory, scholars have also studied whether media messages, particularly those on television, influence viewers' perception of reality, ultimately creating a distorted sense of reality. Noting that there are fewer instances where people are shown smoking on television, Shanahan, Scheufele, Yang, and Hizi (2004) examined whether frequent television watchers, referred to as heavy viewers, determined by the number of hours they watched television, would underestimate how many people actually smoke, but did not find support for this hypothesis.

Respondents who were heavy television viewers actually overestimated how many people smoke. They noted that this response may be attributed to an increase in antismoking messages on television; therefore, "television viewing raises societal risk awareness and concerns about smoking as a social problem" (p. 424). Shanahan and colleagues pointed out that the presence of these antismoking messages may lead people to overestimate the severity of the problem. They noted: "With mixed opinion climate and changing social norms regarding smoking, smokers, and cigarette companies, mass media's role in affecting smoking related public health becomes ambiguous and multifaceted" (p. 426).

In a study on the impact of crime reporting, Reber and Chang (2000) found cultivation effects: The amount of attention paid to local crime in the newspaper and the number of days a week someone watched television news were significantly correlated with fear. They found that 42.3% of respondents associated fear of crime with national media coverage of crime; 31.9% attributed their fear to personal experience; 22.4% said that entertainment programs made them fear crime; while only 19.5% cited local news coverage. However, 75% said that the media paid too much attention to criminal activity. While Reber and Chang did not address this particular finding in relation to cultivation effects, I argue that it can be interpreted as a lack of support for cultivation theory. By suggesting that the media pay too much attention to crime, the respondents indicated that they do not perceive crime in the real world solely based on what they view in the media. They suggested in this statement that media distort reality by paying too much attention, not an appropriate amount of attention, to crime.

Bilandzic and Rossler (2004) suggested that fictional television programs can have an impact on real-world perceptions for two reasons: "the fictional source is *forgotten* and the information is used anyway" or "the fictional source *does not matter*, because what is learned applies to both television and real world" (p. 311). As a result, they noted that the context in which an event is portrayed in a fictional program is crucial in cultivation theory, because "viewers do not treat all information equally, but find some bits more adequate than others for real-world judgments" (p. 312). They pointed to whether an event in a drama is perceived as remote or very close to their own lives as a key factor in determining cultivation effects.

However, Bilandzic and Rossler (2004) also noted that it is not only the realism of the event that is a factor, but whether the relationships exhibited are remote or very close to viewers. For example, they suggested, viewers may feel very close to depictions in soap operas because they recognize the relationships as something they experience in their everyday lives. They explained,

> Elements from fictional fantasy programs may be much closer to a viewer as they portray a human conflict the viewer him-or herself struggles with. In contrast, elements of reality-based television news may be perceived as very remote, because a viewer does not attribute personal relevance to a presidential election in a foreign country. (p. 313)

Bilandzic and Rossler (2004) further suggested that gratifications sought by viewers should be incorporated into audience studies. "It should matter...whether people watch crime shows to be entertained, because they like an actor, or they like the humor of a show, or in order to learn about prevention of crime and to learn what to do if they are assaulted" (p. 314). For example, they noted, a viewer of the television crime genre might be seeking the message that "felons are punished and safety is restored" (p. 314). Therefore, "if this is the message a viewer learns from television, we can argue that he or she could have anticipated the message from the genre, and that he or she watched the genre *in order to* get this message" (p. 314). However, they also noted that viewers can watch programs and learn something they did not seek out. They concluded that, "[e]ventually, beliefs from TV world are *integrated* into real world beliefs" obtained through personal experience and other media messages (p. 317).

Effects on Civic Participation
Keum, Devanathan, Deshpande, Nelson, and Shah (2004) examined effects of media on civic participation, consumer attitudes and consumption, and

associations between consumer attitudes and civic participation. They found that media do not have "largely negative effects on civic participation" (p. 383), and that news media use positively affected civic participation and that television use—"particularly sitcom, police drama, and reality program viewing"—had a negative effect (p. 383). "For entertainment television use, viewing was found to negatively influence civic participation and positively influence status orientation; it worked through the latter to influence status-conscious consumption" (p. 382). They concluded that "news media appear to have stronger and more direct effects on consumer culture and civic participation than entertainment television" (p. 383). Specifically, they found that television use directly affected status orientation positively and civic participation negatively. They attributed the effects from news media use to the "direct, factual mode of most news presentations" and, therefore, that these media messages had "greater sway over audience attitudes and behaviors than entertainment portrayals" (p. 383).

Lee (2005) found that media, and particularly conservative media, can serve to reinforce viewers' political beliefs and, therefore, does not negatively influence civic participation, such as voting. "The *more* consumers consider conservative media important, the *more* they believe their political participation such as voting can make a difference" (p. 424). In addition, "[t]he *more* consumers consider in-depth media important, the *more* they trust the government to do what is right" (p. 424). Lee attributed this to selective consumption—viewers may be selecting programs that reinforced existing beliefs. Lee concluded that none of the media outlets—conservative or otherwise—in the study resulted in an effect of "political alienation (such as non-voting)" (p. 426).

Studying the Impact of Violence
Using cultivation theory, Lett, DiPietro, and Johnson (2004) studied college students and found that negative emotions were associated with television-news viewing following the September 11, 2001, terrorist attacks on the World Trade Center. In addition, increased television viewing also led to increased negative emotions about Islamic peers among

college students. However, heavy viewers were "more positive toward Islamic individuals in general" (p. 44). Lett and colleagues attributed this to television-news coverage that portrayed the "terrorists as extremists and separate from mainstream Islam" (p. 44).

Sotirovic (2001) looked at the impact of exposure to violent images on audiences and concluded that the more perspectives of crime and criminals that are shown in the media, the more these depictions will stimulate more complex thinking about crime, which would support preventive policies, rather than punitive policies. Sotirovic (2001) pointed out:

> People who are more exposed, and pay more attention to, complex media content, represented by the traditional hard-news media format, are likely to have more-complex thinking about crime... [E]xposure and attention to the simple infotainment format of various reality-based, pseudo-news, talk and news-magazine shows limits complexity of thinking and promotes fear. (p. 324)

Other researchers have also looked at the effect of crime reports on fear, and how that translates, if at all, into active influence on crime policy. For example, Potter and Smith (2000) found that graphic depictions of violence impacted whether a person experiences fear. The more graphic the depiction, the more fear it produced in viewers.

In addition to promoting fear, presentations of crime can also contribute to the way people process information about crime. Pfau, Moy, and Szabo (2001) found that prime-time television programs are "at least partly responsible for negative public perceptions of the federal government" (p. 439) and, by extension, its laws. They found support for the claim that prime-time television programs influence public confidence. Sotirovic (2001) found that preference for preventive policies that include rehabilitation and treatment is mediated by a more complex thinking process. Support for punitive policies, including the death penalty and long prison sentences, was a result of fear, which is identified as an affective process.

Cultural-studies scholars, among others, would point to the weaknesses of many of these studies, particularly the ones that seek to isolate a behavior that is not performed in isolation. In most experiments seeking media effects, a group is studied and members' television viewing behavior is isolated to a particular type of programming. However, the aggression that is found through this process could be attributed to many other social and cultural factors that could not be isolated for the study. This sociocultural context is central to cultural studies, as I discuss in the next section.

CULTURAL STUDIES

The field of cultural studies views audiences as actively engaging in a process of interpretation, not as passive recipients of information and messages. Fiske and Dawson (1996) noted that Gerbner's cultivation theory acknowledges the importance of analyzing content in popular culture, but that it does not view the "audience as a potential agent of social change" (p. 310).

> By casting the audience as those who were acculturated by the system it still modeled them as the recipients of effects. Like other effect-oriented models, it never saw the audience as an agent in the social circulation of meanings in which television plays such an important part. (p. 310)

The goal of cultural studies is not to isolate sociocultural events and study a particular aspect of television viewing. The cultural studies approach seeks to reveal how television viewing is incorporated into other social and cultural frameworks (Fiske, 1987; Seiter, 1992; Marchetti, 1989; White, 1992). That framework has guided this research. As Allan (1998) noted,

> Cultural studies (can) be understood as being inclusive of a variety of different approaches (conceptual and methodological) which endeavour to explicate the cultural dynamics of everyday experience in relation to the naturalization of social divisions, and hierarchies, especially those of class, gender, race, ethnicity and sexuality. (p. 106)

The purpose of this research is to help reveal assumptions that have been naturalized in our society about crime and criminals through media texts. Allan (1998) pointed out that cultural-studies scholars have looked at discourse in various media messages:

> Cultural studies researchers have identified the ways in which the news media systematically extend and reinforce the interests of economic and political elites…Whereas news discourse is presented by its makers as an objective, impartial *translation* of reality, it may instead be seen to be providing an ideological *construction* of realities. (p. 106)

Critical-Cultural Studies

My research uses a critical-cultural studies approach to examine the discourse about crime during a specific historical period. Critical-cultural studies theory is often used to explore how society is reflected, explicitly and implicitly, through media representations. Craig (1999) explained,

> For critical communication theory, the basic "problem of communication" in society arises from material and ideological forces that preclude or distort discursive reflection. Communication conceived this way explains how social injustice is perpetuated by ideological distortions and how justice can potentially be restored through communicative practices that enable critical reflection or consciousness-raising in order to unmask those distortions and thereby enable political action to liberate the participants from them. The critical tradition is plausible from a lay point of view when it appeals to commonplace beliefs about the omnipresence of injustice and conflict in society, the ways in which power and domination can overcome truth and reason, and the potential for discourse with others to produce liberating insight, demystification, perhaps even the realization that one has been "had." (p. 147)

In the process of analyzing media representations of criminals, I refer to criminological and sociological theories in this research to provide a basis for my analysis, and discuss the cultural and political climate in American society between 1998 and 2004 in order to place the representations in a historical context, because various factors influence how media messages are interpreted. The American judicial system theoretically follows a philosophy that people must pay for their crimes, primarily through serving prison sentences. Once that debt to society is paid, the system allows them to return "fully" to society. Yet, in reality, that is unlikely, or at least not easily accomplished, due to the connotation that the "criminal" label carries. Reassimilation into society is often difficult, due in part to a "once a criminal, always a criminal" ideology that is commonly reinforced in media messages. Sloop (1996) addressed this connotation:

> While we can claim culturally that individuals must take responsibility for their individual behavior, the force of past discourses in defining how we will conceptualize, say, the African-American prisoner or the female criminal will strongly mold how we will allow this person to act autonomously. We can claim autonomy for the criminal, but it is an autonomy constrained by cultural interpretations that influence how individual prisoners are represented and how they then constitute themselves...Once placed into action, past discourses concerning the prisoner continue to influence present perceptions of the prisoner. (p. 195)

It is with this focus that Sloop (1996) looked at articles in popular mass-media magazines and newspapers, as well as television and film, to determine how depictions of criminals have changed since the 1950s. Sloop explained the following:

> Because "prisoners," like most objects of discourse, become familiar to the public through fragmented representations, the cultural understanding of prisoners is developed from reading *People* magazine in the waiting room of the dentist's office, from viewing CNN before supper, or from conversing with friends. The mediated image has more rhetorical force than do federal statistics on how prisoners are understood culturally. (p. 194)

Sloop identified the 1950s as a time when rehabilitation was stressed, but several publicized prison riots in the 1960s resulted in the perception that prisoners were violent and unable to be rehabilitated. In the 1970s, he found that white prisoners were again perceived as redeemable while black prisoners were perceived as irrational. As Sloop suggested, the connotation of "the criminal" has not been static over time, but fluid. That connotation can lead to support for specific crime policies, as Sasson (1995) suggested.

Popular Culture and Power
Researchers have examined issues of power and status in media, specifically news media. Haas and Steiner (2001) discussed the role of power and status in the *Akron Beacon Journal*'s campaign to improve race relations. One article in the five-part series published by the newspaper documented racial and economic inequalities, but as Haas and Steiner noted: "Highlighting the historical differences in power and status that give rise to conflicts and rank-ordering the salience of differing interests between the already-powerful and the relatively powerless could therefore have been useful" (p. 129).

As Rhodes (2005) pointed out, news outlets have historically used an Us versus Them narrative to frame stories. She noted how this occurred during the coverage of the civil-rights movement in the 1960s: "The press customarily framed stories about the civil rights movement within binary oppositions that reproduced the standard values of American journalism: good versus evil, justice versus lawlessness, and North versus South" (p. 32). As with representations of criminals in fictional television series prior to 1997, in the 1960s, television-news-coverage representations of the civil-rights activists, particularly the Black Panthers, were "sporadic and brief," as Rhodes noted, citing "one or two stories a month through mid-1967." As a result, the binary narrative was dominant.

In addition, researchers have analyzed issues of power and status in entertainment media. Popular-culture texts represent, as Fiske (1996) suggested, a forum for those on the bottom of the social hierarchy to surface in the dominant. They can represent "processes of change by which older dominant currents (are being) transformed into residual ones, and emergent ones (are being) pushed up from the depths and in from the margins to challenge for a place in the dominant" (p. 13). They represent a site for social power negotiation through media representations. Turow (1991) also addressed the power of the media, particularly fictional representations:

> The messages of mass media, as well as arguments about the messages, speak to issues of position and power in society. Who gets depicted, what about them gets depicted, why, with what consequences, at what time, and in what situation—these are questions creators of all cultural models answer in the course of their work. (p. 164)

As such, popular culture is an important site for examining representations of criminals because it is where social norms are reinforced, and therefore, where social power is negotiated, as Good (1989) pointed out. "According to Althusser's anti-existentialist argument, power is effected through individuals' willing subjugation to ideology, which defines them and locates them within a social structure" (p. 60). Through representations in popular culture, we see that power is not fixed, and, as a result, there is always the potential for a shift in social power. Popular culture is a natural site to study the negotiation process, as masses of people are reached and contradictions in ideology are evident. Popular-culture studies consistently deal with the concept of power.

Gramsci (1971) presented culture as tied to political factors of influence through hegemony, which naturalizes power. However, Gramsci suggested that people are not forced into submission, but instead adopt the ideology and values (e.g., capitalism) of a dominant ruling class, because processes of hegemony naturalize those values, presenting them as common sense. Within this process, however, Gramsci acknowledged that power can shift and conflict can occur in this process of coercion. Duffett (2004) described hegemony as "a series of struggles focused on specific cultural sites that can reconfigure the social and cultural landscape" (p. 493):

> Hegemony represents a movement that shifts public discussion onto a terrain that secures leadership. It demarcates a set of consensual ideas that maintains the subordination of particular groups

and values. Rather than being imposed by force from above, it involves the active seeking of consent from ordinary people by persuading them to see themselves and their position in a way that makes them comply with their own subordination. Oppositional voices are negotiated rather than denied in this approach; their interests are taken into account in a process that simultaneously positions them in a nonthreatening role. (p. 493)

In this way, hegemony can be seen as "a way of searching for access points for struggle" (Good, 1989, p. 61). Marchetti (1989) further explained,

> The hegemony of the ruling factions, therefore, is never absolute, but always has to be fought for and reimposed on a daily basis. Ideological hegemony finds expression through "common sense," the very mundane ways in which people make sense of the world. (p. 185)

Marchetti (1989) suggested that "texts need to be looked at as contradictory entities, polysemic in nature, which themselves allow for a range of possible readings" (p. 185).

Die Hard: Identifying Audience Power and Activity

Fiske and Dawson's (1996) study of homeless men who viewed the film *Die Hard* offers insights into the reasons audiences select entertainment programs that contain violent images. They noted that the men who participated in the study "were selective viewers of the movie—and what they chose to pay most attention to were representations of violence… directed against the social order" (p. 301). Among other factors, Fiske and Dawson (1996) examined why genres with violent images are popular:

> When homelessness is a structural and systemic deprivation of the weak by a society which is also theirs, and whose material security they feel ought to be one of their rights, then the conditions are ripe for the taste for violence to develop. The violence may be actual or symbolic, it may be initiated by the social order to control the homeless, or by the homeless against the social order. (p. 303)

I view criminals as fitting this description of a "structural and systemic deprivation of the weak by a society which is also theirs." In the case of criminals, their weakness may not necessarily be attributed to homelessness, but to economic inequalities, as depictions in the television series *Oz* suggest. As a result, people who feel economically disadvantaged may have a similar response to the homeless men, and may develop "a taste for violence." Fiske and Dawson's (1996) description of homeless men's response to society can also apply to economically disadvantaged people who may not be homeless. Their description may explain, in part, the popularity of the television crime genre for more than 50 years, but particularly since the 1990s.

After watching the homeless men, Fiske and Dawson (1996) concluded that the men rarely acted violently, but they did sometimes block sidewalks to force pedestrians to change their paths and would sit on park benches, preventing others in the park from using the benches. They viewed these acts as a way for the men to exert some power over those who were more advantaged in society:

> Society...deprived them of all means of asserting their rights and identities except their bodies, and they so used their bodies' abilities to occupy physical space as a way to assert their right to a position in the social space. The body is where violence is put into practice, so when social relations are reduced to the physicality of bodies, it is hardly surprising that one of the most accessible ways of engaging in them is by violence. (p. 303)

Fiske and Dawson (1996) traced the selection of the film *Die Hard* to the homeless men's desire to voice their "sense of opposition and hostility to the particular forms of domination that oppress them...These representations must contain not only violence, but also markers of ethnic, class, age, or national difference that are portrayed not as natural essences, but as structural agents of power and disempowerment" (p. 304). Fiske and Dawson noted that the type of conflict portrayed in these representations is multidimensional:

> It is a conflict between the bodies of individual males, it is a conflict between law and order and social disruption, it is a conflict

between good and evil, and simultaneously, it is a conflict between social centrality (or the dominant norms) and social subordination or marginality. Symbolic violence is a concrete performance of social inequality, and its popularity suggests that it can offer the subordinated both a representation of their own fighting ability and an articulation of their resentment toward the social order that oppresses them. (p. 304)

Previous Studies of Crime Representations

Various studies have examined representations of crime, criminals, and legal authorities. In a content analysis of reality shows portraying crime, Oliver (1994) found that violent crime and solved cases were overrepresented, when compared to statistics. In addition, she found that whites were more likely to be portrayed as police officers than as criminal suspects, but blacks and Hispanics were more likely to be portrayed as criminal suspects than as police officers. Police officers were shown in the series to engage in aggressive behavior more often than were criminal suspects. She also found that police officers were more likely to use aggression toward black and Hispanic suspects than toward white suspects.

Studies about depictions of crime and criminals in news reports or other reports of actual crime cases focus on representations based on race. Dixon, Azocar, and Casas (2003) conducted a content analysis of race representations of crime in network news and, unlike Oliver's study on reality shows, found that "[w]hites were more likely than African Americans to be portrayed as perpetrators, victims, and officers" (p. 516), suggesting whites are most represented overall. In addition, "African Americans were much more likely to be portrayed as perpetrators than as either victims or officers" (p. 516) when they are represented. Still, they concluded that "network news accurately portrays the racial composition of perpetrators in society" (p. 516).

Early studies of fictional representations of crime, criminals, legal authorities, and the criminal justice system on television show how the genre established specific themes that still exist. Cawelti (1975) noted that the first programs in the television genre drew from narratives in

19th-century popular literature. Literature depicted "benevolent outlaws like Deadwood Dick" or "romanticized the violence of actual western badmen like Billy the Kid, Jesse James and Wild Bill Hickock" and "[t]ypically in these stories the outlaw was represented as a decent person who had been unjustly treated by the rich and powerful, or by women" (Cawelti, 1975, pp. 76–77). Cawelti described how Westerns on television emphasized these same law-and-order themes, and how those elements continued in later genres, including detective stories in the 1970s and police shows in the 1980s. Parenti (1980) also pointed out how police shows presented a good-versus-evil scenario between legal authorities and criminal suspects—police officers sometimes engaging in aggression, yet, even those aggressive actions were presented as justified. Violent behavior alone does not make the police evil, as presented in the programs.

More recent studies about the fictional crime genre have acknowledged an Us versus Them depiction, but scholars point out that social problems and solutions to those problems are also now addressed in the genre. Rapping (2003) discussed how television programs about crime construct specific expectations in audience members about how social issues should be resolved. She noted,

> [T]he televised courtroom and its generic dependents—the endlessly proliferating talk shows, reality tabloid shows, legal dramatic series coming "straight from the headlines"—have become the major arenas through which Americans now come to understand and debate charged social issues of every stripe. (p. 106)

She sees this development as furthering "a right-wing political agenda, driven by the increasingly punitive legal policies that now dominate the thinking of those who make and enforce the laws governing criminal justice institutions and procedures" (p. 107).

Recent television studies have also examined portrayals of the racial backgrounds of criminals. In a study of prime-time programs airing in 1997, which included all genres depicting portrayals of crime, Tamorini, Mastro, Chory-Assad, and Huang (2000) found that depictions of blacks and Latinos were similar to those of whites "in the roles they held and the attributes associated with those roles" (p. 649). In the programs they analyzed, murder was the most common reason for arrest: 53% of white suspects, 90% of black suspects, and 60% of Latino suspects were arrested on murder charges (Tamorini et al., 2000).

Researchers have also examined portrayals of police officers, criminals, and citizens in reality programs. In an analysis of crime-based reality shows, such as *COPS* and *America's Most Wanted*, Fishman (1999) noted the difference in the presentation of crime fighting in the two series. It is depicted as a collaborative effort between legal authorities and citizens at large in *America's Most Wanted* and as an individual act by police officers in *COPS*. Where the programs are similar, she pointed out, is in presenting criminals as deviant. Williams (1993) also examined *America's Most Wanted* and determined that it emphasizes the danger criminals pose, particularly to families.

Prosise and Johnson (2004) found that the authority of police was emphasized in two crime-based reality shows: *COPS* and *World's Wildest Police Videos*. They pointed to depictions of law enforcers who are "in total control and always in the right" (p. 81). In addition, "[w]hen a citizen-suspect attempted to assert his rights in one segment on *WWPV*, he was met with an aggressive response from officers" (p. 81, emphasis mine). They found that police officers were "humanized through the use of actual names and portrayed as courageous defenders against the hordes of the criminally insane," but that the "voice of the citizen-suspects is given little credibility" (p. 81). Aggression, they found, was also exhibited in *COPS*. Prosise and Johnson recounted that in one episode, a "request for clarification of the reasons for stops are dismissed and met with increasing aggression by police" (p. 81). Further, they pointed out that the two series "feature police acting with limited knowledge about suspects. *COPS* does not have an all-knowing narrator. Instead, the officers describe the reasons for stopping and interviewing suspects, or they describe the nature of their call" (p. 84, emphasis mine). Prosise and Johnson noted that the reason for most stops emphasized in the segments is "officer intuition" (p. 84). They concluded that "these programs work to legitimize police actions, even controversial police practices" (p. 85).

Grabe (1999) examined 6 months of news-magazine programs and focused on representations other than race. Grabe found that 83% of programs depicted crime stories and that 38% of the segments presented were crime stories. She specifically identified a good-versus-evil theme in reports. She found "law enforcement officers were cast as the good force (78% of cases) fighting against evil criminals in the classic battle between these two forces" (p. 163). In addition, "the victim was in most cases (91.3%) the helpless good person whom the criminal preyed upon. The criminal took the prominent role as the evil force in 93.5% of cases" (p. 163). Further, "[m]ore than 95% of the portrayed criminals were presented as guilty" (p. 163). Regarding causes of crime presented, Grabe found that "the criminal was presented as having sole responsibility for violating society's moral values" (p. 163). In addition, Grabe found, individual causes of crime were stressed more often than social causes, such as poverty, which was identified in only 1% of the reports. However, psychological instability in the perpetrator of crime was found in 91% of the stories presented.

Neuendorf, Atkin, and Jeffres (2000) examined how perceptions of guilt or innocence were influenced by news coverage in court cases. They specifically examined coverage and perceptions of the O. J. Simpson trial in 1995, and found that "*regardless* of racial identity, attitudes toward affirmative action were strong predictors of evaluations of O. J. Simpson's innocence, as were perceptions of the prevalence of crime and crime fighting." (p. 261). For example, they found that

> perceptions of O. J. Simpson as innocent are correlated with a belief in the quality of local media and a higher perceived reality of television, beliefs that affirmative action is still needed in America and that crime is a major problem in the country today, and a general sentiment that the world is "mean," with a higher chance of being a victim of violent crime and a perception that more individuals make their living in law enforcement. Also, those who report a perception that Blacks have the 'worst' media images are more likely to see Simpson as innocent. Blacks, non-Whites generally, and those of lower income are also more likely to attribute innocence. (pp. 258–259)

Fiske (1996) also looked at perceptions of guilt and innocence conveyed in video images of actual crimes. Those images became part of a discourse about the events, he noted. In discussing the amateur-made video of the Rodney King beating by white Los Angeles police officers, he said that during the trial of the officers, the video was used by defense lawyers to "put into words the fears of white America: they made the movements of Rodney King's body on the ground into signs of a Black refusal to comply with the white social order" (p. 132).

Fiske (1996) also identified a professionally shot video by a Los Angeles television station of Reginald Denny, a white truck driver who was beaten by black youths during the riots that followed the acquittal of officers in the King trial, as an example of how discourse is controlled by what is visual. He pointed out that the Rodney King video "did not show (and could not, because the camera was not there) the car chase, his refusal to stop, and his refusal to lie down when first ordered out of the car" (p. 151). Yet, "The Reginald Denny video, on the other hand, omitted what it could have shown—other Black people rescuing Denny, driving him to the hospital, and saving his life" (p. 151).

The third video Fiske (1996) analyzed included security-camera images of the killing of Latasha Harlins, a black teen who apparently argued with a Korean store owner before turning and walking out of the store; the owner shot her in the back of the head. The images were used by the judge during the store owner's trial to justify the killing. The store owner received a sentence of 400 hours of community service and a $500 fine, but no jail time. Fiske noted: "It was not only Korean storekeepers who were threatened by Latasha Harlins and the gangs: in Judge Karlin's discourse 'family values,' and the whiteness encoded in them, were too" (p. 160).

The programs I analyzed were selected because they present different perspectives than what has been depicted in the genre in the past. These new perspectives are not always the dominant representation, and I analyze them in the context of the series. The new representations, as I show beginning in chapter 4, are presented alongside more traditional representations of crime, criminals, and criminal justice.

CHAPTER 2

AMERICAN SOCIETY: 1998–2004

Since I will analyze representations of crime and criminals in the crime genre, including what media messages say or imply causes crime, what scholars in the fields of criminology and sociology claim as potential causes of crime is relevant. In this chapter, I examine research conducted on the causes of crime. Theories fall into two categories: individual psychology and socially based. I discuss how each theory supports beliefs about the effectiveness of rehabilitation and appropriate crime policies.

As I discuss, between 1998 and 2004, moderate and conservative policies dominated American crime law during the administrations of Democratic President Bill Clinton and Republican President George W. Bush. I also examine a shift in recent years among criminologists, who have encouraged rehabilitation and preventive crime policies over punitive policies. In her 2004 presidential address to the American Society of Criminology, Francis Cullen cited 12 scholars who had "saved rehabilitation." He cited popular belief among criminologists in the 1970s that "nothing works" to rehabilitate criminals, a philosophy that was made popular in the field following the publication of Robert Martinson's book, *What Works? Questions and Answers About Prison Reform*. Cullen said that political conservatives "were more than pleased to join in this effort" and that they "viewed rehabilitation as allowing corrections officials to be overly lenient—as justifying offenders' coddling and early release from prison when stringent penalties were needed" (p. 6). Cullen cited the work of Petersilia, described in this section, among others, as moving away from the existing paradigm that "nothing works" to showing what can work to rehabilitate criminals.

In addition, in this chapter, I review specific crime policies enacted in America between 1998 and 2004 and classify the policies as supporting a conservative ideology or liberal ideology. I also review public-opinion polls about crime conducted between 1998 and 2004 and examine how opinions changed over time, at least according to polls.

INDIVIDUAL PSYCHOLOGY THEORIES

Individual-psychology theories about crime view crime as related to human nature, conscious choice, and biological or chemical imbalances. For example, following individual-psychology theory, crime can be perceived to be related to human nature, "where people, especially children, are naturally hedonistic and selfish, [and therefore] antisocial" (Bryant, 2000, p. 315). Psychological theories also include those that focus on cognitive factors that suggest that people will consciously engage in criminal acts "if they think that the expected benefits will outweigh the expected costs" (Bryant, 2000, p. 315). In addition, psychological theories can focus on biological factors related to psychophysiological and biochemical causes specifically related to levels of serotonin, a neurotransmitter. Researchers have suggested that "[s]erotonergic dysregulation may result in a decreased ability to inhibit certain externalizing behavioral patterns and may reflect a difficulty in behavioral inhibition" (Bryant, 2000, p. 298). Following this theory, people may engage in illegal behavior, but not necessarily because they are consciously choosing to.

Specific studies that have pointed to psychological factors as a cause of crime include a study of 255 prison inmates by Slaton, Kern, and Curlette (2000), who identified three profiles among prisoners. They concluded that individual psychology is a "viable approach for assessing the criminal personality in the 21st century" (p. 101). Profile 1 consisted of the largest group, approximately 50% of those studied. These inmates were categorized as people who were not able to "solve life's problems in a socially interested direction" (p. 104). The prisoners were labeled as independent and unpredictable, and Slaton and colleagues determined that they likely consciously chose to engage in criminal activity and, therefore, would be difficult to rehabilitate. Profile 2 represented about 33% of the group. These inmates had the highest level of education of the three groups, and were mostly involved in nonviolent crimes, such as shoplifting and forgery. Slaton and colleagues identified this group as the most likely to be rehabilitated and specifically suggested that they be identified early upon entering prison, so that they could be taught problem-solving skills. Profile 3, consisting of the remaining 16% of inmates studied, had been imprisoned multiple times, used psychotropic medications, and had more mental-health visitations than those in the other two groups. Slaton and colleagues suggested that inmates in Profile 3 were psychologically impaired, and would be difficult to rehabilitate.

Scholars have used individual-psychology theory to establish treatment and rehabilitation programs for criminals. Cognitive approaches to treatment include Rational Emotive Behavior Therapy, created by Ellis, which encourages people to view behavior and emotions as within their control to change, and that dysfunctional behavior is due to irrational thinking. A second cognitive approach is Logotherapy, developed by Frankl, which Shrum (2004) described as "health through meaning" (p. 228). It suggests that without a "'will to meaning'" people seek a "'will to pleasure' that often leads to addictions, or a 'will to power' that often leads to violence" (p. 228). A third psychological treatment involves journal writing.

Conservative, Punitive Crime Policies
Various psychological theories about crime are used to justify a conservative political ideology about crime policies. Conservative crime policies are based on the belief that crime is caused by individual choice or by psychological illness. The belief is that "criminal behavior must have some pathological sources"...[and crime is attributed to] "criminogenic genes, glands, body types, minds and personality traits" (Bryant, 2000, p. 310). Conservatives generally support punitive crime policies. Punitive policies include mandatory sentences, the death penalty, and eliminating the possibility of parole after a third offense (Sotirovic, 2004). Conservatives "assume that the ideal society is one in which authority is unquestioned....[F]ear of crime is promoted by focusing attention on heinous crimes and emphasizing the 'failures' of rehabilitation, probation and parole" (Bryant, 2000, p. 309). Offenders are "demonized" and "punishment in the name of deterrence is stressed" (Bryant, 2000, p. 309).

While running for president in 2000, during a debate with his Democratic opponent, then vice president Al Gore, George W. Bush said that he supported the death penalty, not as a way to seek revenge, but because it is a deterrent. At a time when many states were calling for a moratorium on the death penalty, Illinois Governor George Ryan went a step further, commuting the death sentences of 167 death-row inmates, which will be discussed further in chapter 8. Yet President Bush continued to show support for the death penalty.

Although some policies supported by Bill Clinton during his presidency between 1992 and 2000 were preventive policies that included examining inequalities in society that may lead to crime, he, too, supported the death penalty, a punitive policy, and even returned to Arkansas while campaigning to attend the execution of a mentally disabled man. This may have been prompted by the doomed 1988 presidential campaign of Democratic nominee Michael Dukakis, who did not support the death penalty. In a debate with challengers, Dukakis was asked what he would do if his wife was raped and murdered, and was widely criticized for his unemotional response. He was further seen as soft on crime because he supported a prison furlough program as governor of Massachusetts. One convicted murderer, Willie Horton, raped a woman while released. Likely in an attempt to combat the soft-on-crime image often associated with Democrats, Clinton stressed his tough-on-crime stance regarding the death penalty. Further, Clinton supported mandatory sentencing laws, referred to as "Three Strikes and You're Out," a punitive policy, which imposed longer prison sentences for certain offenses and eliminated the possibility for parole after three offenses.

SOCIALLY BASED THEORIES

Social factors are also viewed by some criminologists and sociologists as contributing to crime. Socially based factors include economics, family environment, and societal structures.

Economic Factors and Family Environment

Economic-based theories view crime as a response to incentives, based on expected increased earnings, weighed against the risk of being caught and convicted, the extent of the possible punishment, and the opportunities available to engage in legal activities (Bryant, 2000). This can start at an early age, as well, as Fergusson, Swain-Campbell, and Horwood (2004) found when they reviewed data on 1,265 children from a 21-year study. They found an association between low socioeconomic status and high rates of violent and property crime among adolescents. Fergusson and colleagues cited socioeconomic factors—namely "family adversity," including abuse, peer pressure, and individual conduct and school issues (truancy)—as main causes of crime in children (p. 963).

Lykken (2000) also identified family environment as a key factor in determining causes of crime, but he attributed some causes to psychological factors as well. He defined psychopaths as "people whose genetic tendencies, including their temperaments, make them so difficult to socialize that the kinds of parents and neighborhoods that succeed in socializing the vast majority of youngsters do not succeed with them" (p. 588). He found that a combination of factors, not just one single factor, can contribute. Lykken attributed the rising crime rate that began in the 1960s—to a level that represented a 300% increase in 2000—to change in socialization, or as he describes it, unsocialization. Primarily, he cited fatherless children as developing a sociopathic personality, which led to increased crime.

Hoffmann (2003) reviewed data from a national U.S. survey of adolescents, and also identified a lack of parental supervision as a predictor of delinquency. Further, Agnew (2001/1985) cited the blockage of pain-avoidance behavior at an early age—primarily in dealing with a painful environment either in the home or at school—as a source of frustration and delinquency. Klevens, Roca, Restrepo, and Martinez (2001) found parental history and background to be a key predictor of crime committed by male offenders between the ages of 18 and 30. Compared to a control group of nonoffenders from similar neighborhoods and backgrounds, they determined that these offenders had parents with a low educational level and family members who had been involved in crime. They often had absentee parents, and had been physically abused. The strongest predictors that the men would be involved in crime were identified as "lack of supervision, perceiving the primary caregiver as rejecting, having less than a sixth grade education and daily family conflict" (p. 79).

However, family members have also been identified as key factors in the rehabilitation of criminals. The incarceration period may also be a time when inmates and their families are motivated to improve family relationships. Klein, Bartholomew, and Bahr (1999) noted that "[i]nmates talk about the lack of family support for many prison inmates and the need to connect with someone after release" (p. 297). As a result, "[i]nmates who learn how to repair and maintain their family relationships have reduced disciplinary problems within the prison system and are less likely to accept the norms and behavior patterns of hardened criminals" (Bayse, AllGood, & Van Wyk, 1991, p. 292, as cited in Klein et al., 1999).

Societal Factors: Strain, Social Learning, Control, and Labeling Theories

Several theories—namely, strain, social learning, control, and labeling theory—suggest that propensity to commit crime develops through socialization. Strain Theory suggests that crime results when "others prevent you from achieving your goal and others take things you value or present you with negative or noxious stimuli" (Bryant, 2000, p. 324). It is based on "the discrepancies between culturally prescribed goals and the individual's possibility to reach these goals by culturally accepted means" (Skardhamar, 2003, p. 40). In addition, "the resources and opportunities needed to achieve the goals are not equally distributed among the population, while the goals are applied to all, hence many will not have true possibilities to be successful" (Skardhamar, 2003, p. 40). Applying Strain Theory to Norwegian prisoners, Skardhamar (2003) found that they have difficulty assimilating once released from prison. He found that their inadequate living conditions narrowed their opportunities to live a crime-free life.

Criminologists Mantle and Moore (2004) also discussed approaches to crime that focus on situational factors of criminality. They said that "discourses and policies of toughness and cure can be linked to a loss of respect and care for people who break the law" (p. 309). Instead, they sought an approach that addresses social causes as well as individual causes.

> [S]train and rational choice approaches to criminality both focus on the similarities between offenders and conforming members of the community and eschew the pathologising differentiations of individual positivism. Also, both theories point to the influence of situational factors—the rational choice perspective in regards to the criminal event and to decisions taken by the offender relating to their involvement in crime; strain theory in its attention to the structuring of opportunities for legitimate advancement. (p. 308)

They concluded that "emphasis on citizenship, supported by rational choice theory" should be adopted, following strain theory (p. 309).

Social-Learning Theory views people as engaging "in crime, primarily through their association with others...They are reinforced for crime, they learn beliefs that are favorable to crime, and they are exposed to criminal models" (Bryant, 2000, p. 326). Control Theory states that "all people have needs and desires that are more easily satisfied through crime than through legal channels" (Bryant, 2000, p. 327). According to Skardhamar (2003),

> the basis for control theory is not why people commit crimes, but rather why people do not. The assumption is that people are being held within the limits of the law by, first and foremost, internal control, but also to some extent by external control. Most people have something to lose by violating the social norms (p. 41).

Bryant (2000) noted that Labeling Theory states,

> Individuals who are arrested, prosecuted, and punished are labeled as criminals. Others then view and treat these people as criminals and this increases the likelihood of subsequent crime...Labeled individuals may have trouble obtaining legitimate employment, which increases their level of strain and reduces their stake in conformity...[They] may find that conventional people are reluctant to associate with them, and they may associate with other criminals as a result...[and] may eventually come to view themselves as criminals and act in accord with this self-concept. (p. 329)

Labeling Theory in particular offers an explanation for why prisoners have a difficult time reassimilating into society after release from prison. Marbley and Ferguson (2004) addressed the issue of reintegration into society following imprisonment, and called for expungement (i.e., removal of a conviction from an individual's criminal record) to be used as a way to assist convicts after their prison sentences:

> With full reinstatement, the message is clear to prisoners that society is prepared to forgive. Moreover, the criminal gangs who

recruit their membership from those prisoners and probationers who believe society has marked them for failure are disempowered and will no longer have a reservoir of candidates ready to join. (p. 81)

Marbley and Ferguson suggested that by removing the label of "criminal," individuals can break the cycle of crime.

Scholars have found that how criminals perceive themselves and their lives following imprisonment can be key to successful reintegration. Using self-reports of prisoners released from prison, Burnett and Maruna (2004) found that the "level of prisoner optimism might have an impact on their success upon release" (p. 395). They said that "hope may actually condition the effect of social problems (for example, with employment or personal relationships) on individual outcomes":

> In other words, the impact of these social issues on the probability of reconviction depends in part on the level of hope held by an individual prior to release. Participants with high hope scores seem better able to cope with the problems they encounter after they leave the prison walls. (p. 398)

A high level of hope is more likely if the "punishment" of the criminal ends with a prison term. If even after prisoners are released there is a negative connotation—a stigma—attached to them, this labeling can potentially lead to recidivism. Petersilia (2003) pointed to how "people who are labeled 'ex-prisoner' are discredited, marginalized…excluded from a variety of housing and employment opportunities" (p. 226). As a result, Petersilia pointed out, "[s]uch marginalization also has the long-term effect of weakening ties to law-abiding citizens and strengthening connections to the criminal world more generally" (p. 226). Winick (1998) also suggested the following:

> [O]fficially labeling a person "criminal" may actually become a self-fulfilling prophecy, reinforce a person's antisocial behavior, and undermine the potential of any treatments he is offered. The labeling process itself may function to provide these individuals

> with an excuse for giving in to their criminal urges. As a result, it may be more difficult for offenders to exercise the self-control that society would like to encourage. (as cited in Petersilia, 2003, p. 227)

In criminology, this stigma associated with being an ex-convict can impact future behavior, and is referred to as criminogenic effects. Petersilia (2003) suggested,

> It is possible that the offender did not change as a result of being in prison, but society's and the criminal justice system's *response* to him did. We have shown that employers are reluctant to hire ex-prisoners; landlords are hesitant to rent to them; and families and neighbors are reluctant to reconcile with them. The criminal justice system also treats ex-prisoners more harshly, increasing their probability of arrest and incarceration. If society's response makes it more difficult for the offender to resume (or establish) a noncriminal lifestyle, imprisonment may still be said to have produced criminogenic effects and increased crime in the community. In this case, the imprisonment effect is simply delayed rather than immediate. (p. 224)

Petersilia (2003) pointed out that working to assist prisoners reintegrate into society is necessary, "not only because it will be good for prisoners returning home, but because it will ultimately be good for their children, their neighbors, and the community at large" (p. 247):

> Ideally, we would like to send those to prison who are dangerous and have a high probability of continuing in crime if left in the community and not incarcerate those who are not dangerous and will likely be made worse from the experience—or, as is often said, we wish to imprison those "who are bad, not just those we are mad at." But today, most authorities, even some hard-line prison administrators, admit that a significant fraction of people being sent to prison today (possibly as many as a fifth to a quarter) should be diverted to specialized drug treatment programs or other well-structured alternatives to incarceration. (p. 225)

Petersilia (2003) suggested that soon politicians may seek to create sentences that do not collectively address crime:

> The one-size-fits-all characteristics of current mandatory sentencing schemes mean that the system is simultaneously too lenient and too harsh. On the one hand, prisons are full of low-level, nonviolent, first-time drug offenders who historically would have gotten probation. On the other hand, we have violent offenders who often serve less time than warranted because the corrections system has neither the resources nor the staff to incarcerate these persons for their full term, treat them while in prison, or monitor them sufficiently at release. (p. 231)

Crime policies that acknowledge society's role in blocking opportunities for people are supported by liberals. As Bryant (2000) explained, liberals assume that

> the ideal society is one in which there is equality of opportunity and a general consensus to accept differences in rewards as the outcomes of fair competition…Though naturally inclined to peaceful and mutually supportive relations with others, people whose opportunities for enlightenment and achievement are blocked—by the organizational and operational shortcomings and cultural biases of social institutions—are at risk of falling into crime as they try to cope with the stresses imposed on them. The institutional shortcomings that cause stress, and therefore crime, are to be remedied by legal and social reform. (p. 311)

As a result, those who follow a liberal ideology would support preventive crime policies that include addressing injustices in societal structures—such as poverty, health care, and racism, which may lead to blocked opportunities—as a way to prevent crime. Liberals see crime as caused by social, not individual, factors, and therefore support rehabilitation and treatment of offenders. Preventive policies include assisting prisoners improve their economic conditions, offering educational programs, gun-control laws, and increasing the number of police patrols in the United States (Sotirovic, 2004).

48   THE PEOPLE ARE REPRESENTED

President Bill Clinton signed the Brady Bill—named for Jim Brady, who was shot during the 1981 assassination attempt on then president Ronald Reagan—into law in 1993. The legislation included a waiting period to buy a handgun, mandatory background checks, and the ban of assault weapons. This is considered a preventive crime policy supported by liberals; in contrast, conservatives support the right to bear arms and oppose gun-control legislation. Clinton also supported adding police patrols.

While most of the crime policies supported by President George W. Bush between 2000 and 2005 were conservative, punitive policies, during the 2000 presidential campaign, George W. Bush discussed InnerChange, a prison ministry program he created for criminal rehabilitation. This preventive program, according to GeorgeWBush.com, is a "24-hours-a-day, Bible and value-based prerelease program, aimed at helping inmates achieve spiritual and moral transformation." Inmates begin the program up to 18 months prior to release and up to a year after leaving prison.

TYPES OF CRIMES COMMITTED

Between 1998 and 2004, according to the Bureau of Justice (ojp.usdoj.gov), the number of violent crimes continued to decrease, as it had in the previous 30 years. Of the people arrested in 2002 for murder, 10,285 were male, 1,108 were female, and the sex of 4,420 was unknown, presumably omitted from the report upon arrest. Among those offenders, 5,356 were white, 5,579 were black, 274 were listed as other, and the race of 4,604 was unknown. The types of crimes committed have also changed in the last 3 decades. In 1973, 47.7% were violent crimes, and that number steadily decreased for the next 30 years. In 1985, 45.2% were violent, and in 1995, 46.1% were categorized as violent. Yet, by 2002, only 22.8% of all reported crimes in the United States were violent.

The DOJ statistics also show that property crime has steadily decreased since 1973. Reported as "victimization per 1,000 households," in 1973, there were 519.9. In 1985, it dropped to 385.4 and dropped further in

American Society 49

1995 to 290.5. In 2002, it was only 159. According to the DOJ's 2002 Uniform Crime Reports, one violent crime occurs in the United States every 22.1 seconds; an aggravated assault every 35.3 seconds; a murder every 32.4 minutes; and property crime every 3 seconds. In 1993, there were 15,125 murders, but that figure dropped to 8,933 in 2002, down 40.9%. In 1993, 96,877 robberies were committed; in 2002, that decreased to 69,405, down 28.4%. In 1993, drug-abuse crimes totaled 710,922, and that rose by 2002 to 974,082, up 37%. DUIs totaled 984,141 in 1993, and that dropped to 879,210 in 2002, down 10.7%. According to the 2002 Uniform Crime Reports (ojp.usdoj.gov), adults constituted 83.5% of arrests in 2002. Males constituted 77% of arrests, most often drug abuse and DUI, including 82.6% of violent-crime arrests and 69.3% of property-crime arrests. Whites constituted 70.7% of all arrests, most often for DUI; 26.9% of all those arrested were black, most often for drug-abuse violations.

PUBLIC OPINION

In order to determine public concerns and the extent of public support for specific crime policies between 1998 and 2004, I reviewed polls in the 30th edition of the *Sourcebook of Criminal Justice Statistics 2002*—which is a compilation of more than 100 sources by the U.S. Department of Justice and Federal Bureau of Justice Statistics. Lewis and Wahl-Jorgensen (2005) noted that public-opinion polls generally involve citizens responding to existing policies. "When people are shown expressing political views, it is most likely to involve giving—or failing to give—support for the policies or actions of political leaders. When we are given a political voice, in other words, we tend to be shown following rather than leading" (p. 105). However, the polls I reviewed include questions about the major problems facing the country and what respondents see as appropriate crime policies. Therefore, the poll results offer information not only about existing policies but also about additions or changes that respondents said are needed. Notably, a majority of Americans polled support rehabilitation of criminals and preventive rather than punitive crime policies for the correctional population. This population is estimated in 2002 at 6,732,400, consisting of 3,995,165 on probation, 665,475 in jail, 1,367,856 in prison, and 753,141 on parole.

Americans' Main Concerns

I specifically looked at responses to polls in the *Sourcebook* that received the highest percentage during the two decades. In 1984, as the country's deficit rose, the largest percentage, 12%, cited excessive government spending and the federal-budget deficit as the biggest problem America faced. A decade later, in 1994, 37% cited crime and violence as their main concern. In 2000, 16% said education was the biggest problem, specifically the quality of education in America. In 2001, 13% cited ethics, morals, and family decline, which could be attributed to the President Bill Clinton–Monica Lewinsky affair that was heavily reported in the previous year. Not surprisingly, in 2002, following the September 11, 2001, terrorist attacks on the World Trade Center, 22% cited terrorism as the country's biggest problem, and a year later, 35% said they feared war or nuclear war and believed that America's biggest problem was international tensions. In 2004, 27% again cited international tensions as the biggest problem.

Confidence in the Justice System

In 1994, at the same time that Americans said the country's biggest problem was crime and violence, only 15% of Americans cited strong confidence in the criminal justice system. In 2004, that percentage jumped to 34—more than double. And, confidence in the police to protect citizens from violent crime has risen in the last decade as well. In 1995, 20% said they had a great deal of confidence, and 30% said they had quite a lot of confidence. In 2003, 20% again said they had a great deal of confidence, while 40% said they had quite a lot of confidence in the police. Police officers were also viewed by those polled as honest and having high ethical standards. In 2003, 14% said police had very high ethical standards, and 45% cited high standards, compared to only 9% responding "high" and 37 responding "very high" in 1994. This increase in perception of

American Society 51

high ethical standards may have been due to increased public awareness about the role of law enforcement officers during the World Trade Center attacks on September 11, 2001, and their continued role in protecting Americans since that time.

Crime Policies
A majority of Americans polled have consistently supported addressing social problems as the best way to combat crime. In 1990, 57% said the best way to combat crime was to attack social problems, while 36% cited more law enforcement. In August of 1994, 51% cited social problems and 42% supported more law enforcement. Yet, in 2003, 69%—two-thirds of respondents—cited attacking social problems, while only 29% called for more law enforcement. These polls show that Americans recognize the role of society and social problems as a motivator for crime.

Death Penalty
When asked in the case of a charge of murder whether they prefer to impose the death penalty or life in prison with no possibility for parole as the sentence, there was no change in the last decade in the percentage of people who supported the death penalty, but more people selected life in prison, rather than "don't know." In 1994, 50% preferred the death penalty; 32% life in prison, and 18% said they do not know. In 2000, again, 50% preferred death, 37% preferred the life sentence, and 11% said they do not know. By 2004, 50% still supported the death penalty, but almost as many supported the life sentence, with 46% selecting that option and only 4% saying they do not know. When asked if they believe that the death penalty acts as a deterrent to the commitment of murder, and that it lowers the murder rate, fewer responded yes in 2004 than in 1985. In 1985, 62% said it was a deterrent, 31% said no, and 7% did not know. In 1991, only 51% said it was a deterrent, 41% said no, and 8% were not sure. By 2004, 35 believed it was a deterrent, 62% said it was not, and 3% did not know.

Between 1998 and 2004, most respondents supported liberal crime policies. In 2000, the respondents were almost evenly divided over support for the death penalty; in 2003, more than two-thirds said attacking social problems was the best way to combat crime; and in 2004, nearly two-thirds said the death penalty did not act as a deterrent to other criminals. The shift in public support for liberal crime policies may be attributed to increased public discourse about inequalities in the American justice system.

9/11: America Responds to Terrorist Attacks
It is not surprising that following the terrorist attacks on September 11, 2001, terrorism, war, and international relations were the biggest concerns among Americans polled. However, it is also important to note that in 2001, among those polled, most—69%—still believed that attacking social programs was the better way to combat crime, even more so than adding police officers, which was Clinton's approach while President. This suggests that while crime, and specifically terrorism, was a concern on an international level, by 2002, Americans recognized that social issues were also a key cause of crime. Those polled indicated that respondents supported preventive measures and liberal policies over punitive measures and conservative policies.

RECIDIVISM AMONG SEX OFFENDERS

To illustrate the interconnectedness of beliefs about causes of crime, effectiveness of rehabilitation, and appropriate crime policies, in this section, I discuss public discourse about sex offenders. I point to examples of how mainstream media messages perpetuated a "moral panic" about sex offenders, in the process of identifying a national threat. As described by Tavener (2000), who examined television talk shows, moral panics consist of several components:

> Concerned with the overall moral, emotional, and physical health of the body politic, our cultural and political leaders identify numerous social problems as cause for concern. Panics are neither single nor isolated. They form part of a larger field of panics which together represent the current threats to the nation as particular to the present moment. They shape our understanding of

present-day social conflicts as constituting a radical rupture with the past, and implied in such a rupture is the narrative of return. If we are to find our way as a nation, we must return to the past of our forefathers. (p. 68)

Tavener further noted, "Moral panics articulate the symbolic threat that the lower classes and minority groups pose to the communality of the nation" (p. 68). Tavener (2000) suggested that "nationalistic rhetoric prepares the way for new public policy that, more often than not, creates new sites of criminality as well" (p. 68). She cited the "war" on drugs and Clinton's "three strikes" crime bill as "evidence of the power of moral panics to create consensus and legitimate repression which are clothed as rational and progressive social reform" (p. 68). Media play a role in this perpetuation, she noted: "Moral panics are rhetorically framed and circulated by a media that has the power to portray events, both near and far, as up close and personal" (p. 68). Tavener concluded that "psychic stress...comes from living in a society that celebrates egalitarianism even as it reinforces its hierarchies of value, wealth, status, and power" (p. 83).

In the next sections, I discuss scientific research that has been conducted regarding recidivism rates for sex offenders, and illustrate how media discourse has contributed to the erroneous perception that recidivism rates are "high." While that term is relative, I will show that public perception differs greatly from scientific data on this issue. Further, I discuss court rulings about legislation requiring community notification of sex offenders once they are released from prison. As scholars suggest, this legislation was proposed by politicians in response to public outcry for protection from what is perceived as a national threat. The result of notification legislation, researchers point out, is that sex offenders are further alienated from the community upon release from prison, because law-abiding citizens fear that they or their children will be the next victim.

Public Perception of Sex Offenders

The perception in U.S. society is that sex offenders have a recidivism rate higher than that of many other kinds of offenders. Therefore, they are seen as unable to be rehabilitated, and pose a serious threat to people in society, specifically children. As a result, understandably, a tough-on-crime policy has been sought to protect society. However, the goal by politicians has been not to keep sex offenders imprisoned longer, but to notify people where they are in society. Current crime policy in the United States calls for relatively short prison sentences for sex offenders, and requires them to register with their local counties once they leave prison.

A 2003 study conducted by the U.S. Department of Justice, Office of Justice Programs, Bureau of Justice Statistics, indicates that prison sentences for sex offenders convicted of rape or sexual assault are short. The average prison sentence for sex offenders was 8 years, with 3.5 years actually served prior to release. The average prison sentence for child molesters was 7 years, with 3 years served on average. However, the DOJ study does not support the notion that sex offenders have a high recidivism rate, or that they cannot be rehabilitated. The study, described by the department as "the largest followup study ever conducted of convicted sex offenders following discharge from prison" found that "within three years following their 1994 state prison release, 5.3% of sex offenders (men who had committed rape or sexual assault) were rearrested for another sex crime," according to the U.S. Department of Justice website (http://www.ojp.usdoj.gov/bjs/abstract/rsorp94.htm). If all crimes were included, 43% of sex offenders were rearrested. These statistics indicate that recidivism is high—but not for additional sex offenses. Five percent is a relatively small number, and certainly much smaller than the popular perception that has been created in society that virtually all sex offenders reoffend.

Additional scientific studies support the DOJ study findings, but also raise questions about the accuracy of data available on sex offenders. Pyschologists Turner, Bingham, and Andrasik (2000) studied 200 sex offenders who had been released from the Florida Department of Corrections. They found a lower recidivism rate among men who had completed a treatment program compared to those who were not required to undergo treatment. Four percent of those who completed treatment recidivated within 5 years; 14% of those not receiving treatment reoffended. In addition, psychologists Lang, Pugh, and Langevin (1988) studied 22 pedophiles and 29 men convicted of incest who had completed a treatment program. In a follow-up study, they found that 7% of incest offenders reoffended; 18% of pedophiles reoffended within 3 years of completing the treatment.

Criminologists Lowenkamp and Latessa (2005) studied residential treatment programs in Ohio and found that among low- and low-moderate-risk offenders, there was an increase in recidivism among those who participated in the program. However, the program was determined to be effective among 70% of moderate- and high-risk offenders, with reduced recidivism "in magnitude and frequency with these two groups of offenders compared with the lower risk offenders" (p. 284).

Reviewing the effectiveness of a treatment program in New Jersey, Zgoba, Sager, and Witt (2003) found that the 10-year reconviction rate for sexual offenses was 8.6% for offenders who had completed treatment at the Adult Diagnostic and Treatment Center, which is part of the New Jersey Department of Corrections. Prisoners can choose to complete the sentence in this treatment program instead of among the general prison population. Among the general prison population of sex offenders, 12.7% had reoffended within the 10-year period. They also found reoffense rates for nonsexual offenders to be 25.8% for ADTC participants and 44.1% for the general prison population of sex offenders. However, Zgoba and colleagues cited a potential flaw in many recidivism studies: They acknowledged that they only had access to reconviction data, and based their findings on this information. More accurate data could be rearrest figures, rather than reconviction figures.

In a study assessing four methods, Sjostedt and Langstrom (2002), forensic psychiatrists in Sweden, found only one of four measures to be better than chance. In addition, Falshaw, Bates, Patel, Corbett, and Friendship (2003) found that some methods used to collect reconviction data did not accurately reflect sexual behavior by sex offenders. For the study, data was collected on a group of 173 offenders who had completed the Thames Valley Sex Offender Groupwork Programme, a community treatment program. They reviewed reconviction information from a police database, an offenders index, and the program files. Each method revealed different rates of recidivism. Using the offenders index, reconviction rates could not be calculated in 12% of the group; in the remaining cases, sexual reconviction was calculated at 3%. Using the police database, 19% could not be identified, and the reconviction rate was 9% for the remaining cases. Using records from the Thames Valley program, 6% had been reconvicted of a sexual offense, 7% were sexual reoffenders, and 16% were labeled as recidivists. Sexual reconviction included conviction, reoffending was redefined as engaging in an illegal sexual act (but may not have included rearrest), and recidivism was defined as engaging in "offence-related behaviour, legal or illegal, with a clear sexual motivation" (p. 211). These classifications, they also acknowledged, are debatable, and they suggest that clarification of recidivism rates may also be warranted to result in more accurate findings.

In 2004, Bates, Falshaw, Patel, Corbett, and Friendship conducted another follow-up study of 183 men who completed the Thames Valley Sex Offender Groupwork Programme, and found that 5.4% were reconvicted of at least one sexual offense after treatment; half of these included a contact sexual offense. Another 1.1% reoffended, but had not been reconvicted. An additional 9.2% exhibited behavior that was considered recidivism, but in those cases the researchers determined there was no evidence "that any act of sexual abuse had taken place but the behavior was clearly risky" (p. 34). "Risky" behavior identified included forming friendships with children, having unsupervised visits with his own child against a court order, and not signing the Sex Offender Register. They concluded that "sex offenders can take much longer periods of time to re-offend than other kinds of offenders" (p. 35). Psychologists Barbaree and Marshall (1988) studied 170 male sex offenders, and also found that over a longer period of time, the recidivism rate increased. Of the 170, 20.7% had reoffended, and among 58 who had completed a treatment program, 13% reoffended. Recidivism rates increased as the follow-up time period was extended. Dividing the follow-up period into three categories, they found that 12.5% reoffended in the first 2 years,

38.5% reoffended between 2 and 4 years later, and after more than 4 years, 64.3% had reoffended. They found predictors of recidivism to be sexual deviance, but social status, which included socioeconomic status and IQ, was not a significant predictor of recidivism.

Evaluating arrests in Illinois in 1990, Sample and Bray (2003) found that those arrested for robbery had the highest probability of being arrested within 5 years, at 74.9%. The rearrest rate for burglary was 66%; nonsexual assault was 58%; and larceny was 52.9%. Sex offenders were likely to be rearrested for any offense within 1 year at a rate of 21.3%; 37.4% after 2 years; and 45.1% after 5 years. The offense-specific rearrest rate of sex offenders who committed a sexual offense was 2.2% after 1 year, 4.8% after 3 years, and 6.5% after 5 years. As a result, they found that the reason that is often given for encouraging surveillance of sex offenders—that they are more likely to reoffend than other offenders—is unsubstantiated.

Mainstream Reports of Recidivism Among Sex Offenders

To determine how mainstream media outlets report about sex offenders and recidivism—and to illustrate how a high rate of recidivism among sex offenders was reinforced even though scientific evidence does not support this claim—I conducted a Lexis-Nexis search of the combined terms "recidivism" and "sex offenses" for the 2 years following the release of the federal government's study in 2003. My search turned up only two reports citing the 5% recidivism findings in the federal DOJ study, in the *Star Tribune* in Minneapolis, Minnesota, on May 3, 2004 (Furst, 2004), and in the *San Francisco Chronicle* on July 12, 2004 (Doyle, 2004). Additionally, a July 3, 2004, article in *The Seattle Times* cited a separate state study that over a 20-year period, 70% of inmates convicted of sex offenses were at "the lowest risk of reoffending" (Martin, 2004, n.p.). Mainstream news reports continue to emphasize high recidivism rates, but not specific scientific findings about recidivism rates for sex offenses. By emphasizing high recidivism rates among sex offenders, mainstream news organizations create a sense of danger that sex offenders are "on the loose." For example, A *CBS News* report on the company's Web site on June 25, 2001, began by stating the following:

> The Colorado State Supreme Court may have given over a thousand rapists and child molesters a get out of jail free card, with rulings Monday that limits [sic] the length of parole of offenders sentenced in particular years. The rulings came in the cases of five sex offenders who argued they were wrongly sentenced to parole terms longer than their prison sentences. ("Sex Offenders Could Go Free," n.p.)

In this report, information was included from people interviewed about the high recidivism rate. Corrections Director John Suthers said: "It's not good news from a community safety standpoint. One thing we know about sex offenders is you don't cure them, you manage them. To manage them you need to supervise them." The piece concluded by citing "studies," not named or explained further, as showing "that as many as one out of every two sexual predators, once freed, repeats their crime." Although, it did also cite a 1983 study by the federal Bureau of Justice Statistics that "found that sexual offenders and rapists tended to commit the same crime again less frequently than other violent criminals." However, the more recent DOJ study released in 2003, indicating only a 5% rate, was not included.

Major news reports also tend to focus on single cases and present them as examples of a larger problem, a common technique employed by journalists to engage the audience by showing that the issue has a personal impact on people. However, in the process of reporting crimes by sex offenders in this way, reports have emphasized the high recidivism rate, creating a misconception in the culture. For example, a *USA Today* article in March 25, 2005, stated: "The arrest of a convicted sex offender this week in the kidnapping, rape, and murder of a 9-year-old Florida girl underscores a national problem, experts say: Authorities don't have enough money to identify, treat and monitor the sex offenders most likely to repeat their crimes" (Memmott, n.p.).

An April 21, 2005, edition of the political-commentary program *Hannity & Colmes* on Fox News Channel also followed this format of focusing on a single, high-profile crime. Residents at a Winter Park, Florida, apartment building protested outside the building "in order to pressure the landlord to convict two registered sex offenders who were living there." The protest, Hannity stated, was in response to the murders of 13-year-old Sarah Lunde and 9-year-old Jessica Lunsford, both of Florida. Hannity stated,

> The thing we're discovering here, Barry, more than anything else is we're discovering that the recidivism rate is so high I do not want a sex offender next to my house with children. I do not want one in my neighborhood, and I want to be informed by my government that one lives there, because what happened to Mark should never happen to another father and mother in this country again.

In addition to personalizing the stories, journalists often use extreme cases to illustrate the impact of crime. For example, a June 18, 2005, report on *World News Tonight Saturday* on ABC focused on an extreme case of child molestation, but never cited an actual recidivism rate, except to include an interview with someone who stated it was very high. Anchor Bob Woodruff introduced the piece by citing a "California man *could be* responsible for a staggering 36,000 cases of child molestation" (emphasis mine). Reporter Pierre Thomas explained: "Police raided [convicted child molester Dean] Schwartzmiller's home in May and made a stunning discovery, seven notebooks listing 36,000 boys' names. Next to the names, codes [appeared] to indicate how the children were molested." They interviewed John Clark, of Immigration and Customs Enforcement, who said, "There's a recidivism rate with child molesters that's phenomenal. They do seem to just continue on." A specific recidivism rate was not included, but Woodruff did emphasize that "there are about 500,000 registered sex offenders in the US," and Thomas stated, Schwartzmiller "was one of more than 100,000 sex offenders who are unaccounted for." Little evidence is presented to suggest that the man actually committed 36,000 cases of child molestation. In the report, even the immigration officer said it could be one-tenth of that, and rightly emphasized that it would still be a staggering number of offenses, but the inflated and highly speculative number was used to introduce and frame the report in this context, in order to grab the attention of the audience. In the process, the facts are vague and distorted.

Strengthening Legislation Regarding Sex Offenders
In recent years, legislators have sought ways to strengthen laws regarding sex offenders, by extending notification to the Internet, and even going beyond notification. In an article in the *St. Petersburg Times* on April 20, 2005, following the high-profile crimes against Jessica Lunsford and Sarah Lunde, Florida legislators said they wanted to include minimum mandatory sentences of 25 years in prison for child molesters. According to the proposed legislation, following release, the person would be monitored electronically for life (Johnson, 2005). However, Democratic Rep. Shelley Vana, who supports life-in-prison sentences, argued that the electronic monitoring did not protect anyone. Another Democratic Representative, Dan Gelber, suggested surgically implanting a GPS monitor, and Democratic Rep. Ron Greenstein suggested chemical castration. The bill was sponsored by Republican Rep. Charlie Dean, who did not support these additional measures, according to the article, and said he was "trying to take a more measured approach to tracking the state's registered sex offenders" (Johnson, 2005, ¶17, Retrieved November 18, 2005, from http://sptimes.com).

Based on these reports, it appears that some legislators on both sides of the aisle are guided by public perception, not scientific studies and evidence, in deciding what is the most effective crime policy for sex offenders. This example also raises the question of how to define "harsh" policies in society. If recidivism is in fact high, then life in prison seems reasonable, but if it is not, then it seems overly harsh.

Court Rulings on Notification Laws
U.S. courts, including those in Connecticut, Washington, New York, and New Jersey, have repeatedly upheld the constitutionality of notification

laws. One key ruling on the issue of crime policies involving sex offenders was a 1997 decision by the U.S. Supreme Court in *Kansas v. Hendricks*. The court ruled that involuntary civil commitment was not unconstitutional, so convicted sex offenders can be held in a mental-health facility beyond the term of a prison sentence. Writing about the implications of the ruling, LaFond (2000), a professor at The University of Missouri-Kansas, cited the misconception about recidivism in how the public perceives laws about sex offenders. He said:

> Today people in the United States are enraged by sex offenders and the crimes they commit. One primary catalyst to this communal rage is a small number of horrible crimes committed by convicted sex offenders against children, which received wide media coverage. These crimes aroused public anger and generated widespread demands that new laws be enacted to ensure that sex offenders will never victimize again. (p. 153)

By moving the issue of sex offenders to the mental-health system, rather than the criminal justice system, LaFond cited the ruling as being dependent on a "prediction of future harm" rather than on "past harmful conduct" (p. 156), as is the case in the criminal justice system. LaFond cited this as a shift in the "ideology of rehabilitating offenders which came to dominate American criminal law during the 1960s and 1970s" (p. 157) to one in the 1990s that increased the state's authority in an effort to maintain social control. The ruling, LaFond said, emphasizes "the community's interest in safety alone is sufficient to justify civil commitment" (p. 163). As a result, he saw the ruling as creating:

> a slippery slope with a very steep pitch. After *Hendricks* there may be no meaningful limit on what a state legislature can characterize as a mental condition sufficient to support involuntary civil confinement...In short, civil commitment can be used as a "piggy-back" system of social control that can be activated when the authority of the criminal justice system terminates. (pp. 165–166)

LaFond further questioned whether civil commitment gives too much authority to states to act on very little evidence:

> *Hendricks* has empowered the state to use involuntary civil commitment solely as a protective device without requiring proof of mental illness or providing treatment. In so doing *Hendricks* may encourage policy-makers in the U.S.A. to refocus involuntary civil commitment to protect the public from perceived danger rather than to provide help for seriously disturbed individuals. (p. 167)

Following enactment of American notification laws, European countries adopted similar legislation, and European scholars have also criticized the implementation of these laws, suggesting that "sexual offending behavior may be increased if the offender feels socially isolated," according to Irish sociologist McAlinden (2000). She said that notification laws serve to stigmatize the offender, and while she asserted that this may be appropriate "to impress upon them the wrongness of their actions," she also said that treatment programs may be more effective in protecting the public and rehabilitating the offender because they encourage the offender to control the behavior "rather than stigmatizing and socially excluding the offender through registration and community notification" (p. 94). As McAlinden suggested, notification laws for sex offenders can be seen as a form of labeling that could lead to additional crimes for social, not psychological, reasons.

As I have shown, even scholars who support rehabilitation and preventive crime policies acknowledge that some people are so dangerous that they should be removed from society. However, based on scientific research about the recidivism rate for sex offenders, criminologists and sociologists are not convinced that sex offenders have the high recidivism rate portrayed in the media. Ultimately, however, Americans may conclude that strict sentences that include community notification are warranted for sex offenders because of the heinous nature of sex offenses. Yet, the current discourse about sex offenders, as I have shown, is not focused on the nature of the crime as much as it is on high recidivism rates—a notion perpetuated by mainstream media.

In practice, the result of community-notification legislation for sex offenders is community alienation—which may actually perpetuate crime. Returning sex offenders to society, only to label them as dangerous, may prevent them from ever being rehabilitated, particularly because cultural institutions continue to reinforce the idea that sex offenders pose a national threat. This seems to be a contradictory message; the sex offenders are considered dangerous enough to require community notification, but not dangerous enough to be kept in prison. Given the public discourse regarding sex offenders, releasing them from prison on the condition of mandatory community notification appears to serve to perpetuate a moral panic about the threat they pose to law-abiding citizens. Community-notification legislation may have been intended as a way to reduce prison sentences—possibly in an effort to acknowledge that rehabilitation occurred in an individual. However, public discourse about sex offenders, and community-notification requirements, reinforce the Other status for convicted sex offenders.

While I focused in this example on sex offenders, Tavener's (2000) approach to examining moral panics can be applied to television representations of criminals in general. I discuss these representations further in chapter 6. As I will show, the psychic stress resulting from being treated as a social outcast, which Tavener described, is depicted in fictional representations of criminals. This process is shown, in some cases, to lead to criminal behavior—a notion, as I have shown in this chapter, supported by criminologists and sociologists as well communication researchers.

CHAPTER 3

METHODOLOGY

In this chapter, I discuss the method I used to conduct a discourse analysis of crime shows airing between 1998 and 2004. In addition, I review business and regulatory aspects of the television industry that impact content, including ratings, ownership, and FCC regulations. I also provide a summary of each series I analyze in this study.

Crime shows were popular between 1998 and 2004, on both broadcast and cable networks. During this time, CBS aired *CSI* (2000–present), *CSI: Miami* (2002–present), and *CSI: New York* (2004–present), all with a focus on forensic evidence used to determine guilt; *The District* (2000–2004), starring the chief of a Washington DC department; *Without a Trace* (2002–present), portraying FBI investigations involving missing people; and *JAG* (1995–2005) and *NCIS* (2003–present), depicting military investigations and trials. NBC aired four *Law & Order* series. The first half of the original (1990–present) focused on police procedure, while the second half depicted the trial. *Law & Order: Special Victims Unit* (1999–present) depicted the work of police detectives in the unit that dealt with sexual crimes. *Law & Order: Criminal Intent* (2000–present) debuted the following year, and used more of a "whodunit" format, with the suspect only revealed at the end of the episode, not early on as in the original series. *Law & Order: Trial by Jury* (2004–2005) was similar to the original, but focused more on the trial portion of cases than on the police work. On Fox, *24* (2001–present) profiled government agents in the Counter Terrorism Unit in "real time," with 1 hour of the show representing 1 hour of the characters' lives. Each season depicts a 24-hour period. On ABC, *Alias* (2001–2006) profiled the undercover work of CIA operatives, while *Boston Legal* (2004–present), a spin-off of *The Practice*, focuses on the cases involving a legal firm in Boston.

During this time, several cable networks offered original programming that featured crime. On Lifetime, *Missing* (formerly *1-800-Missing*) (2003–2006) depicted FBI agents who investigate missing-persons cases, and *The Division* (2001–2004) traced the work of five female detectives in San Francisco. USA's comedy *Monk* (2002–present) chronicled the life of a former San Francisco police detective who stopped working after his wife died and who developed extreme obsessive-compulsive disorder. He later worked with the department as a consultant. The premium-cable channel HBO also aired *Deadwood* (2004–present), about law and order in the wild West during the late 1800s, and *The Wire* (2002–present) portrayed homicide and narcotics detectives in Baltimore. For David Simon, executive producer of HBO's *The Wire*, the shift was a conscious effort to raise awareness about cultural institutions. Poniewozik (2004) noted:

> [T]he series is only nominally a cop show but rather a story about "how the working class has been betrayed" and how institutions—from companies to police departments to gangs—fail the little guy...One of the problems with the American cop show is that we have demonized the underclass and made them out to be subhuman. (p. 66)

Among all these fictional series that were airing, I selected eight that represented the range of depictions present in the genre during the 6-year period. The HBO series *Oz* and *The Sopranos* were selected because they both starred criminals. In an article in *Television Week*, Chris Rohrs, president of the Television Bureau of Advertising, said that a lot of cultural attention is paid to cable programs, likely because journalists watch these shows, which he called "appointment television." These are programs that people plan to watch on a weekly basis. The sitcom *Seinfeld* used to be appointment television; today, the drama series *The Shield* has that distinction. *The Shield*, which began its fourth season in 2005 and ranks No. 865 in the ratings, has outlasted other series in the genre, including the fourth installment of *Law & Order*, which was expected to be a ratings winner like its three counterparts in the franchise, but failed. So, while ratings for cable programs such as *The Shield* are only a fraction of broadcast networks' ratings, they still attract a lot of attention culturally and have loyal audiences, which in turn is attractive to advertisers and network executives as well.

Police detectives were the focus of *NYPD Blue* on ABC, which offered a view of detectives working in a lower-economic-class section of New York City, while *Law & Order* on NBC provided a portrayal of police in a middle- to upper-middle-class section of the city. Further, *Law & Order* depicted the trial portion of the case, in addition to the police procedures. *Cold Case* on CBS was chosen because it focused on detectives attempting to uncover previously unsolved cases—also a new variation on depictions of police detectives in the genre, which traditionally focused on current murders and other crimes. *The Shield* on FX starred a police officer—but one who was corrupt—so it offered a very different depiction than what had been seen in the genre in the past. I selected *The Practice* on ABC because it was one of the few remaining series that offered depictions of criminal-defense attorneys—rather than prosecutors, as seen in *Law & Order*. Finally, *The Jury*, debuting on Fox in the summer of 2004, offered a new portrayal in the genre, as it focused strictly on jury deliberations. The series included recurring characters—prosecutors and defense lawyers—but they were so minimally seen in the episodes that the main characters were a new set of jurors each week.

I had also originally intended to include *Hack* and *The Guardian*, both of which aired on CBS, in my analysis. However, the shows were cancelled before I began the study, and copies were not available. *Hack* (2002–2004) starred a Philadelphia police officer removed from the force for stealing money retrieved during a drug bust. Labeled as "dark" during the first season (Hiltbrand, 2003), the lighter tone of the second season did not save it from cancellation. At the end of its first season, it ranked 94th (Hiltbrand, 2003). The drama focused on Mike Olshansky (played by actor David Morse), who was removed from the police force after he took drug money while investigating a crime. He worked as a cab driver, but continued to assist his former partner, Marcellus Washington. *The Guardian* (2001–2004) starred a Pittsburgh attorney sentenced to community service after a drug conviction. It averaged 10.5 million viewers in its final season (Elber, 2004). Both *The Guardian* and *Hack* continued the depictions seen in *Oz, The Sopranos,* and *The Shield*, telling crime stories from a new perspective, in these cases, by criminals who previously worked as police officers and lawyers, and then returned to that work, either formally or informally, during the series as a way to reform their lives.

In selecting programs for this study, I took into account the business aspects of the industry as well as the content of each series, as both have an impact on representations on television, as I discuss in the next section. Ultimately, I chose series that collectively offer a range of portrayals about crime and criminals that air on broadcast, basic-cable, and premium-cable channels.

THE BUSINESS OF TELEVISION

While my focus is on the representations of crime and criminals on television between 1998 and 2004, as Gitlin (1972) suggested, it is also important to note that television programs are part of a business. "The mass media in capitalism are private properties before all else. Their prime self-conscious function is profit-making" (p. 338). Media organizations are corporations first and foremost. Whether they deal with news-media productions or entertainment-media productions, the goal is the same: profit. While this research focuses on the cultural impact of representations of criminals on television, the structure of the medium influences television-program content and impacts cultural representations. Turow (1989) addressed the impact of the business structure of television on content:

> [T]elevision creators work under systems of creativity and constraint that encourage continuity with the establishment as well as deviation from it. The result of the complex cross-organizational headaches would seem to be mixed: TV's creations are not platforms for the democratic presentation of a wide gamut of ideologies. But neither are TV's programs mere channels that transmit the established powers' versions of their world through prime-time stories. (p. xviii–xviii)

The television industry is impacted by ratings, crossownership, and FCC regulations, as I discuss in the following sections.

Ratings

Ratings equal profit in the television industry, and in the last decade, crime shows have garnered large audiences. Ratings translate into profit for networks because they determine how much a commercial spot can be sold for during a specific television program. The higher the ratings, the higher the cost of the commercial. The success of crime shows in the 1990s has sparked "franchises" that included several spin-offs of the original series. Since 1990, NBC has had ratings success with the *Law & Order* franchise created by Dick Wolf that includes the original, *Law & Order: Special Victims Unit*, and *Law & Order: Criminal Intent*. The crime franchise enabled NBC to become the ratings leader, along with other popular series, including *ER, Seinfeld, Frasier*, and *Friends*. However, by 2004–2005, the franchise showed signs of weakening, as *CSI*, another crime-based show that developed into a franchise, led CBS to garner the largest television audience. By this time, NBC's three popular sitcoms were no longer airing, and a fourth *Law & Order* series, *Trial by Jury*, failed after one season, resulting in NBC dropping to third place in overall ratings (Lowry, Grover, & Brady, 2005). The network ended the season in fourth place.

The forensic-focused *CSI* was created by Jerry Bruckheimer, producer of several television series, including the reality show *Amazing Race*, and the films *Top Gun*, *Beverly Hills Cop*, *Flashdance*, *Pearl Harbor*, and *Black Hawk Down*, among others.

CSI was the most watched drama, according to an article in *Broadcasting & Cable*, and helped CBS rise to ratings-leader status (Benson & Romano, 2005). As Poniewozik (2004) explained, the series was seen as both progressive—moving beyond past genre elements—and traditional by mainstream media critics:

> *CSI* and its cohort [*CSI: New York*] have taught TV new visual tricks, raised its production standards and perhaps shown the dinosaur networks a way to survive the swarm of nimble cable competitors…But they have also—cop show after doctor-cop show after military-cop show—made it more homogeneous. (p. 63)

Bruckheimer has successfully spun off *CSI* into two additional series, *CSI: Miami* and *CSI: New York*. Bruckheimer also produces two other popular shows in the genre for CBS, *Cold Case* and *Without a Trace*. Further, he developed two new crime shows for the 2005–2006 season. *Close to Home*, which aired on CBS, was described on the official CBS website as a series about an "aggressive prosecutor with a near perfect conviction record who tries the cases that take place in her own backyard." *Just Legal*, which aired on the WB, was described as "a lighter," more comedic depiction of "a down-on-his-luck lawyer and an idealistic teenage partner" (Benson & Romano, 2005, n.p.). Even though these new series by Bruckheimer were not officially a franchise, his shows have proven successful, so he continued to get opportunities from many networks to develop new series. The success of his past shows was seen as an indicator that he would have success with future shows as well. Bruckheimer's and Wolf's winning formula has influenced the content of television programs because they have seemingly created a model for others to follow to ensure they will produce a hit series. In the case of these two programs, however, the formula did not work. *Close to Home* and *Just Legal* only aired for one season. Still, the result in recent years has been that the crime genre has

Methodology   71

grown in popularity, and in the process, some positive, progressive representations have emerged. These progressive representations pose questions about criminals and the justice system that broaden the discussion about crime, including whether rehabilitation works, and the underlying causes of crime, which will be discussed further in chapters 5–8.

Vertical Integration
In addition to ratings success, crossownership also influences the content of programs on television. Media companies strive for vertical integration, where they own several media outlets in various mediums. As a result, fewer companies own more networks. Crossownership enables companies to use all outlets to crosspromote programs. Examples of vertical integration include Viacom. Viacom owns the broadcast networks CBS and UPN, and several cable networks, including Showtime, Flix, The Movie Channel, The Sundance Channel, MTV, MTV2, CMT, Spike TV, Nickelodeon, VH1, Comedy Central, Nick at Nite, TV Land, and BET. Through Paramount Television and CBS Enterprises, it produces television programs. It owns several radio stations through Infinity Broadcasting. The company's Paramount Pictures produces movies. It also owns the publishing company Simon and Schuster, and has businesses that produce for the theatre. Viacom owns *Cold Case*, which I analyzed in this study.

Disney owns the broadcast network ABC, and the cable channels Lifetime, A&E, E!, SoapNet, ESPN, The Disney Channel, ABC Family, and Toon Disney. Its entertainment company, Buena Vista, produces television shows and music. Walt Disney Studios produces movies, and is the parent company of Touchstone Pictures, Hollywood Pictures, Miramax Films, and Dimension Films. Disney also owns several radio stations, produces for Broadway, and publishes through Hyperion Books. Disney owned *The Practice* and *NYPD Blue*, which I included in my analysis.

NBC Universal owns the broadcast networks NBC and Telemundo, and the cable networks Bravo, Sci Fi, and USA. It also produces television and radio shows as well as movies through Universal Pictures and Focus Features. NBC Universal owns *Law & Order*, which I examined in this study.

Time Warner owns the cable channel HBO, as well as the Internet company America Online, the film company New Line Cinema and Time Inc., which produces *Time* magazine. Time Warner Cable offers cable, phone, and high-speed Internet services. It owns Warner Bros. Entertainment, which produces for movies, television, and video. It also owns Turner Broadcasting System, which includes the cable channels TNT, TBS, Turner Classic Movies, The Cartoon Network, and CNN. Two series I analyzed—*Oz* and *The Sopranos*—are products of the premium-cable channel HBO. *Oz* ended its run in 1997; *The Sopranos* ended its run in 2007.

News Corporation owns the broadcast network Fox, and the cable channels FX, Fox News Channel, Fox Sports Network, The National Geographic Channel, and The Speed Channel. The company produces movies through 20th Century Fox, Fox Searchlight, and Fox Studios. The company also produces programs and provides news to radio stations. It publishes *The New York Post* newspaper, *The Weekly Standard*, *TV Guide*, and *Inside Out* magazines, and books through the publishing companies Harper Collins, ReganBooks, and Zondervan. Of the eight fictional series I included in this study, two were produced by News Corporation companies. *The Jury* aired on Fox in 2004, and *The Shield* airs on the basic-cable channel FX.

Encouraged by crossownership, additional new episodes, beyond the traditional 22 per season, are being produced (Benson & Romano, 2005). This move is in response to fan complaints of too many reruns in a season. Network executives hope to retain viewers for the duration of the season—which stretches from September through May. However, there is also a direct business incentive for executives to produce more shows: They can sell shows for syndication at a higher price if there are 100 episodes already produced. The increased crossownership in the industry has made reaching 100 episodes quickly a goal. According to Benson & Romano (2005) in *Broadcasting & Cable*,

> When the shows were under separate ownership, the networks had no vested interest in seeing them succeed. Now with vertical

integration putting all the networks under the same roof as the production units, it is in the networks' best interest to rack up the episodes as fast as possible. They can get there in four years with 26 episodes versus five years with 22 episodes. (n.p.)

It is clear that the business benefits of vertical integration have an impact on the content of television programs, particularly as more programs are being produced, and where products can be crosspromoted through various channels.

FCC Content Regulations
Regulation by the Federal Communications Commission also impacts what is seen on television. According to the commission's Web site, FCC.gov, the commission is an independent United States government agency established by the Communications Act of 1934 to "regulate interstate and international communications by radio, television, wire, satellite and cable." The Media Bureau of the commission "develops, recommends and administers the policy and licensing programs relating to electronic media, including cable television, broadcast television, and radio in the United States and its territories. The Media Bureau also handles post-licensing matters regarding Direct Broadcast Satellite service." The Video Division within the Media Bureau regulates television. The FCC can regulate the content, and can ban language that is determined to be obscene for broadcast networks. According to the FCC Web site,

> The Communications Act prohibits us from censoring broadcast matter and, therefore, our role in overseeing the content of programming is very limited. We are authorized to fine a station or revoke its license if it has, among other things, aired *obscene language, broadcast indecent language* when children are likely to be in the audience, broadcast some types of *lottery information*, or solicited *money under false pretenses*...Obscene speech is not protected by the First Amendment and cannot be broadcast at any time. To be obscene, material must meet a three-prong test: (1) an average person, applying contemporary community standards, must find that the material, as a whole, appeals to the prurient

interest; (2) the material must depict or describe, in a patently offensive way, sexual conduct specifically defined by applicable law; and (3) the material, taken as a whole, must lack serious literary, artistic, political, or scientific value.

The two lesser categories of offensive content, indecent and profane broadcasts, are both restricted by the FCC to air between 10 p.m. and 6 a.m. "The Commission has defined broadcast indecency as language or material that, in context, depicts or describes, in terms patently offensive as measured by contemporary community standards for the broadcast medium, sexual or excretory organs or activities." To determine whether language meets these criteria, according to the FCC, "the standard is that of an average broadcast viewer or listener and not the sensibilities of any individual complainant." The Web site further states that indecent content is content that does not meet the definition of obscenity, and therefore, is protected by the First Amendment and cannot be banned, but it can be restricted "in order to avoid its broadcast during times of day when there is a reasonable risk that children may be in the audience." Content is considered profane, according to the FCC, when it includes "language that denot[es] certain of those personally reviling epithets naturally tending to provoke violent resentment or denoting language so grossly offensive to members of the public who actually hear it as to amount to a nuisance." It is similarly restricted to air during evening hours, but cannot be banned.

These regulations and restrictions apply to the content on broadcast channels, but the FCC does not have jurisdiction over cable TV, and therefore, it cannot ban the content on cable channels, such as the premium-cable channel HBO and the basic-cable channel FX. The FCC Web site notes, "cable TV channels are available only by subscription and cannot be received over the air, and they are subject to different FCC rules than broadcast stations." In 2004, legislators discussed whether the FCC should have the ability to regulate cable content in the same way it regulates over-the-air content. As reported in a May 16, 2004, article in *The San Francisco Chronicle*, Rep. Joe Barton, who heads the

Methodology 75

House Energy and Commerce Committee that oversees the FCC, told attendees at the National Association of Broadcasters' convention, "If I can see it on my TV and my grandson can click and watch a channel, whether it's satellite, over-the-air or cable, the same rules in terms of decency should apply" (Curiel, 2004, ¶4, Retrieved November 18, 2005, from http://www.SFGate.com). However, the article also noted that media executives felt that the FCC began to harshly enforce regulations following the February 2004 Super Bowl, when during the half-time show, Justin Timberlake tore off a piece of Janet Jackson's costume and exposed her breast during the performance that was broadcast live. When interviewed for the *Chronicle* article, Attorney Robert Corn-Revere, who filed a petition on behalf of 24 media organizations asking the FCC to "reconsider its ruling against NBC, which was reprimanded for airing a Golden Globes broadcast during which the singer Bono used a seven-letter expletive as an adjective," said, "There really is a separate constitutional standard for regulating one medium, and the courts up to this point have uniformly held that indecency regulations are unconstitutional when applied to cable."

Not bound by FCC regulations, cable series have offered new depictions in the crime genre. Rather than seeking status-quo portrayals that appeal to advertisers, cable programs have expanded the representations, particularly those of criminals in the crime genre. Seeking to differentiate itself from the rest of the industry, particularly broadcast programs, HBO's slogan is "It's not TV, it's HBO." While cable programs have lower ratings than broadcast-network programs, the cultural impact of these programs extends beyond ratings, ownership, and content regulations. Many cable programs are highly discussed in mainstream publications, such as newspapers and magazines, in part because they offer new representations that are described in mainstream publications as groundbreaking. For example, *The Shield* on the cable station FX, while not garnering a huge audience, does have a significant cultural impact because there is so much discussion about the program in the mass media. Its impact extends beyond the viewing process into a mainstream discourse in newspapers and magazines about the show and its content.

SERIES SUMMARIES

I decided to analyze how crime, criminals, and the American justice system is depicted in eight fictional programs, two reality programs, and four documentaries that aired between 1998 and 2004. I analyzed the fictional programs *The Practice*, *The Shield*, *NYPD Blue*, *Cold Case*, and *Law & Order* (which place legal authorities as the main characters); *Oz* and *The Sopranos* (placing criminals as the stars); and *The Jury* (showing crime from the perspective of jurors); the reality programs *COPS* and *America's Most Wanted*; and the documentaries *Capturing the Friedmans*, *America Undercover: Gladiator Days: Anatomy of a Prison Murder*, *Deadline*, and *In the Jury Room*. The selections were based primarily on the content of each program and the focus evident by the main starring roles. The series were selected because they represented the range of depictions evident in starring roles in the genre at the time. A further practical consideration was whether enough episodes of the programs were accessible and could be viewed.

A summary of each fictional series I analyzed follows. The reality series are discussed are discussed further in chapter 8 and the documentaries are examined in chapter 9.

The Sopranos

The Sopranos, an HBO original series that first aired in 1999, was created by David Chase, who previously worked as a director and writer on *The Rockford Files* in the 1970s and *Northern Exposure* in the 1990s. *The Sopranos* tells the story of a New Jersey-based mob family run by Tony Soprano. Emphasis is on the traditional suburban family life of Tony Soprano, as well as his life as the boss of a Mafia family.

Tony is plagued by anxiety attacks from a panic disorder, for which he is treated by a psychiatrist, Dr. Jennifer Melfi. In the pilot episode, Tony has recently taken over as head of the Mafia family business, which his father once headed. As leader, Tony must decide how to run his organized-crime business, and in the process, experiences dissent among the ranks of his mob family, which includes Tony's cousin Christopher Moltisanti, and Tony's consigliere, Silvio Dante. He also has to address problems associated with traditional family life: disciplining his children, A. J. and Meadow; helping his children get into college; dealing with problems in his marriage to Carmela, primarily surrounding his own infidelities; and responding to his mother's complaints of neglect. Having a hard time balancing these situations, Tony turns to Dr. Melfi for help, but he is secretive about it; he knows it will be viewed as a weakness, both to his crime family and his traditional family.

In its first season in 1999, *The Sopranos* was nominated for more Emmy Awards than any broadcast network program (CNN, 1999). It has also won Golden Globe awards, as well as a Peabody, broadcasting's highest honor. By the finale of the fourth season in 2002, 12.5 million viewers tuned in weekly, representing a bigger audience than any broadcast program in that time slot (Turegano, 2003). Yet, *The Sopranos* has been criticized by Italian American groups who view the series as perpetuating negative stereotypes about Italians and their connection to the Mafia, which will be discussed further in chapter 6.

Oz

Oz, which aired on HBO in 1-hour episodes from 1997 to 2003, was the first original series produced by the network. Set in a state prison, although not specifically in any one state, the series chronicles the lives of several inmates and their interactions with others, in and out of the prison setting—including other inmates, family members, prison administrators and corrections officers, medical personnel, and clergy. This prison drama depicts the lives of inmates specifically in the "Emerald City" section of Oswald (Oz) State Prison. Em City is a test program designed by a prison administrator to help inmates learn to live as part of a community. Group "leaders" of inmates in the general population of the prison who are seen to have the potential to do well in Em City are selected by administrator Tim McManus to live in pods (glass-enclosed cells) located in a communal portion of the prison where they can roam freely, work out in a gymnasium, visit the library, and meet with the prison priest and psychologist/nun. They are offered much more freedom than their "gen pop" counterparts.

The main characters belong to specific groups in *Oz*, including The Brotherhood of Aryans; The Irish; The Others; The Homeboys; The Latinos; The Muslims; The Italians; and The Gays. Members of each group were selected to live in Em City. A 1997 *New York Times* review pointed out that the conflicts among groups in *Oz* reflect those in society. "The prison population is a nightmarish mirror of the outside world's ethnic rivalries" (James, 1997, ¶6, Retrieved November 18, 2005, from http://nytimes.com). Prison staff includes Governor James Devlin, Warden Leo Glynn, Em City Administrator Tim McManus. Two Roman Catholic clergy are also main characters: Psychologist Sister Peter Marie Reimondo, and Chaplain Father Ray Mukada. Many of the correctional officers engage in unethical, and sometimes illegal, behavior. Ratings for *Oz* averaged just under 4 million viewers (Levin, 2003).

Reviews of *Oz* range from "gruesome" to "powerfully acted." According to Slate.com,

> The 60-minute episodes are organized not around some aspect of rehabilitation, but around murder—the only thing that is progressive about Emerald City, as best the viewer can tell, is that the prisoners are allowed to walk about at will, which allows them to murder and rape every six minutes or so. The series' creators understand that people don't possess the will or interest to watch a television series about real penal reform, or to address the underlying moral and economic conditions that help fill the prisons. What people want is the spilling of guts. (Goldberg, 1997, ¶10, Retrieved November 18, 2005, from http://Slate.com)

A *New York Times* review by James (1997) cited the creators' intention to "shock" viewers:

> Set almost entirely in the prison, a high-tech horror with glass-walled cells, "Oz" can also be unpleasant to watch, it is so gruesome and

claustrophobic. Yet over the first few weeks, as the series moves beyond its introductory shock value, it becomes more serious, disturbing and gripping. (¶3, Retrieved November 18, 2005, from http://nytimes.com)

Oz was created by Tom Fontana, who also wrote several of the episodes. In a 2001 article in *The New York Times*, Peden (2001), quoting Fontana on the series, wrote:

> There are lessons and there are morals to the stories in "Oz"... It's like, look at what we do to each other. I mean, it's really about the world: it just happens to take place in a prison...There are genuine moments of redemption, several of them involving major characters. (n.p.)

He echoed this concept in a January 2, 2003, article written by Levin (2003) in *USA Today*, when he said:

> I'd like to think years from now that people will see past the surface shock of it and see hopefully the deeper truths we've been dealing with...The struggle to survive on a day-to-day basis, whether you're in prison or facing Saddam. There is a faceless population in the U.S. that deserves more recognition and attention than it gets by most of us on the outside. (n.p.)

In 1982, Fontana began his career as a writer for *St. Elsewhere* (1982–1988), an NBC series that profiled a group of doctors in a Boston hospital. He also created the acclaimed 1993 series *Homicide: Life on the Street* (1993–1999), which aired on NBC and chronicled the work of Baltimore detectives. One character from the series, Detective John Munch, played by Richard Beltzer, appeared in other series, first in crossover episodes on *Law & Order* at the same time *Homicide* aired. He is now a starring character on *Law & Order: Special Victims Unit*.

The Jury
In 2004, Tom Fontana created *The Jury*, a short-lived summer series that aired on Fox for one season and was cancelled due to poor ratings. *The Jury*

profiled deliberations of a New York jury each week. Fontana also wrote several of the episodes. Each 1-hour episode begins with jurors being led into the deliberation room. Parts of the trials are revealed through flashbacks that reference testimony that the jury deliberates. Set mainly in the deliberation room of a New York City courthouse, trial testimony in each case is revealed in flashbacks as the jurors debate/discuss the evidence. After a verdict is reached and read by the judge, at the end of the episode, a flashback scene shows what really happened at the time of the crime, ultimately revealing whether the verdict was "right." Throughout the program, a Web address is also posted for the audience members to cast a vote, and the audience verdict is posted on the screen just moments prior to the "official" jury decision in the program.

Recurring characters include defense attorney Melissa Greenfield, prosecuting attorney Keenan O'Brien, prosecutor John Ranguso, and Barry Levinson as Judge Horatio Hawthorne. Levinson is also executive producer and a writer for the series. However, the "main characters" in each episode are the 12 jurors. Each week, a new jury is introduced. Jurors are the dramatic stars of the episodes, but because they are not recurring characters, emphasis is not placed on their personalities but rather the content of their deliberations.

Reviews for *The Jury* were mixed; it was called both "inventive" and "disappointing." A *New York Times* review by Stanley (2004) stated,

> What is striking about "The Jury"...is that even though its approach is inventive, visually, the series is startlingly similar to such shows as *"CSI,"* "Without a Trace" and *"Cold Case,"* highly polished crime shows produced by Jerry Bruckheimer. "The Jury" uses many of the same cinematic techniques—grainy flashbacks, fast-motion photography, luridly enhanced color—to tell its stories. It's the Bruckheimerization of television crime shows: a homogenization of style that has already overtaken malls, bars and business hotels. All the shows look good, but they are all starting to look alike. (n.p.)

USA Today cited it as "one of the most excruciatingly boring hours ever to trickle by on TV" (Bianco, 2004, n.p.). However, Pennington's

(2004) review in *The St. Louis Post-Dispatch* noted, "[T]he show is anything but a talky new take on the '12 Angry Men' theme. With quick cuts taking us into court, to the crime scene, to interrogations and elsewhere around New York to illustrate the often abrasive debate, the pace of 'The Jury' is often head-spinning, especially in the early going" (n.p.). Pennington described it as "an anthology series—even a throwback to Golden Age dramas such as 'Naked City'" (n.p.).

Because the series was created by Tom Fontana, who had received critical acclaim with *Homicide* and *Oz*, critics cited expectations that *The Jury* would find the same success. "Considering its pedigree, 'The Jury' carries high expectations. Although far from a failure, what actually arrives is more ordinary than extraordinary; interesting and worthy of attention, but not immediately dazzling" (Pennington, 2004, n.p.). However, *The Jury* and *Oz* aired on different networks, one on a broadcast network and one on a premium-cable channel, and were guided by different business structures and content regulations. Fontana's previous series *Homicide: Life on the Street* benefited from airing on the same network as the successful *Law & Order*. He was able to include crossover storylines, with *Homicide*'s Detective John Munch providing an opportunity for the established series bringing attention to a then-new series. No such crossover opportunity existed with *Oz* and *The Jury*.

Law & Order
Law & Order first debuted on NBC in September 1990 and continues to air original episodes. At the time it first aired, its distinction from other shows in the genre was that it combined two dramatic elements. Where traditionally programs in the genre followed either police detectives who identify the suspect in a crime or the prosecuting/defending attorneys who try the cases, not both, *Law & Order* shows *both* the police story and the legal proceedings of the same case in each episode. In the first half hour of each episode, two New York City detectives investigate a crime, and in the second half, two attorneys prosecute the suspect. *Law & Order* is set in upscale sections of New York City. The crimes

depicted are committed primarily by middle- to upper-class residents. The program is plot driven, based on the individual cases presented in each episode. At the center of each show are the lives of the suspect or suspects.

The audience learns more about the nonrecurring characters, namely, the criminals, than it does about the police detectives or the lawyers working the cases for the district attorney's office. *Law & Order* episodes usually begin at a crime scene, with the police detectives being briefed from the first responding police officers at the scene. The detectives investigate and then turn the evidence over to the District Attorney's Office, who then proceeds to prosecute the case, all within the 1-hour episode. During each episode, the focus is not on why a crime occurs, but rather on how it occurs.

The program has undergone many casting changes during the 18 years it has been on the air, with no original cast members now remaining. In most series, this would have a profound effect on the program, likely diminishing its popularity. However, the impact of the casting changes has had little effect on the content of the shows, as *Law & Order* does not focus on the personal lives of any of its star characters.

Ratings for the series have consistently been good, even in its later years. The series was 13th in the ratings in the 1998–1999 season, and 11th for the 1999–2000 season (classictvhits.com). Cable reruns of *Law & Order* (on TNT) are also popular, ranking 7th, 13th, and 15th in February 2005 ratings (Zap2it.com). Still, the ratings for original episodes have slipped in recent years. *Law & Order* scored its smallest audience in 5 years in September 2004. However, the success of the original series has led to a *Law & Order* "franchise," as it has been spun off into three additional installments. *Law & Order: Criminal Intent* focuses on establishing the suspect in a murder, while *Law & Order: Special Victims Unit* shows both the police detective work and trials of people suspected primarily of sexually related crimes. Critics say that each one offers something different, something more. "Whatever the risk of hastening viewer fatigue, each new (*Law & Order*) show further enriches the world all the series share. Even as they snugly coexist in New York City, they expand that realm" (Moore, 2005, n.p.). However, viewer fatigue may have led to the demise of the fourth series in the franchise, *Law & Order: Trial by Jury*, which aired in 2005. It focused on court proceedings in criminal cases, but was to include Jerry Orbach's Detective Lennie Briscoe character as a crossover from the original series. Orbach died of prostate cancer in 2004, before the new series aired. He appeared in the first few episodes and his part was recast. The show only lasted one season, and is the first of the franchise not to extend beyond its original season.

NYPD Blue

The popular police drama, ABC's *NYPD Blue*, which first aired September 21, 1993, concluded its run in 2005. Created by Stephen Bochco and David Milch—who also created *Hill Street Blues*, airing in the 1980s—the series centers around detectives in the 15th Precinct of New York City, an area that includes Hell's Kitchen, Little Italy, and the surrounding area. The plots, shown in 1-hour episodes, involve the personal lives of the main characters as much as their professional lives—and often the two intersect. In the final season, main characters were: Detectives Andy Sipowicz and Greg Medavoy, both original characters; Detectives John Clark and Baldwin Jones; Rita Ortiz; Laura Murphy, newly added character who joined the cast after other actors departed the series; and Squad leader, Lt. Thomas Ball, also a new character. A March 2005 article in *The Toronto Sun* credited *NYPD Blue* as being a forbearer for *The Sopranos* (Brioux, 2005).

It was a Top 10 show throughout its first season, but ratings slowly slipped as, according to reports, "renewed restrictions and increasingly conservative political climate cost it some of its edge" (Griffith, 2005, n.p.). Over the course of its run, it won 20 Emmy Awards, including 27 nominations in its first season (Brioux, 2005). The series was ranked 12th in ratings during the 1998–1999 season, and 17th during the 1999–2000 season (classictvhits.com).

Newspaper media critics recognized that *NYPD Blue* pushed the boundaries of what was acceptable in broadcast programming. Griffith (2005) noted,

> There have always been shows and televised moments that hovered around the boundary of what the censors allow, but "NYPD" was truly blue, ushering in an era of permissiveness, language, nudity and reality that other shows quickly imitated, usually less successfully. It went far beyond the titillation of '70s "jiggle TV" like "Charlie's Angels" and, later, the tasteless drivel of shock jocks, to combine adult attitudes toward sexuality with realistic depictions of police work. The show was always racy and edgy but never gratuitous. (n.p.)

As a result, controversy has surrounded this series, particularly when it first aired, and advertisers protested the nudity and coarse language (Keveney, 2004). The character of Detective Andy Sipowicz was also controversial because he openly exhibited racial prejudices. As such, a new representation of police detectives appeared on network television.

Cold Case

Cold Case, a 1-hour drama on CBS, was created by Jerry Bruckheimer. The series debuted in the 2003–2004 season and it remains a hit program for CBS. Laurence (2003) credited Bruckheimer with combining themes traditionally seen in the genre with new special-effects techniques:

> Produced by Jerry Bruckheimer, "*Cold Case*" is slicker than "*Murder, She Wrote*" ever was, peppered with Bruckheimer's trademark camera tricks and a few gimmicks of its own. But its theme, a detective chasing down forgotten murder cases, is an old, cozy and comfortably familiar one. (n.p.)

The most watched new drama when it debuted, *Cold Case* has been described by critics as working "so well because it's such a twisty murder mystery that always features enough suspects to keep you guessing" (Thompson, 2004, n.p.). The review continued: "And in a cool visual gimmick, we see the suspects and survivors of each *Cold*

Case as they were then and as they are now. The gimmick gives *Cold Case* an added layer no other TV crime show has" (Thompson, 2004, n.p.).

This Philadelphia-based drama created by Meredith Stiehm, a former writer on *NYPD Blue* and *ER*, follows investigations by two detectives who work on "cold" cases—ones that had been closed because they reached a "dead end." When a recent crime or a witness comes forward, the case is reopened (and the two detectives always solve the case this time around). The main character Lilly Rush works with a team of detectives, including Lt. John Stillman and Detectives Scotty Valens, Will Jeffries, and Nick Vera. This program focuses on previously unsolved crimes, so it begins with a flashback to a previous crime. Each episode follows the same format: the crime has already occurred, but no clear suspect has emerged. During the reinvestigation by the cold-case team, the reason the crime was committed is ultimately revealed. In the course of solving the crime, the detectives uncover what led to the crime, and as a result, the nonrecurring criminal characters are as much a focus in this program as the recurring detective characters.

The program has been popular since it first aired. During the first week of March in 2004, during its first season, *Cold Case* won the night with 16 million viewers (Ryan, 2004). It continues to garner a large audience.

The Shield

Another series depicting police work is *The Shield*, originally airing in 2002 on the basic-cable channel FX. It continues to air original, 1-hour episodes. In the pilot episode of *The Shield*, created by Shawn Ryan, who was a writer on *Nash Bridges* and *My Two Dads*, the context in which the criminals operate is set. They are in a part of Los Angeles described in the voice-over narration as "the most dangerous part of the city," and a place that "some people call a war zone."

As the series opens, there has been a decrease during the previous 6 months of murders, rapes, and robberies, attributed to main character Vic Mackey, played by Michael Chiklis, and the efforts of his Strike

Force Team—which includes Shane Vendrell and Curtis "Lemonhead" Lemansky. The result is that the community, families, mothers, and children, can feel safer. A "rogue" cop, Mack often breaks the law in the process of his work. When Mack shoots and kills his team member who opposed his tactics in the pilot episode, he covered it up as a crime committed by a drug dealer. His supervisor, squad Captain David Aceveda, knows he is a bad cop and is investigating him, but also sees that Mack is effective, which makes the team look good, which in turn makes the department look good, and that makes the supervisor and the mayor look good. Mackey's "unorthodox" ways are portrayed as wrong, but to some extent, necessary. Through this series, how crime impacts Mackey, and how he believes it should be dealt with, is presented. It is a police detective's view, but, unlike the police characters in *Law & Order*, *Cold Case*, and *NYPD Blue*, he is a rogue, corrupt police detective. As a result, there is ambiguity about whether his is an appropriate process. Poniewozik (2004) said the following about the series:

> FX's *The Shield*—about politics, corruption and nobility in a dangerous LA precinct—has its share of grisly, surprise-twist murder investigations, but above all, it's a multifaceted story about how we want (as opposed to how we claim we want) police to use power at a time of anxiety. (p. 66)

The series has received industry acclaim. It won the first basic-cable prime-time Emmy award for lead actor in a drama for Michael Chiklis. Also, for the first time, a basic cable series received Emmy nominations for writing and directing, according to fxnetworks.com. According to Goodman (2003) in *The San Francisco Chronicle*,

> There's no doubt…that "*The Shield*," one of the best dramas on television, can expand on the can-you-believe-this? shock of the first season, when the scripts went way, way beyond "edgy" and Chiklis' career-defining tour-de-force performance was one of those visions you couldn't shake. There's more meat on "*The Shield*" than it was given credit for last season. (¶8, Retrieved November 14, 2005, from sfgate.com)

Owen (2003) credited *The Shield* with giving FX a more prominent role in the industry.

> [*The Shield* gave] the Fox-owned basic-cable channel an identity. Before "The Shield," FX was known as a home for reruns of prime-time series and the lowbrow humor of its original comedy, "Sons of the Beach." After "The Shield," FX is seen as (a) place for creative visionaries, risk-takers whose fare is too edgy for the broadcast networks. FX has found a niche, building its brand as the basic cable answer to HBO. (¶2, Retrieved November 14, 2005, from Lexis-Nexis)

In its first season, *The Shield* was among the top five on basic cable, with 3.2 million viewers tuning in from 2.1 million homes (fxnetworks.com). Of those viewers, 2.1 million were adults between the ages 18 and 49, a coveted demographic for advertisers.

The Practice

The 1-hour drama *The Practice* first aired on ABC in 1997, and depicts defense lawyers in Boston and their interactions with their clients. *The Practice* follows the professional and personal lives of attorneys who primarily work on criminal-defense cases. When the series begins, a team of lawyers join Bobby Donnell's law practice. Most of the cases involve an ethical dilemma the lawyers face in the course of balancing their obligations to defend their clients, the law, and their own consciences. The dramatic element of the program often focuses on the difficulty of satisfying all three. They all struggle to establish this new firm, and in the process, wrestle with moral dilemmas that emerge from their work with suspects, and in some cases, convicted, or admitted, criminals.

Dylan McDermott played main character, Bobby Donnell, who started the firm, hiring Rebecca Washington (played by Lisa Gay Hamilton), Lindsay Dole (Kelli Williams), Eugene Young (Steve Harris), Ellenor Frutt (Camryn Manheim), Jimmy Berluti (Michael Badalucco), Jamie Stringer (Jessica Capshaw), and receptionist Lucy Hatcher (Marla Sokoloff). Lara Flynn Boyle portrayed prosecuting attorney Helen

Gamble. *The Practice* won an Emmy in 1998, when it was up against *Law & Order* and *NYPD Blue*.

In the final season of *The Practice* in 2003, several main characters, including the character that the series centered around—Bobby Donnell—were written out of the series when the actors portraying them were fired from the show by creator and Executive Producer David E. Kelley, who cited financial constraints placed on him by the network, ABC. Fired along with McDermott were Washington, Williams, Sokoloff, and Boyle. The show was also the most expensive series produced by 20th Century Fox Television, at $6.5 million in 2003 (Keveney, 2003). With the change in cast in 2003, the cost dropped to $3.5 million (Rohan, 2003). To replace the outgoing cast members, two new characters—Alan Shore played by James Spader and Tara Wilson played by Rhona Mitra—were added.

In the early days of *The Practice*, ratings outranked *Law & Order* and *NYPD Blue*. During the 1999–2000 season, it ranked 9th, ahead of *Law & Order* (#11) and *NYPD Blue* (#17). Through 2001, it remained a Top-10 show (Keveney, 2003). Yet, the demise of the show in 2004 was ultimately attributed to a ratings drop, in part due to the loss of the popular *Who Wants to Be a Millionaire* as a lead-in and the timeslot move from Sunday at 10 p.m. to Monday at 9 p.m. in January of 2003 (Keveney, 2003). Eventually the show was moved back to its 10 p.m. slot, but it only remained on the air through the 2004 season, when it was spun off as a new series, *Boston Legal*, starring the character Alan Shore.

Reality and Documentary Programs
In addition to the fictional programs, I wanted to explore whether real-life depictions mirrored those seen in the fictional depictions, and also analyze what might account for the success of crime shows during this particular 6-year period in the 1990s and into the new millennium. I suspected it was due to viewers' desire to feel reassured that criminals were being punished and that law and order would prevail, which may have been heightened as coverage of real-life crime dramas increased during this time with the emergence of newly established 24-hour news channels. CNN, the

first 24-hour news channel, first aired in 1980, and CNN2 launched in 1982. The name was changed to CNN Headline News in 1983 (wikepedia.com). In 1981, the first business-news channel, Financial News Network, aired, and in 1991, NBC purchased FNN, and it later became CNBC (nbccableinfo.com). In 1996, Fox News Channel and MSNBC, jointly owned by Microsoft Corporation and NBC, first aired.

CSI, unveiled by CBS during the 2001 television season, is a natural continuation of extensive forensic discussion in the news within the decade, particularly during the highly publicized 1995 O. J. Simpson trial, along with the 1996 JonBenet Ramsey murder case, an unsolved case. These two stories frequently filled 24-hour news channels' airtime. In subsequent years, several other high-profile criminal acts were discussed heavily on cable news channels:

1996: The bombing at the Atlanta Olympics resulted in the deaths of two people and more than 100 wounded.

1999: The Columbine High School shooting in Colorado resulted in the death of 13 people and the suicides of the two student shooters.

May 2001: Actor Robert Blake's wife was killed, and he was charged with the murder. The trial resulted in an acquittal in March 2005.

September 2001: Terrorists bombed the World Trade Center in New York City, killing nearly 3,000 people.

June 2002: 14-year-old Elizabeth Smart went missing in Utah, and was found alive 9 months later in March 2003, with the assistance of a tip from an *America's Most Wanted* viewer.

December 2002: Young mother-to-be, Laci Peterson, who was 7 months pregnant, disappeared from her Modesto home the day before Christmas. Her husband, Scott, was charged with the murder and convicted November 2004.

March 2004: Martha Stewart was found guilty of lying to prosecutors about a stock transaction. She later served more than 5 months in prison and an additional 5 months under house arrest.

July 2004: Lori Hacking, in her mid-20s, went missing in Utah. She was found dead in October in a landfill. Her husband pled guilty to the murder in April 2005.

2005: Michael Jackson was found not guilty of sexually molesting a teenage boy.

The result of these high-profile cases and trials is that the public became much more familiar with the judicial process than it had been before. Americans also shared a common narrative about justice. Court cases have always been part of storytelling in fictional television, and these real-life cases were gripping, in part because of the nature of criminal cases. The truth is often not clear, and as a result, it is something that can be debated. This enabled 24-hour news channels, with a lot of airtime to fill, to spend day after day discussing the cases. Analysts offer different opinions about the cases and how the evidence should be interpreted. Court cases also take a long time to complete, so they can be covered by the media for weeks, months, or even years. They become a narrative that viewers can follow as events unfold, very similar to the way a fictional narrative unfolds. The format and structure of these real-life court cases is an easy one to recreate in a fictional format because many of the elements are already present: there is mystery, conflict, and often unusual human behavior—all also key elements of compelling television.

As Rapping (2004) suggested, television viewers are able to witness "major" events through the broadcasts on 24-hour news channels:

> The Clarence Thomas confirmation hearings, the O. J. Simpson trial, the wedding and funeral of Princess Diana: all these events were witnessed by a global audience swept up in a long-running, round-the-clock spectacle around which swirled endless dialogue and debate about what the television news magazine producers refer to as "societal issues" and "the human condition." (p. 261)

Rapping pointed to how these events are selected because they have "legs," and can run for several days, or even weeks. In the process of broadcasting these events, she said viewers were forced to "deal with serious social injustices, at least for the brief time they held our undivided attention" (p. 262). She viewed these broadcasts as having a "socially positive and enlightening impact" and cited changes in sexual-harassment legislation following the Hill-Thomas hearings and discussions about how race (and I would add economic class) impacted the justice system following the O. J. Simpson trial and the airing of the videotape of the Rodney King beating by Los Angeles police officers.

Like the 24-hour news channels, the cable network Court TV also rose in popularity in the late 1990s. Kleinhans and Morris (2004) cited the O. J. Simpson trial in 1995 as "the decisive moment for Court TV's growth and change" (p. 163). During the ensuing years, producers of fictional programs created many crime dramas that still remain popular today. Kleinhans and Morris identified criteria used by Court TV executives to select from among real trials to be televised on the network—that they were newsworthy, addressed social issues, and were watchable and entertaining—and these elements are also present in current fictional dramas. Kleinhans and Morris (2004) cited Court TV's use of text on screen as part of its appeal, and called the network's programming a hybrid of soap opera and sports. The trials on Court TV, like on soaps, include: bizarre stories, which they acknowledge are often even more bizarre than on fictional soap operas, and likable and recurring characters. Like sporting events, they air live and include an uncertain outcome between two battling sides—and offense and a defense. Broadcast networks also continue to air real courtroom cases on *The People's Court*, *Judge Judy*, *Judge Hatchett*, and *Texas Justice*. Ouellette (2004) examined how *Judge Judy* supports a neoliberal philosophy by training "TV viewers to function without state assistance or supervision as self-disciplining, self-sufficient, responsible, and risk-averting individuals" (p. 232).

To determine how the real depictions of crime reinforced or deviated from the fictional depictions, I analyzed the reality series *COPS* and *America's Most Wanted*, which are discussed further in chapter 8. I was also interested in comparing the fictional and reality depictions to those in documentaries. I identified four documentaries that aired on television between 1998 and 2004. *Capturing the Friedmans*, depicting the investigation, trial, and conviction of a high school teacher in Long Island, aired on HBO, as did *Gladiator Days: Anatomy of a Prison Murder*, part of HBO's America Undercover series, which portrayed the prison stabbing of one inmate by another. ABC's *In the Jury Room* documented jury deliberations of a man on trial in Ohio for murdering his wife and her friend. As part of its *Dateline* series, NBC aired the documentary *Deadline*, which traced Illinois Governor George Ryan's decision to commute the death sentences of 167 inmates on death row in 2000. The documentaries are analyzed in chapter 9.

Process

Episodes

To examine how the representations of crime and criminals changed or progressed during the 6-year period between 1998 and 2004, I randomly selected six episodes of each of the fictional and reality television programs from episodes available in original or repeat broadcast airings, or the Museum of Television & Radio library. In some cases, when more than six episodes were needed to reach "saturation," additional episodes were analyzed (Strauss & Corbin, 1998, p. 136). The goal in sampling was to reach saturation for each program when "no new information seems to emerge during coding" (Strauss & Corbin, 1998, p. 136). Strauss and Corbin (1998) acknowledged that "there always is that potential for the 'new' to emerge. Saturation is more a matter of reaching the point in the research where collecting additional data seems counterproductive; the 'new' that is uncovered does not add that much more to the explanation at this time" (p. 136).

I viewed six episodes of each series, but additional episodes were consulted when necessary to confirm a plot point that was explained in a previous or future episode, or if something about the plot was not clear. This was necessary in analyzing *Oz, The Practice, The Sopranos*, and *NYPD Blue*, which had continuing storylines. Also, while I viewed six episodes for the analysis, and referred to these six episodes for the study, I was familiar with several shows prior to conducting my analysis. I was a casual watcher of *The Practice, The Sopranos*, and *Oz*. In the early stages of developing this study, I conducted a pilot study on *Oz*, for which I viewed an additional six episodes. In addition, I had watched *NYPD Blue* and *Law & Order* in the early days of the series, but had not been a viewer for several years prior to conducting this study. However, I did conduct pilot studies of these two series in the process of developing this study. I did not refer to the content of the episodes viewed for those studies in this analysis, however, because the episodes I viewed aired prior to 1998. Before conducting this research, I had never watched *Cold Case*, *The Shield*, *The Jury*, or any of the four documentaries. I was familiar with the concept of *COPS* and *America's Most Wanted*, but had never watched full episodes of these series before I began the study.

A total of 65 hours were viewed for this research: six episodes of nine, 1-hour long series; six episodes of one, 30-minute series; and four, 2-hour documentaries. Only a limited number of episodes were available from the archives of The Museum of Television and Radio and New York City. There, I viewed episodes of *The Shield*, *NYPD Blue*, and the documentary *Gladiator Days*. The remaining episodes were videotaped as the episodes aired in their original runs or in reruns in syndication. If the shows were not original-run episodes, where I knew they ran within the time period I was interested in analyzing, I consulted network Web sites, which provided an episode guide, to confirm the airdates.

Scholars who have conducted textual analysis of television programs, and specifically those addressing ideology and discourse, have analyzed single episodes to illustrate how ideology is revealed (White, 1992; Glynn, 2000; Gitlin, 1985). However, I followed van Dijk's (1998) structure for conducting media discourse analysis for this study, and referred to more than one episode. I included six episodes of each text in order to be able to incorporate the complex process that is necessary to dissect the texts, and reveal ideologies and discourse. As White (1992) pointed out, it is important to take into account the intertextuality when analyzing media texts; she explained that even within a television series, representations in one episode can be contradicted in another. In looking at six episodes of each program I was able to look beyond the single episode to explore each text in depth and determine patterns that were evident.

Points of Analysis

For the fictional, reality-based, and documentary television programs, I began by looking specifically at the point at which the episodes took place, and analyzed them to determine depictions in three key areas: whether the criminals were portrayed as redeemable/able to be rehabilitated; the range of crime causes depicted, and if societal structures were presented as a cause; further, if crimes were portrayed as individual acts, I examined whether they were shown to be impacted by personal relationships; and whether punitive or preventive measures were celebrated in dealing with crime.

I used van Dijk's (1998) "ideological square" model to complete the analysis, identifying the Us versus Them relationship presented in the text (p. 33). I determined whether the text emphasized "our" good properties/ actions; emphasized "their" bad properties/actions; mitigated "our" bad properties/actions; or mitigated "their" good properties/actions. Following van Dijk's suggestions for carrying out an ideological analysis of media discourse, referred to as Critical Discourse Analysis, I:

a. examine[d] the context of the discourse
b. analyze[d] which groups, power relations, and conflicts were involved,
c. look[ed] for positive and negative opinions about Us and Them,
d. spell[ed] out the presupposed and the implied, and
e. examine[d] all formal structures that (de)emphasize polarized group opinions. (p. 61)

The key areas van Dijk cited to include in analysis, which were incorporated into this study, are backgrounds, context, ideological categories, polarization, the implicit, and formal structures. These are defined as

a. *Backgrounds*: Includes "facts about the historical, political or social background of a conflict, its main participants, the grounds of the conflict and preceding positions and arguments" (p. 62).

b. *Context*: Defined as analysis of the genre and the setting in which the events take place within each episode in the genre.
c. *Ideological categories*: Determined by "socially shared representations of groups about themselves and their relations to other groups" (p. 62).
d. *Polarization*: Defined as how the ideologies presented "reproduce social conflict, domination and inequality...represented as Us vs. Them. This polarization is at the basis of much ideological discourse, that is, as the strategy of positive self-presentation and negative other-presentation" (pp. 62–63).
e. *The implicit*: Examines ideological opinions, which van Dijk suggests are often "implied, presupposed, hidden, denied or taken for granted" (p. 63).
f. *Formal structures*: They may "emphasize or de-emphasize information or opinions about Us and Them; [include] sound structures in talk (e.g. intonation, stress, volume, 'tone', applause, laughs);... the overall (schematic) organization of the discourse (e.g. argumentation); lexical choice; and variation in the description of Us. Vs. Them." (p. 63).

In addition, to determine where depictions in the television series located the cause of crime, I referred to the frames used by Sasson (1995) in his study to assess how Americans talk about crime. I found these frames identified by Sasson useful because they covered the range of crime causes identified by criminologists and sociologists, as discussed in chapter 3. He asked members of a neighborhood-watch program to read newspaper op-ed articles about crime, and then state what they perceived to be the causes of crime presented in the articles, choosing from the following frames:

a. *Faulty System*: People commit crimes because they can get away with them, and it is the failure of social-control agencies that contributes to crime;

b. *Social Breakdown*: Crime is caused by the breakdown of the family and neighborhood, on an individual level, with responsibility falling to parents and neighbors as individuals;
c. *Blocked Opportunities*: Poverty, poor education, bad housing, lack of health care, unemployment, and discrimination result in crime;
d. *Media Violence*: Violence in movies, television, and music contributes to crime; and
e. *Racist System*: Arrests and sentences are unfair toward African Americans, who are more likely to be targeted for arrest, with sentences, including the death penalty, unfairly administered to minorities.

When he analyzed the responses, Sasson (1995) found that 55% of respondents cited faulty system, 36% social breakdown, 33% blocked opportunities, 5% media violence, and 10% racist system. In the discussions with residents, he determined that faulty system was a strong response, and blocked opportunities was a weak response, with most participants arguing for "a more punitive criminal justice system" (Sasson, 1995, p. 161). The strongest frame, however, in the discussions, was social breakdown, which Sasson saw as an area for potential to move to more discussions of blocked opportunities. Blocked opportunities, as Sasson suggested, is the liberal version of the neutral social breakdown. Both frames identify social problems, including poverty and racial discrimination, as the cause for crime, but social breakdown focuses more on individuals being the cause of crime, and not structures, as is the viewpoint in blocked opportunities. "With respect to crime, television news...cultivates the notion that it is individual criminals and not society who are ultimately responsible. It therefore tends to reinforce the popular wisdom that says crime is a matter of individual 'choice'" (Sasson, 1995, p. 152).

Between 1998 and 2004, the television crime genre showed a wide range of representations of criminals' backgrounds and motivations that pointed to both individual causes and social causes of crime, as I discuss in the next five chapters.

CHAPTER 4

LEGAL AUTHORITIES: POLICE OFFICERS, JUDGES, AND LAWYERS

Beginning with *The Lone Ranger* in 1949, criminals were portrayed as deviant in the television crime genre, and societal "leaders" were portrayed as responding to the criminals. That depiction continued through 1996, until the HBO series *Oz*, starring criminals, debuted in 1997. Westerns served as the "first frontier" in the television crime genre, and many of the same genre elements in the early Western series are evident in contemporary programs. To combat destructive forces in society, Western heroes ride to the rescue; police authorities now do the same. Among the most popular Westerns in the early years of television were *Bonanza*, which ran on ABC from 1959 to 1973, and *The Lone Ranger*, also airing on ABC from 1949 to 1957. *The Lone Ranger* portrayed the "masked man" trying to maintain law and order within his community. An element of this series that remains today in programs such as *Law & Order* is the anonymous nature of the law enforcer. Concealing the identity of the Lone Ranger was an integral part of this narrative. While in *Law & Order* the identities of the law enforcers are not concealed, they are essentially unimportant; numerous casting changes have not diminished the popularity of the series, mostly because little is revealed about the personal lives of the law enforcers. Their personal stories are not essential, only the work that they do—much like *The Lone Ranger*. These *Law & Order* characters are universal; they are, in many ways, *every* law enforcer. The focus is on the procedures they follow and the role they serve in society, collectively, not individually.

Cawelti (1975) described *The Lone Ranger* as "bringing law and justice into the life" of a Western community (p. 1). *Bonanza* portrayed law and order on the "Ponderosa," the ranch owned by the Cartwright family. They are the "good guys" who sought to do the right thing in Virginia City at a time when lawlessness reigned. Many of the themes that I explore in the contemporary genre in the next three chapters echo *Bonanza*. In one episode, Adam Cartwright was mistaken for a criminal look-alike. In the process of clearing his own name, he discovered that the impostor had been killed by other outlaws. Adam solved the crime, but discussed how people are assumed guilty based on appearances, and that it took very little evidence to jump to the conclusion that someone is guilty. In another episode, Joe Cartwright helped a man who had worked on his ranch but turned to a life of crime. After killing 16 men, the rancher was being hunted by the father of one of the murdered. Joe sympathized with the murderer, even though the man admitted to the crimes, because Joe saw that there were circumstances that led to him becoming a criminal. When the man told Joe that his crimes were all he had to be proud of, Joe sympathized with him. Vigilantes prevailed during that time, but Joe challenged this approach, because he believed that law and order should not be carried out by individuals, particularly for revenge.

The themes evident in this Western series reemerged in the genre during the next 50 years, particularly between 1998 and 2004, the years I studied. This chapter explores how the series I analyzed that star legal authorities—*Law & Order, NYPD Blue, The Shield, The Practice,* and *Cold Case*—do not present one unified message about criminals and legal authorities, but a varied representation. As a result, the representation of legal authorities, criminals, and crime fighting has expanded from a singular Us versus Them focus. I specifically examine depictions of unethical and illegal behavior by legal authorities as they apprehend, prosecute, and defend criminals, and analyze how such unethical behavior is either mitigated in the series to construct criminals as the reason for the improper behavior, or emphasized to suggest that legal authorities are morally ambiguous. First, I will provide an overview of the crime genre from 1952 to 1997 and identify the common themes that existed prior to 1998.

THE CRIME GENRE: 1950s–1990s

Dragnet, airing on NBC from 1952 to 1959 (and returning from 1967 to 1970), is remembered for the "just the facts, ma'am" attitude displayed by main character Sgt. Joe Friday. This is similar to the tone depicted today in *Law & Order* and *NYPD Blue*. The police detectives present a "tough-as-nails" attitude, and in the process, a dedication to their job of maintaining law and order in society. *Perry Mason*, airing on CBS from 1957 to 1966, depicted the legal system from the perspective of a defense attorney who revealed—in dramatic fashion—that an innocent man had been arrested for the crime. The series was known for this recurring element, and today, reports of real court cases refer to "Perry Mason moments," or the lack of them. For example, a 2003 report on the Modesto, California, murder trial of Scott Peterson, accused of killing his wife and unborn child, on Court TV's Web site carried the headline: "Peterson players promised Perry Mason prelim, but will they deliver?" Similar headlines appeared elsewhere throughout the trial, including in an August 24, 2004, report on KTVU's Web site, which read: "No 'Perry Mason Moment' During Frey Cross-Examination," referring to testimony by Peterson's girlfriend Amber Frey. In an April 2005 *Newsweek* article on the Michael Jackson molestation trial, an analyst described testimony that Jackson's accuser was not allowed to leave Jackson's Neverland ranch for a week as "a Perry Mason moment." In the fictional series, the result of this "moment" was a sense of closure for the audience; good always won and the truth was revealed. As Rapping (2003) pointed out, audiences also began to expect these types of moments:

> Television drama depends foremost on "closure," what Bertolt Brecht once cynically described as "Happy endings/Nice and tidy." While it is true that "closure" can be achieved by any number of definitive conclusions, including, for example, an acquittal of an innocent defendant—the mainstay of early legal series such as Perry Mason and Matlock—the rising anti-crime/criminal mentality of post-sixties America created an audience of viewer-citizens who were increasingly demanding a particular kind of closure: the conviction and punishment of the evil offender. (p. 10)

Naked City, which aired between 1958 and 1963, was described by The Museum of Broadcast Communications as blending documentary and fictional genres.

> *Naked City*, which had two incarnations between 1958 and 1963, was one of American television's most innovative police shows, and one of its most important and influential drama series. More character anthology than police procedural, the series blended the urban *policier* a la *Dragnet* with the urban pathos of the *Studio One* school of television drama, offering a mix of action-adventure and Actors' Studio, car chases and character studies, shoot-outs and sociology, all filmed with arresting starkness on the streets of New York. The series was inspired by the 1948 "semi-documentary" feature, *The Naked City* (which borrowed its title from the photographic collection by urban documentarist/crime photographer Weegee). (museum.tv)

The 1960s also marked the first time a series starred a "criminal." *The Fugitive*, which aired on ABC from 1963 to 1967, starred a man on the run from police—but he was portrayed as innocent. It would be nearly another 35 years before convicted criminals would star as recurring characters on television, in *Oz* and *The Sopranos*. However, in the 1960s, the focus was still on the legal authorities. The 1960s did bring new elements to the genre, particularly the use of teamwork to solve crimes. Crime-fighting teams depicted in the 1960s included *The Avengers, Mission: Impossible,* and *The Mod Squad*. The three undercover cops on *The Mod Squad* were hipper than the serious police officers of the 1950s. Miller (1997) discussed the impact of the popular series *The Avengers* on the crime genre.

> We could subdivide the series into its own narrative pattern: science fiction, policing, treason, loss of identity, and power-hungry elites operating across horror, fantasy, comedy, soap opera, special-event television, quality drama, the spy story, crime series, thrillers, the fantastic, melodrama, British film noir and auterist text. (p. 95)

During this time, fashion played a key role in series such as *The Mod Squad* and *The Avengers*; clothing and style served to signify that these crime fighters who were part of the Los Angeles Police Department were not like crime fighters in previous television series. Gone were the trench coats. In their place were more casual clothes, including jeans, such as in *The Mod Squad*, and trend-setting outfits in *The Avengers*, such as mini-skirts, body suits, knee-high boots, and a lot of accessories, including jewelry and wide belts. It was the first time that women were depicted as crime fighters, and their attire helped to affirm that they were not the same type of crime fighters as the buttoned-up Sgt. Friday. In addition to these aesthetic changes, the narrative changed during this time, too. Miller (1997) pointed out the change in *The Avengers* as deviating from classic detective fiction because it had a "depthlessness."

> [Rather] than seeking motivation through temporary occupancy of the criminal mind or a reconstruction of its psychic imbalances, perversities are simply dealt with when encountered. They are narrative information capable of turning pleasures into obstacles and vice versa, not hermeneutic clues to the repressed truth of wrongdoing. Nor does the team persuade a court of law or any

organization that the truth has been established: they have executive power. (p. 104)

In the 1970s, the genre returned to the format of following a lone detective, reminiscent of elements seen in *The Lone Ranger* in the 1950s. However, as Cawelti (1975) suggested, the detective story presented storylines with a singular focus, while the Western offered more varied storylines. The 1970s-era television programs, such as *Columbo, Kojak, The Rockford Files, Baretta,* and *Quincy, M.E.*, were vehicles for an individual detective solving somewhat sanitized crimes, mostly murders, presented in a melodramatic, unrealistic way. The crimes were not depicted graphically, and the murders were never shown to the audience; they had already happened when the hero character arrived on the scene. Even though the focus of crime programs shifted from the work of police teams to that of a single detective, Cawelti (1975) drew parallels between the Western and the detective story in both character and patterns of action. "One of the major organizing principles of the Western is to so characterize the villains that the hero is both intellectually and emotionally justified in destroying them" (p. 14). He also said of the detective story that the ideology of the "good guys" versus the "bad guys"—outlaws of society—presented in the Western has been recreated in the television crime genre over the last 5 decades, with the same underlying principles represented: maintaining law and order in society, with clear distinctions of good versus evil.

The setting may have changed, but the plot and the characters of the Western and the early cop shows are essentially the same. Actual murders in these popular detective series in the 1970s were never shown, and neither were gritty depictions of violence. The narrative followed a "whodunit" format. The heroes worked alone, often as private detectives, not within a government agency or department. Even if they were members of a police squad or prosecutor's office, they were seen as working alone; teamwork was not a popular notion, as it had been in the 1960s. At this time, storylines centered around the lone detective, also serving as the dramatic heroes, with little or no attention centered on the victim or the criminal. Often in these depictions, the criminal is revealed only in the last minutes of the program.

In the 1980s, police dramas were popular, but representations of the single detective hero, popular in the 1970s, remained as well. Rather than one dominant depiction of legal authorities existing, as had been the case in earlier decades, varied portrayals were shown. Essentially, "the clash of civilization ('law and order')" (Cawelti, 1975, p. 36) on the frontier in the Western is recreated on the streets of urban areas in police crime stories. The core elements of the Western remain in the 1980s, with an outlaw "other" and his culture depicted as unacceptable. As Cawelti (1975) pointed out, "if the Indian represented a significant way of life rather than a declining savagery, it would be far more difficult to resolve the story with a reaffirmation of the values of modern society" (p. 38). Instead, Indians and outlaws represent "rejection of the town and its way of life" (Cawelti, 1975, p. 54). In the police dramas, such as *Hill Street Blues, Wiseguy,* and *Cagney and Lacey*, the criminals serve this role. Gitlin (1985) pointed out that *Hill Street Blues*, in its first season in 1981, broke many of the conventions of the crime genre. *Hill Street*, described as the first "postliberal cop show," was successful, Gitlin (1985) suggested, because it "immersed itself in major popular cross-currents—far more than the law-and-order shows that hit the airwaves at the same moment" (p. 307). While reality crime shows in the form of *COPS* and *America's Most Wanted*, both on Fox, also first aired in the late 1980s, and, theoretically, offered more realism than series in the 1970s, the genre continued to offer sanitized and even comedic depictions as well, including in *Magnum p.i., Murder, She Wrote,* and *Moonlighting*. During this time, the genre began to include many depictions of crime and criminals, rather than just a single focus on police procedures.

In the 1990s, police teams, rather than individual detectives, returned on the law-enforcement side, in the form of defense attorneys, police detectives, and prosecutors. *Law & Order* and *NYPD Blue* portrayed police-detective teams and *The Practice* depicted a team of defense attorneys. Viewers of these programs often knew "whodunit." The drama was grounded in the notion that justice must be done; punishment must be carried out. The dramatic development centers around catching the criminal, who is identified (at least by the authorities) very early on, and with certainty. Denis Franz's Andy Sipowicz on *NYPD Blue* is intent on forcing suspects to admit they committed the crimes he is investigating, similar to the format of *Perry Mason*, as the climax of *NYPD Blue* is also the revelation that the suspect was caught and will be punished under the law.

Conventions of the genre demand that the actions of the legal authorities engaged in the process of trying to apprehend the criminal, even when illegal, were often not portrayed as their fault. Instead, the criminal is portrayed as having necessitated the action, as Parenti (1980) suggested. Parenti (1980) found in a study of cop and crime shows "that police actions habitually violate the constitutional rights of individuals... '[T]he message communicated is that evil may be subdued by state-sponsored illegality'" (p. 177). Crimes committed by authorities in the act of trying to protect society are justified in many series in the genre today. Nonetheless, this depiction of justified illegal behavior by police is no longer the *only* depiction.

Depictions of the types of crimes committed in the programs I analyze are realistic, as shown by actual crime statistics I noted in chapter 2. Most crimes depicted in the programs I viewed were committed by males; actual crime statistics in 2002 show that of the people arrested for murder, 10,285 were male, 1,108 were female, and the sex of 4,420 was unknown, presumably omitted from the report upon arrest.

However, the types of crimes depicted are not always proportional to actual statistics. For example, murders appear to be overrepresented in the television crime genre compared to statistics. Most crime shows depict legal authorities solving, prosecuting, or defending people suspected of murders. Most crimes I viewed in *Oz, The Sopranos, NYPD Blue, Law & Order*, and *Cold Case* were murders. (Although, *Oz, The Sopranos, The Shield*, and *The Practice* also showed crimes related to business deals, and *Oz* portrayed substance-abuse-related crimes.) In 1993 there were 15,125 murders, but that figure dropped to 8,933 in 2002, down 40.9%. Statistics also show that other types of crimes continue to decrease. Property crime has also steadily decreased since 1973. DUIs totaled 984,141 in 1993, and that dropped to 879,210 in 2002, down 10.7%. However, drug-related crimes have increased since 1993—at that time, drug abuse crimes totaled 710,922, rising by 2002 to 974,082, up 37%.

The dominance of the crime genre on television does not reflect the overall decrease in crime in society reflected in these DOJ statistics. Actual crime statistics show that most crimes have decreased since 1973. Still, based on research by criminologists and sociologists described in chapter 2, the specific depictions about rehabilitation, the causes of crime, and crime policies in the fictional series can be categorized as realistic, even if some of the plots include unlikely scenarios.

POLICE PROCEDURE

Law & Order

Law & Order, which first aired on NBC in 1990, and continues to air new episodes, presents the work conducted by both the police officers and state prosecutors. While presenting the process of solving crimes, *Law & Order* depicts police corruption, but rarely by main characters. This is evident in one episode in season 14 (2003). A bar fight ended with one man being killed. The suspect, Walter Grimes, was a white man in his 40s who had spent the previous 20 years in prison for a murder he did not commit. He had recently been released from prison after being exonerated through DNA evidence. After the bar fight, the leader of the New York Exoneration Project, Rodney Fallon, said that unlike other convicts, Grimes was not a criminal before he went to prison, but that the experience in prison "shaped him."

However, Executive Assistant District Attorney (ADA) Jack McCoy was not convinced, and when he looked at Grimes' records, he discovered that before going to prison for 20 years, Grimes had been a suspect in the murder of a woman, Julie Sayer, but was never charged in the crime because the police officer investigating the case at the time, Ken Daniels, was told by his supervisor to "kick" the case, because Daniels beat up Grimes in an effort to intimidate him during the interrogation and make him talk, and Daniels' supervisor wanted to avoid a lawsuit. Daniels then framed Grimes for another murder, that of Leanne Testa, by planting the evidence. Daniels said he had to "make it right" that the Julie Sayer case did not proceed because of him. Once this information was brought to the ADAs' attention, they decided to charge Grimes for the murder of Julie Sayer. Grimes ultimately accepted a plea deal, which the prosecutors supported because otherwise Daniels would still have to testify; they believed that his testimony would be tainted by the fact that he had framed Grimes in the Testa case. Grimes was given credit for the 20 years he had already served in prison and was sentenced to an additional 5 years in prison. He also pleaded guilty to killing Donner in the bar fight and received an additional 7 to 15 years to be served consecutively with the Sayer sentence. In this episode, the corrupt police officer, Ken Daniels, was presented as an Other among police officers. His actions were not condoned by the recurring characters—portrayed as honest and upstanding members of the police department.

Another episode in season 14 involved a corrupt family/divorce-court judge who was favoring the clients of lawyers who bribed her to side with them. When police gathered enough evidence to arrest her, she said that the nature of the family cases, which were open to interpretation, made it easy for her to cover up her crimes. In determining divorce and custody settlements, most cases were subjective. She also claimed that her crimes did not hurt anyone. However, when the ADAs investigated, they discovered that in one case the judge ruled in favor of a mother who was an alcoholic, and the children suffered as a result. They had been kicked out of two schools because of bad behavior and the daughter would often cut herself to get her mother's attention.

In these episodes, the audience is encouraged to identify with the main characters—the police detectives and the ADAs—who expose corruption, not the corrupt police officers and judges, who are nonrecurring characters. The audience is further encouraged to view the corrupt people in the profession as rogue members—aberrations who are the exceptions, not the norm. As such, the series suggests that when corruption among legal authorities occurs, it is exposed and dealt with, and therefore "justice" is not affected by this corruption. This notion is further reinforced in the episodes because the suspects are revealed to be guilty of *something*. In the episode where Grimes was wrongfully incarcerated, he may not have been guilty of *the* crime he was incarcerated for, but, as depicted in the episode, he was still guilty. Moreover, the depiction suggests, had he not been framed for the crime he did not commit, he would have gone free, even though he should have been incarcerated because he had murdered someone else.

NYPD Blue

NYPD Blue, first airing on ABC in 1993, and concluded its run in 2005, depicted both official and unofficial procedures of police. In episodes I analyzed, improprieties by police were not as extreme as planting evidence. Nonetheless, there were several examples of harassment, with police holding suspects in a cage in an interrogation room and using other tactics to intimidate them to make them "give up" information. For example, during season 5, Detective Andy Sipowicz discovered that a young girl was killed by her mother's boyfriend while he was high on crack because the girl wet the bed, and Andy yelled at the mother's sister to coerce her to provide him with any information she had about her sister. When the sister broke down in tears, Andy realized he had gone too far and touched her arm in an apologetic way at the end of the interrogation.

At times, the officers also resort to physical violence. In a later scene in the episode with the young girl who was killed, when the boyfriend was brought in, Andy, who was morally outraged by the man's behavior, smacked the man in the head twice in an effort to intimidate him. The tactic worked, and the man implicated the mother in the crime. (At this point, the mother had already been given immunity because the boyfriend was suspected of the crime, but after finding out the truth, the ADA, who is married to Sipowicz, rescinded the immunity offer.) In another episode in season 5, Diane Russell and her partner, Jill Kirkendall, were investigating a case involving a pedophile; while interrogating him, Kirkendall smacked him across the face because, she said, he was not responding with any useful information. Then she smacked him again. Diane also told him they would kill him and bury him in Nassau County if he did not cooperate. The squad supervisor, Lt. Fancy, who had been listening in from outside the room, stormed in to stop the harassment. Again, the tactic had worked; the man was trembling in the corner of the room and said he would provide all the information he had.

As in *Law & Order*, in *NYPD Blue*, the unethical and criminal acts by police officers—the same acts for which suspects are often arrested on assault charges in the programs—are presented as necessary. The tactics are effective, and the ends justify the means. They rationalize that their actions are the lesser of two evils; it would be worse for the guilty to be set free. Therefore the actions are portrayed as acceptable, or at least understandable. As evidenced by the episode of *Law & Order* where the police officer framed the suspect for the murder he did not commit, allowing a guilty man to go free is presented as a worse "crime" than those in which the police engage in order to achieve a greater good—protecting society. The officers never exhibit any guilt or remorse for their actions. The police officers' bad behavior is mitigated—presented as being a response to worse behavior by criminals. Therefore, the damage caused by the police officers' criminal actions is minimized, while the damage caused by the criminal suspects' actions is emphasized.

NYPD Blue offered messages about the role of police officers similar to those in earlier series in the genre—including in *Hill Street Blues*, also created by Stephen Bochco, and the even earlier *Dragnet*—as the narrative focuses on the process of police work. Also like *Hill Street Blues*, *NYPD Blue* ventured into narratives that suggest that police work can have a negative effect on the officers' personal lives. It deviated from the focus of *Dragnet* in this way, as *Dragnet* never portrayed the personal lives of the officers. However, in all three series, the focus remained solely on the police. Little was discussed or understood about the criminals, beyond what was necessary to reveal to present a coherent plot. *NYPD Blue* depicted personal problems that police detectives themselves encountered as a result of their job of protecting society. The personal price they paid was naturalized as part of the job, and the police detectives were portrayed as another "victim" of the criminal. The series shows how the personal and work lives of the officers consistently intersect with negative results. For example,

- In the early days of the series, Detective Andy Sipowicz suffered from alcoholism. Job stress was often revealed as the cause of his drinking.
- In a later episode of the series, in season 5, Sipowicz discovered that he had prostate cancer. When he talked to the doctor about his illness, he used the same terms he used in his investigations. For example, he said there was a "lack of evidence" that he had cancer, and that he "pursued" his suspicions with a second doctor. This serves to reinforce that the police detective approaches everything—even things in his personal life—in the same way he approaches his work. They are all equally important, and he follows the same "procedure."
- In another episode in season 5, Detective Bobby Simone investigated the murder of a woman who lived in a building he owned. The suspects included the woman's nephew, who frequently visited her at the building, and the building manager, who was part owner of the building. The episode ignored any conflict of interest resulting from Simone investigating the case, and his ownership of the building appeared to have no impact on the investigation. The episode illustrated an association between his work and his personal business dealings, but there were no financial consequences to him as a result of the murder occurring in a building he owned.
- Also in season 5, Bobby and fellow detective Diane Russell (who also battled alcoholism in the series) planned to marry at City Hall on their lunch break, after several cancellations due to work. However, the cases they were working on kept them from meeting. At first they even planned to postpone the wedding another day. The message consistently was that criminals are to blame for the

difficulties. Nevertheless, at the end of the work day, just as the City Hall office was closing, they decided not to let work interfere again, and they married.

In each of these examples, the detectives are shown struggling with personal issues because of their job. The officers, as dramatic heroes of the program, are situated as people dedicated to capturing criminals, even if their personal lives must suffer in the process, and even if they must sometimes resort to unethical and illegal behavior. Because of the sacrifices the police make, the audience can admire them and adopt the "tough-on-crime-and-criminals" notions they expound in the series.

The Practice

ABC's *The Practice*, which first aired in 1997, is set in a Boston law firm of criminal-defense attorneys. In this series, as is the case in the series starring police officers, the lawyers are also depicted as unethical. For example, in one episode in season 6, the character Lawrence O'Malley, a cannibal who called himself Hannibal Lecter, after the character in the movie *Silence of the Lambs*, was defended by attorney Bobby Donnell. The client claimed he was a cannibal but not a murderer. After O'Malley was found not guilty of murder, Bobby's wife, Lindsey, also an attorney at the firm, began to receive crank phone calls. Both Bobby and Lindsey were certain that it was O'Malley calling and hanging up because he had developed an obsession with Lindsey, calling her Clarisse—also a reference to the movie—during the trial. After the prosecutor's office tried to have O'Malley declared insane and institutionalized, the judge denied the petition, chastising the prosecution for trying to take O'Malley off the streets by any means after failing to get a conviction.

Later, O'Malley visited Lindsey at her home. She shot and killed him as he stood in the doorway of her apartment. He did not have a weapon and did not threaten her; he just appeared at her apartment, which frightened her. In a subsequent episode, Lindsey was put on trial for murder in the first degree and she claimed self-defense. The other attorneys in the firm defended her, claiming that she acted out of fear because she suffered from "battered woman syndrome" due to her previous encounters with former clients: one had stalked her and another stabbed her. However, a jury rejected that defense and convicted her of murder.

Clients are frequently depicted as insane and out of control in *The Practice*. During the trial, Lindsay's defense was that she "snapped." She was not the only attorney depicted as responding violently to criminal clients. It was revealed that Bobby had himself previously been charged with conspiracy to commit murder when one of his clients was killed; that client had also stalked Lindsay Dole. (Bobby was acquitted in that case.) In each of these scenarios, the violent act was portrayed as something Bobby and Lindsay could not control. The criminals that these attorneys defend were portrayed as dangerous. Their behavior, as cannibals and stalkers, was depicted as deranged. Therefore, when the attorneys respond with violent acts themselves, it was mitigated as a necessary evil act. The defense attorneys are not situated as criminals even though they committed criminal acts, like the clients they defend. The attorneys were portrayed as good people forced to respond violently to violent criminals. The defense attorneys explain, repeatedly, that they were required to carry out their role in the justice system by defending them, even when they found them morally reprehensible. The client criminals were portrayed as morally reprehensible, but the attorneys were not portrayed as morally reprehensible for defending them, or even killing them.

The attorneys also feared further violence by their clients. For example, in season 7, Lindsay was incarcerated for a month while her murder case was appealed, but the conviction was ultimately overturned, and she returned to the firm temporarily. However, she soon decided she did not want to continue to work as a criminal-defense attorney. Instead, she wanted small, routine (i.e., nonthreatening) cases, and decided to start her own practice to do so. She was shown as not wanting to associate with criminals anymore, because, in essence, it led her to become a criminal, and she did not want to encounter a similar situation again. Her decision to leave the firm to focus on noncriminal cases implied that if she remained a defense attorney, she felt she would be likely to commit another crime in response to a client's frightening behavior.

In the series, the actions of the prosecuting and defending attorneys were also often unethical—and even illegal—which influenced, and ultimately manipulated, the outcome of a case. An example can be seen in an episode in season 7, during which a woman, who kidnapped a baby 16 years prior, hired attorney Jimmy Berluti to visit the woman who had been wrongly accused (but never convicted) to say that she knew that she was innocent. She also wanted Jimmy to visit the girl's real mother to let her know that her daughter was not harmed. Jimmy accepted the case and visited the mother. He then contacted the wrongly accused woman, a white, lower-middle-class waitress in her 40s. Meanwhile, the real kidnapper, an upper-middle-class, white suburban mother in her 40s, got cold feet because the biological mother they already visited had informed police. The kidnapper told Jimmy not to follow through with telling the accused kidnapper, but he had already called her in to his office, and while there she was picked up by the prosecutor's office, who still believed she was the real kidnapper and that *she* had hired Jimmy to visit the real mother. When the waitress confessed to police because she was exhausted by the prosecution's lengthy questioning, legal ethics required Jimmy to tell the waitress he represented the real kidnapper, but it was impractical. He feared the message it would send to other clients if he revealed information to another person involved, in this case as a suspect. Jimmy visited the judge, a woman in her 60s (with whom he had a romantic relationship) and told her *ex parte* that he represented the real kidnapper. She said he had to get the real kidnapper to come forward if he wanted to clear the waitress. She said it was improper for him to be speaking to her about it.

However, she also said in court that she was disgusted by the prosecution's tactics in the confession, and made the prosecutor, Helen Gamble, stand in the corner with her face to the wall, to humiliate her. Still, the judge allowed the confession to stand because the waitress did not ask for a lawyer and made the statement voluntarily. When the waitress read in the paper that Jimmy was representing the real kidnapper, she asked him to go to police and tell the truth, but he said he could not, saying he believed he was protecting the process. A new female attorney who recently joined the Donnell firm joined Jimmy on the case and decided to go to the real kidnapper to plead with her to do the right thing and come forward to save the other woman. The kidnapper agreed.

In this way, as Rapping (2003) suggested in her analysis, the series is working "not to *escape* reality, but to reconstruct it in such a way that viewers are purposely confused about the actual message about law and justice it presents" (p. 45). The episode of *The Practice* with the waitress is an example of how Jimmy's actions could be read as wrong, but he was convinced that to be a good defense attorney he must fully defend his client. His obligation was to his client, not the truth. He also stresses that legal ethics are not the same as human ethics. His responsibility to the waitress as a human being was different than his responsibility to her as a defense attorney for someone else in the case. The attorneys in *The Practice* often feared their clients would harm them, or others, and therefore the attorneys agonized over their duty to defend or protect the clients, as was the case with Jimmy in the episode with the waitress, and a desire for a fair outcome. Jimmy tried—again through unethical tactics—to maintain confidentiality with his client, but still reveal the truth, by going to the judge *ex parte*. She, too, refused to breach her role in the system by acting on the information he was presenting to her.

The Practice primarily raised questions about the system that the lawyers have to operate in, not the actions of the lawyers themselves, because the lawyers were presented as serving the unpopular but necessary role of defenders. The series promoted the idea that every client deserves representation in court, and once an attorney accepted a case, he or she had to use virtually any means necessary to protect that client from prosecution. Guilt and ethics were irrelevant factors, so they cannot be considered. This depiction of defense attorneys was unlike the depiction in *Perry Mason*, where good always "won" and the truth was revealed. In *The Practice*, the guilty were sometimes set free, and the innocent were convicted—and the defense attorneys sometimes suffered emotionally and physically for their involvement in the process. Crime was presented as out of the control of the criminal, and as a result, also out of society's control to prevent it. *The Practice* depicted the criminals as posing a threat, not just to society, but specifically the legal authorities.

The Shield

The FX series *The Shield*, which first aired in 2002, depicts the police work of the Los Angeles Strike Force Team, headed by Vic Mackey. However, in this series, it is not the case that all the police detectives, who are the main characters, represent "us," or society, while the criminals in society represent "others," as is the case in *Law & Order* and *NYPD Blue*. In the series pilot, the audience learns that *The Shield* offers a very different message, as Mack engages in criminal behavior in order to apprehend suspects, and is threatened with the possibility of punishment for his crimes after a member of his team confirmed Mack's crimes to department Captain David Aceveda. In response, Mack orders the murder of the detective. This sets the tone for the series. Aceveda is the "good cop" and Mack is the "rogue cop." The struggle between good, represented by Aceveda, and evil, represented by Mack, is played out in this series. Aceveda strives to restore order to the police squad, while Mack tries to restore order to the city of Los Angeles, but uses illegal and criminal means. In the process, Mack uses violence, threats, and fear to deal not only with the drug dealers he is seeking to remove from the streets, but also with informants and other detectives. Throughout season 1, he committed many criminal acts:

- He stabbed a suspect with the pin of his badge, and punched other suspects, to try to coerce information out of them.
- He covered for other officers who had committed crimes. In one segment, he helped a high-ranking police official cover up the fact that the official ran over a child and killed him. He also covered for another officer who shot a suspect. In that episode, he donned a disguise, posing as a gang member, and held up a van of police officers who were transporting the evidence of the officer's gun used in the shooting, and then framed a gang member for the crime.

Legal Authorities 115

- He killed a drug dealer in cold blood, without provocation.
- He even used violence and threats against his own team members. He shot a fellow police detective on his Strike Force Team, after the detective reported to Aceveda that the team was involved with illegal activity. The detective said he would help Aceveda prove that Mack was a dirty cop. After the shooting, Mack framed two drug dealers for the killing.

These actions are clearly more violent than the transgressions exhibited by the officers in *NYPD Blue* and *Law & Order*, but as in the earlier two series, they are portrayed as necessary to maintain order and to achieve the greater good of protecting society. However, while *Law & Order* and *NYPD Blue* identify the behavior as inappropriate, in *The Shield*, Mack does not perceive his crimes as crimes. In an episode in season 1, he explained to his team members the danger the supervisor posed to the work the team was trying to do. Mack said Aceveda was "trying to stick us in a cage with the same animals we fight everyday." In the context of the series, Mack does not view himself as an "animal,"—that is, a criminal—even though Mack's actions include murder and deception, and he is similar to the criminal drug dealers he chased down.

The delineation of good and evil characters is blurred in *The Shield*, as Mack is not the only legal authority character depicted as having flaws. Even though Aceveda sees Mack as an enemy (he is unaware that Mack wanted to have him killed), in one episode in season 1, Aceveda called on Mack to employ his rogue ways when Aceveda saw no other way of solving a crime. In the episode, a man addicted to crack cocaine sold his daughter on the Internet to get money to buy drugs. When the police attempted to locate the girl, Aceveda asked Mack to step in to interrogate the man, knowing that Mack would beat the information out of the man if he felt he "had to," which he did. As a result, at the same time the series depicts the struggle between good and evil through the two characters of Mack and Aceveda, it also raises questions about how to define what is "good" and what is "evil." While Aceveda says he is repulsed by Mack's tactics and wants to remove him from the team, there are clearly gray areas for him—in this case, because he saw no other way of resolving the case. His main concern was finding the girl—using any means available.

The series also depicts Aceveda as personally benefiting from Mack's tactics. Crime decreased in the city since the team was created, and Aceveda is applauded by the police department and city officials for this achievement. While Aceveda can be viewed as noble in his desire to bring down Mack, a corrupt cop, his motives are also presented as suspect. Plus, he talks about bringing Mack down, but takes little action in this direction. In the context of the series, Mack is situated as the "rogue" officer, but when Aceveda asks Mack to employ his rogue ways, the squad captain is shown to be no different than Mack. They may differ on how and when Mack's tactics should be used, but neither is shown to fully reject them.

Mack is not the only unethical member of the department. In one episode, also in season 1, Assistant Chief Ben Gilroy used his influence in the police department to perpetrate a real-estate scam by reducing the number of police officers patrolling one particular a neighborhood, so that crime would increase. This enabled Gilroy to buy real estate in the neighborhood very inexpensively. After the sale, Gilroy returned the officers to the neighborhood so crime would decrease, enabling him to sell the property for a much higher price than he bought it at. As far as Gilroy was concerned, no one got hurt. He showed no understanding of how his illegal behavior impacted the people who lived in the neighborhood during the time crime rates escalated. The residents of the neighborhood were a pawn in his scheme, and were not viewed by him as human beings with lives that were affected by his crime. However, the episode does reveal the damage he caused.

While Mack and Gilroy are situated as "others" in the department, in one episode Mack is also shown to be an "other" in his personal life, when his autistic son was denied admission to a private school that has a specialized program for autistic children because one of the school trustees was aware of Mack's corrupt ways and the fact that he was facing stolen-drug charges. Mack was not seen by the school trustee as "one of Them."

He was perceived as an outsider, and not accepted. The trustee believed that Mack was guilty of corruption, and as such, someone who must be kept outside of the private-school circle. Even though Mack had not been convicted of any crime, because he was believed to be corrupt, he was branded an "other."

Interestingly, Mack often uses this very same tactic himself when he is trying to capture criminals. For example, in one episode, Mack knew that a drug dealer would be the likely suspect of a shooting, and he used that perception of guilt to frame the drug dealer and cover up a shooting by another officer. He never considered whether he treated the man he framed "fairly." Yet, when Mack was labeled an "other" by the school community, he felt he was being treated "unfairly." His crimes should have had no relevance on whether his son, an innocent child, was accepted to the school, but in addition to the educational program it offered, as a private school, it also had a certain status, and the trustee showed that he was trying to maintain that status, which did not include associating with criminals.

These portrayals in *The Shield* clearly show that law-enforcement officers are neither all good nor all bad. They sometimes engage in illegal acts, but, they believe, for good reasons. Yet, in *The Shield*, when criminals commit illegal acts, their crimes are never depicted as acts committed by complex and complicated people who can be both good and evil. The criminals are shown to be purely evil; there is no gray area. The question is never raised in the series whether the criminals, like Mack, feel they are committing the crimes for some greater "good," even if it is a distorted sense of good, as is Mack's.

The Shield does not imply that all law-enforcement officers are corrupt and unethical, but it illustrates a need to examine the tactics used by *some* officers. However, the series can also be read as suggesting that criminals are to blame for good cops doing bad things. In this way, *The Shield* may appeal to people who hold similar beliefs to Mack's, and prefer vigilante methods. However, with its complex representations, it may have as much appeal to people who believe that Mack's tactics are reprehensible, serving to confirm the belief that legal authorities abuse their power and police tactics need to be questioned. While the depiction of Mack is open to interpretation by the audience and he could be seen as good or evil, the depictions of the police officers in *NYPD Blue* and *Law & Order*—particularly of the main characters—suggest they are clearly good, because their violent acts are not extreme, and are only used in "rare" instances, and by nonrecurring characters. These acts are an aberration, not normal behavior for legal authorities, and, therefore, are more easily excusable than Mack's may be to some viewers.

Although *The Shield* is not progressive in its representation of criminals, as it follows the traditional themes presented previously in the genre, the series presents crime from the perspective of legal authorities, as most series in the genre before it did. However, it is depicting legal authorities in a new way, in that they are shown here to be morally ambiguous.

Cold Case

Cold Case, which first aired on CBS in 2003, also stars police detectives, this time attempting to solve old cases. *Cold Case* follows a structured narrative each week that begins postcrime, similar to *Law & Order* and *NYPD Blue*. Unlike these earlier two series, however, the narrative focus is primarily on the motivations of the criminal suspects and the events that lead to crime. For example, in one episode in season 1, the detectives investigate the death of an 8-year-old boy. They discover, through interviews, and it is revealed to the audience in flashback scenes, that on the night he died, he had asked his parents if he could go to the local store to buy a notebook for school. His parents were preoccupied, as the house was in chaos with two smaller children for the parents to attend to, so the 8-year-old left the house alone, without his parents knowing. On his way to the store, he encountered a group of African American teens who taunted him and convinced him to steal some glue for them. The boy bought the notebook and stole the glue, which infuriated the owner of the store. He followed the boy out of the store and beat him, leaving him lying in the snow, where the boy eventually froze to death.

Legal Authorities 119

In this example, the rage felt by the shop owner ultimately leads to the killing, but several other factors led the boy to be in the wrong place at the wrong time. The crime is essentially senseless, that is, this crime could have been avoided or prevented:

- if the parents had paid more attention to the boy and gone with him to the store;
- if the boy had not encountered the teens on the way to the store;
- if the teens had not tormented him and challenged him to steal the glue;
- if the boy had not succumbed to the teens' threat;
- if it was not so cold;
- if the store owner had handled his anger differently.

Most crimes on *Cold Case* follow a similar narrative of a senseless or preventable crime. In another episode in season 1, a Jewish father and his son, Benny, fought both over the son's gentile girlfriend, and the fact that the father wanted the son to become a dentist, while the son wanted to be a disco dancer. The father said he would disown the son if he married the girl and did not become a dentist. After the argument at the disco club, the father left and Benny got into another fight with a rival dancer, Paul, who was going to be competing with him in a dance-off at the club that night. Paul pulled out a gun, they struggled, and the gun went off, killing Benny. Paul set fire to the club to cover up the murder. In another episode in season 1, a serial killer/rapist was caught when the detectives discovered his MO—attacking girls who own cats and are involved in book clubs, both seen by the killer as signals they are "alone in the world." He selected victims who were smart and cultured because he resented his upbringing in a trailer park in Trenton, New Jersey.

While these fictional depictions in *Cold Case* offer a new representation of crime and criminals—emphasizing that crime is often random—they also indicate the preventability of crime. As in the episode with the 8-year-old boy, there are many points in these other examples where the crimes could have been averted. In addition, as previously unsolved cases, the circumstances of these crimes—most occurring many years earlier—are often such that the people who committed them have already changed, and are essentially "good" people. The suspect is never obvious in the episodes. It is usually a seemingly "normal" or unlikely suspect—sometimes a family member—who commits the murder, reinforcing the notion that rehabilitation of criminals is possible. In flashback scenes, the suspects and victims are often depicted in happier times. As a result, the suspects are shown to have redeeming qualities.

However, each episode always ends with the suspects being led to jail by police, having been arrested. Therefore, it is implied they will be prosecuted for their crimes. As murderers, presumably most of them will serve a long prison sentence. Yet, a sadness is also conveyed in these depictions, especially in the final scene as the suspect is led away by the arresting detectives. Their faces are superimposed with an image of them at the time they committed the murder, often many years younger. In this final scene, the main detective in the series, Lilly Rush, often has a sad look on her face; she does not revel in having caught the murderer. Also in this final scene, the victim usually appears to Lilly in a "ghost" form. These two visual images together work to indicate to the audience that the circumstances of the person being arrested are unfortunate—because the crime could or should have been avoided. Still, Lilly clearly considers her strongest obligation to be to the victim. As a result, the audience is left with the sense that the outcome is "just." Further, because the criminals are not recurring characters, the audience is not encouraged to identify with the criminal suspects, but they are encouraged to understand—and even sympathize with—them because the main character, Lilly, does. The depictions of criminals in *Cold Case* are more complete than the depictions in *Law & Order, NYPD Blue, The Practice*, and *The Shield*.

Each series promotes a specific way law and order is—and should be—maintained in society. *Law & Order, NYPD Blue, The Practice*, and *The Shield* construct crime fighting as a role for legal authorities—police detectives, prosecutors, and defense lawyers. While these series focus on police work after crime has been committed, *Cold Case* goes a step further, beyond merely apprehending suspects, to suggest that crime is *preventable*. It implies that people should not wait for crime to occur and should not deal with it only by apprehending and punishing suspects after the fact. *Cold Case* presents crime prevention not as the role of police in society, but of individuals who are not police officers. Therefore, it signifies a new representation of legal authorities in the genre.

CHAPTER 5

CRIMINALS

Villains and heroes are central concepts in the television crime genre. Historically, criminals have been portrayed as "villains" in society, while the hero legal authorities have represented "us," or society. For the first 50 years in the genre, "the villain appears as such a taken-for-granted entity, the common-sensical embodiment of everything a society supposedly finds abhorrent" (Marchetti, 1989, p. 192). Still, these characters served a cathartic function for viewers, as Marchetti suggested:

> Frequently...the villain represents utter contempt for all those things American society holds most sacred—e.g., middle-class respectability, the nuclear family, suburban material comfort, law and order, patriotism...[I]t can be argued that, in expressing contempt for these institutions, the villain may be venting the viewer's own frustrations arising from pressure to succeed or fit in. (p. 193)

Fiske and Dawson (1996) further pointed to villains, and particularly violent acts performed by them, as providing an opportunity for audiences who feel oppressed to identify with other oppressed people:

> Certain representations of violence enable subordinated people to articulate symbolically their sense of opposition and hostility to the particular forms of domination that oppress them. These representations must contain not only violence, but also markers of ethnic, class, age, or national difference that are portrayed not as natural essences, but as structural agents of power and disempowerment. (p. 304)

Even while villains were being portrayed as "others" who challenged societal norms, viewers identified with them. At the same time, these villains served to reinforce what was "normal" in society. They were not creating a new "normal," but confirming the existing norm. "[E]verything the villain is not is normal and positive" (Marchetti, 1989, p. 193). Villains "represent a desire to be 'different,' not to follow the norms and strictures which bind our society together" (Marchetti, 1989, p. 193). Therefore, when villains were not abiding by social norms, they were appealing to audiences who, for whatever reasons, felt constricted by those norms themselves. As a result, these representations of criminals in the genre have likely traditionally appealed to segments of society who feel that they do not fit into the American, middle-class mold, either by their own choice, or because society is keeping them outside of society through its structures. The criminal/villain in these texts represents the struggle and negotiation over power that exists within the larger societal structure, as well as smaller substructures, including family units, the workplace, or between friends. Viewers who feel oppressed and outside society (us), therefore, identify with the villains (them), and gain satisfaction vicariously through these characters who rebel against society, and often against authority figures.

Between 1998 and 2004, two series in the genre, *Oz* and *The Sopranos*, offered a new depiction of criminals by portraying what happens to a criminal prior to, and after, a crime is committed. These portrayals provided the criminal perspective on crime, rather than the legal authorities' perspective. A key theme in the series is the importance of personal relationships in either causing or preventing crime. Criminals—traditionally "villains" in the genre who served as antagonists of the main police characters—became the dramatic heroes, the recurring characters that viewers tuned in to watch each week. As such, audiences were encouraged to view the events that unfolded in the way the criminals saw them, not the way the legal authorities saw them.

In this chapter, I explore the representations of criminals in *Oz* and *The Sopranos* and show that they offer more than a singular "Us. versus Them" depiction. This shift suggests that the representations in the genre expanded during this time period. Representations of criminals in these two series locate them as part of families and other groups, primarily based on ethnicity, which, in some cases, influence the individuals who eventually turn to crime. Through these depictions, the cultural connotation of "the criminal" in society is understood. As Seiter (1992) suggested, "connotative meanings land us squarely in the domain of ideology: the worldview (including the model of social relations and their causes) portrayed from a particular position and set of interests in society" (p. 39). As I will show, the need for people to "belong" is a common theme in the series I analyzed. I examine how depictions of individual relationships and membership in small groups are used in these two series to construct criminals either as people who are unable to be rehabilitated, or as complete, but complex and flawed, human beings who have redeeming qualities.

OZ AND EMERALD CITY

Discourses about family are a central theme in the HBO series *Oz*, which is the nickname given to Oswald State Penitentiary, where the series is set. The name of the series is an intertextual reference to the famous 1939 film *The Wizard of Oz*, and the themes in the movie are also evident in the television series. In the movie, Dorothy sought to return to her family from the Land of Oz, although at first she claimed to want to get away from Kansas and her family. She did not think she would miss her family or the life she knew on the farm when she wished to go "over the rainbow." In the television series, several of the inmates in the prison were also trying to get back home to their families. Like Dorothy in the movie, many of the inmates in Oz understood the importance of their family relationships only after those ties were severed.

In the movie, Emerald City within the Land of Oz was perceived as a utopia. Similarly, in the HBO series, a section of the prison called Em City—an experimental community where inmates are given more freedom than those in the general population of the prison, in order to help them become more socialized and assimilate back into society at the end of their sentences—represented a seemingly ideal "community" compared to other areas of the prison. Em City served to recreate group membership in society. The groups in the prison—as designated by the prison administrator, Tim McManus—consisted of: The Brotherhood of Aryans, Irish, Others (McManus' term to refer to people he sees as not belonging to any group), Homeboys, Latinos, Muslims, Italians, and Gays. Each group was represented by four members in Em City. With a gymnasium and a recreational area, Em City was where inmates could congregate, play cards, and watch television (often HBO-produced programs).

Inmates in Em City identified themselves as belonging to a specific group, often by wearing the same clothing they wore in the outside world (allowed in Em City, unlike in Gen Pop). Irish inmate Ryan O'Reily wore green shirts, a cross on a chain around his neck representing his Catholic upbringing, and a green jacket with "Ireland" embossed on the back. Muslim inmate Kareem Said and his followers wore crocheted hats. They showed pride in belonging to these groups by their attire and association with members of the group. The Italians wore tank tops (also referred to culturally as "Ginny T-shirts"). Their clothing also helped the audience identify the groups the inmates belong to, as there was little explicit discussion in the series about the group identification or structure of Em City beyond the early episodes, when the experimental unit and the council of representatives were established. The prisoners were in some cases officially classified as Others by administrators or informally labeled as "others" by inmates in Oz, thus illustrating how people become "others" in society. This was most clearly seen in the character of inmate Augustus Hill, an African American who was also confined to a wheelchair. When Hill discovered that he had been placed in Em City officially as an Other, he challenged the classification, reminding McManus that he interacted with many of the inmates in Em City from many different groups, primarily with the Muslims. McManus did not see him as being part of the Muslims, and said the classification would stand. Hill was powerless to change his Other status, which classified them as not like anyone in the remaining groups, that is, "leftovers."

However, just as Dorothy realized that even though she had her freedom in Oz and Emerald City, she did not have her family with her—and she learned that family was more important to her than her freedom—some prison inmates in Oz discovered that "home" is the real utopia, and they strived to return, having learned the importance of family. By referencing the movie *The Wizard of Oz* in the HBO television series *Oz*, series creator Tom Fontana drew a connection between Dorothy—a quintessential "good and wholesome" character in the American culture—and what was otherwise seemingly the antithesis in the culture, "the criminal." As a result, the depictions in *Oz* enabled the audience to move beyond this cultural connotation of criminals as villains and recognize that criminals may value the same things as law-abiding citizens, particularly the relationships they have with family members and other acquaintances. The series suggested that these relationships often lead to their redemption. In the next section, I show how a group of characters in *Oz* who exhibit redeeming qualities were portrayed opposite characters who specifically did not exhibit these qualities, and a range of criminal representations emerged from the perspective of the criminal rather than of the legal authorities, making it evident that the genre progressed in its construction of "the criminal" in society beyond the previous narrow and incomplete villain/other depiction.

FAMILIAL RELATIONSHIPS IN *OZ*

Ryan O'Reily
When *Oz* began, Ryan O' Reily was a street-tough leader of the Irish group in Em City. By season 2, his status as a leader was in jeopardy when he was diagnosed with breast cancer. He concealed his illness, especially

because it was a "chick's disease," as he referred to it, fearing he would be perceived as weak by inmates, who revere traditional masculine traits. As Ryan recovered in the prison hospital, he fell in love with his prison doctor, Gloria Nathan. His obsession with her led him to convince his brain-damaged half-brother Cyril—who had an IQ of 51—to kill Gloria's husband. When Cyril carried out his brother's orders, he was incarcerated in Oz as well. The relationship between the brothers could be read in two ways. It could indicate that Ryan is motivated by his desire to have his brother near him, that is, imprisoned, and therefore does not see his actions as "hurting" Cyril, which I take to be the preferred reading as presented in the series. Cyril *was* clearly happy to be near Ryan, and because of Cyril's disability, prison was not a torturous experience for him, as it was for many other inmates. Or, it could be read as a relationship based on selfish manipulation, and that Ryan's obsession with the doctor was more important to him than his relationship with his brother.

I contend that the series was depicting Ryan as both nurturing and manipulative, and through these depictions, *Oz* was addressing the complex nature of people, in this case particularly criminals. An example can be seen in one flashback scene, where Ryan was shown to be responsible for the injury that resulted in Cyril becoming brain damaged. In the scene, Ryan got into a bar fight, and Cyril went to his aid. Cyril was pushed by one of the brawlers, and he hit his head, which resulted in the injury. Distraught and guilt ridden, Ryan went on a driving rampage that ended with him driving his car into a group of construction workers, killing one of them. In this depiction of the reason for Ryan's incarceration, he was portrayed as someone who was not an "evil" person before he was incarcerated. Driving his car recklessly following Cyril's accident was portrayed as an act of punishment he inflicted on himself for causing his brother's life-altering injury. That is, the audience was encouraged to see Ryan as having redeeming qualities, including that he had a sense of guilt over what he had done and felt a responsibility to other people, including his family members.

However, the representation of Ryan also included instances where he chose to continue to commit crimes, including killing Gloria's husband, for which he had no remorse at first. This contradictory behavior of a character who had both good and evil traits enabled him to evolve throughout the series, as this struggle between the "two Ryans" was played out. Part of the appeal of the series was likely that this portrayal of a complex character created unpredictability. While the potential for Ryan to be rehabilitated was presented, so was the potential for him to reject rehabilitation. It was particularly through Ryan's interactions with Gloria, a noncriminal character, that an evolution was evident. In one episode of season 2, when Ryan first confessed his love to Gloria, he said: "You always do the right thing, the moral thing. That's why I love you. I've got every reason to live now." He saw in her what he was lacking: morality, or at least consistent morality.

Gloria was shown to be torn by her compassionate and at times affectionate feelings for Ryan, and her hatred for him because he killed her husband. Therefore, like Ryan, Gloria was engaged in an internal struggle, too. This was clearly shown in season 4, when Ryan discovered that the man who raped Gloria after she had left the prison and was walking home had become an inmate in Oz, and he beat the man to death. He wanted to confess to the killing, but Gloria pleaded with him not to because she knew he would be put to death. In this interaction, Gloria acknowledged that Ryan's life was worth saving, and later in season 4, when Ryan talked to Gloria about the crimes he had committed—including killing her husband—she acknowledged that she loved him. In the episode, he told her he wanted to confess his crimes to his mother, but he feared she would stop loving him. Gloria assured Ryan his mother would not turn her back on him. Gloria said: "In my experience, you don't love Ryan O'Reily by choice." Gloria was shown in the series to be both the source of Ryan's desire to transform his life so she would want to be with him, and the person who recognized that he was undergoing a transformation, which encouraged him to continue to change for the better. As a "good and wholesome" character, the audience was able to identify with Gloria, and was encouraged to see Ryan as she did.

Flashback scenes provided the audience with additional evidence that Ryan had redeeming qualities, as they offered a glimpse into Ryan's life prior to incarceration, particularly his family life. He came from a lower-class neighborhood, and his biological mother, Suzanne Fitzgerald (played by Broadway star Betty Buckley) had left the family because the father was abusive. Ryan was then raised by Cyril's mother, whom he believed to be his biological mother. In season 4, Ryan discovered that Suzanne was his real mother, and she began visiting him regularly in prison, which enabled them to reestablish their relationship by talking about Ryan's abusive father and their love for Cyril. Even though Cyril was not her biological son, she was motherly toward him. In those early meetings with Ryan, Suzanne explained that she was not able to contact him for so many years because she was on the run from authorities. In the 1960s, she was involved in a militant war protest that ended with someone being killed. She told Ryan she wanted to confess to her involvement in the killing and turn herself in, but Ryan pleaded with her not to because he feared losing contact with her again. Ryan continued to exhibit a strong attachment to his mother in season 5, after she turned herself in to authorities. As part of her sentence, she began giving singing and acting lessons to inmates in Oz to help them stage a performance of *Macbeth* (which occurred in the series finale in season 6). However, Ryan's affection for his mother and his desire to protect her eventually led to more crime.

In one episode in season 5, he discovered that the Asians in Em City planned to rape and kill Suzanne to retaliate for a crime Ryan had committed earlier against another member of their group. When Ryan confronted one of the Asians, they fought, and Ryan stabbed him. Cyril followed Ryan's lead and ultimately delivered the fatal injury. Cyril was convicted of murder and placed on death row. Suzanne and Ryan continued to bond as they tried to get Cyril's death sentence overturned, citing his diminished mental capacity. After all avenues were explored, Cyril was put to death by electric chair in the series finale in season 6, but Ryan said he could not watch the execution, and went to the gym. Gloria met him there, and to comfort him, she kissed him.

In season 5, Ryan's father, Seamus, was introduced in the series. In a discussion with Ryan's new cellmate, an Irish priest (played by best-selling author Malachy McCourt), Ryan explained that he had been brutalized by his father as a child, but it was the death of his 6-month-old sister, Carolyn, when he was a child himself, that still haunted him. He said Carolyn fell out of her crib and broke her neck. The priest, in Oz for destruction of property and assaulting a police officer, believed that Ryan was carrying guilt over her death—and that it could be the motivation for his self-destructive behavior. He encouraged Ryan to address the issue with his father. When Seamus visited Ryan in prison, Ryan asked him about Carolyn's death, and said he remembered that Seamus shook her violently until she stopped crying. Seamus denied this, and insisted that Carolyn fell out of the crib. The battle between the father and son continued when Seamus later became an inmate in Oz, in season 6. While at first they remained at odds, in the series finale, after Cyril was executed, Gloria told Ryan she would forgive him for killing her husband if he made amends with his father, who was dying in the prison hospital from a stab wound sustained during an altercation with another inmate. Gloria said that through Ryan's relationship with Cyril, she saw that he was good, but she also saw that he could be evil, too. At her coaxing, Ryan went to his father's bedside, held his hand, and said he would not let him die alone. By the series finale, Ryan had recognized that his crimes were self-destructive and damaging to other people, had shown affection for family members and Gloria, and was shown affection by Gloria, a noncriminal character, so the audience was encouraged to see Ryan as rehabilitated.

Tobias Beecher
While Ryan's struggle between good and evil was an internal one, that theme was further explored in *Oz* through fellow inmates Tobias Beecher, who was classified by McManus as an Other in Oz, and Vern Schillinger, the Aryan leader. When the series began, Vern wanted Beecher—a former lawyer incarcerated on vehicular-manslaughter charges for driving drunk and killing a family of three—to become an Aryan follower. Beecher refused, and a rivalry began between the two, escalating in season 3, when Beecher convinced Schillinger's son, Andy, also an inmate in Oz,

to condemn his father's evil ways. Vern decided he had to remove this threat to his power and authority, even if it meant killing his own son. Knowing that Andy was addicted to drugs, he sent him a package of heroin while he was in solitary confinement, intending for him to overdose. Schillinger blamed Beecher for Andy's death, even though Schillinger was responsible. To retaliate, in season 4 Schillinger asked another son, Hank, to kidnap Beecher's two young children—a son and a daughter. Beecher's son was killed during the kidnapping.

Beecher was situated in the series as the "good" and redeemable character, even though he sometimes engaged in criminal behavior. This was because, unlike Vern who was portrayed as purely evil, Beecher felt remorse for his crimes. For example, in one episode, Beecher asked one of the Italians to kill Hank, and Beecher planned to kill Vern himself, to retaliate for the murder of his son; but, after visiting with his daughter and receiving counsel from Muslim leader Kareem Said, he decided to call off the hit. By the time he spoke to the hit man, it was too late, and Hank was already dead. Beecher ordered the crime out of anger, seeking revenge, but because he tried to stop it and showed that he understood that it was wrong, he was perceived as potentially redeemable, while Vern, who never questioned whether killing was wrong, was not portrayed as redeemable. Another example of this was evident in one episode in season 6, when Beecher was to go before the parole board, but first asked to meet with the family of the girl he killed in the drunk-driving accident that resulted in his imprisonment, against the advice of Sister Peter Marie, the prison psychologist (played by Rita Moreno), who feared that the parents would try to block Beecher's parole. Beecher even required that the meeting be part of his parole. During the meeting, Beecher told the parents that he understood what he did to them because his son and wife had died since he has been in Oz because of destructive things he had done. Beecher demonstrated that he was able to understand the chain of crime, and the consequences of crime. As with the interactions between Gloria and Ryan, Beecher was depicted in *Oz* as a redeemable character because noncriminal characters saw him that way. In addition to Beecher's interactions with Sr. Peter Marie, this was evident in season 4, when Beecher's parole lawyer developed an attraction to him, and they began a romantic relationship.

The series depicted women who dealt professionally with criminals as forming a romantic attachment to them, which could be seen in two ways. The women could be seen as being emotionally manipulated by the male criminals, as the men do benefit from having these noncriminals view them as redeemable. The lawyer who fell in love with Beecher could help him get paroled if she could convince the parole board that he was no longer a danger to society. The doctor who had romantic feelings for Ryan supported his cause to get his brother Cyril off death row. Or, the relationships between the female noncriminals and the male criminals in *Oz* could be seen as genuine emotions that emerged when the women saw that the men interacted in a loving way with their family members. The women saw these men as trying to rehabilitate their lives, and evidenced by the fact that they work in the correctional system, that was presumably a personal goal.

By the end of the series, Beecher did kill Schillinger, the result of an accident involving trickery by his boyfriend in Oz, inmate Chris Keller, a character who also never showed that he was redeemable. In the series finale, Vern and Beecher performed in the prison production of the play *Macbeth*, and Keller, who was in charge of providing the props during the play, switched the prop knife with a real one, which resulted in Beecher killing Vern. The unintended deaths continued later in the episode, when Beecher and Keller argued over Keller's deception: Keller expected Beecher to be happy that he helped him kill Vern, but Beecher was furious. Keller saw Beecher as being free of the man who had caused him so much pain, but Beecher was haunted by the guilt—something Keller did not understand. As the two tussled, Beecher accidentally knocked Keller off the second-story balcony of the Em City area, killing him too. This final struggle between Beecher and Keller could be seen literally and metaphorically as a struggle between good and evil. Presumably, "good" won, but given the previous events in the series, it was implied that the cycle of crime would continue because there would be retaliation for Vern's death, by the other Aryans.

Even the characters portrayed as evil and unable to be rehabilitated, such as Keller and Vern, did show in the series that they were operating under some moral code, and that they *do* distinguish between what they consider to be "understandable" violations of the law and reprehensible ones. For example, in season 2, a Catholic priest, imprisoned for 10 years after molesting children from his parish, was released from Oz, but he returned, having no other place to go. Inmates rejected the priest, including Schillinger, who lured the priest to the gymnasium, where the priest was nailed to the floor. Schillinger said, "Any laws I've broken do not deserve to be laws." Here, it was clear that even Schillinger recognized *something* as wrong. Keller, too, showed that he operated under a moral code, albeit a distorted one. He often committed crimes to protect Beecher. Keller, like Ryan and Beecher, was shown in the series to commit crimes because he was protecting someone he loved. However, unlike Ryan and Beecher, he died having never recognized that his good intentions did not make the crimes acceptable. As a result, Keller never exhibited the transformation that Ryan and Beecher did, even though they were all shown affection and form relationships. In this way, rehabilitation was depicted as a choice made by the criminals. They chose to acknowledge their destructive behavior and not continue the cycle of crime. It was also implied in the series that the types of crimes committed that led to incarceration are key in determining whether rehabilitation will be pursued. Ryan and Beecher were incarcerated because of reckless behavior, not because of a conscious choice to kill. Keller and Vern, however, were depicted throughout the series as people who chose to kill and showed no remorse for that choice, making them less redeemable.

The Prison Staff
While the Oz prison staff often served to reinforce the notion that rehabilitation was possible for inmates who chose to pursue it, the staff struggled to hold onto that belief. At one point in *Oz* in season 6, McManus, the prison administrator who created Em City and had always believed that prisoners could be rehabilitated, questioned whether rehabilitation

was really possible—and if it was worth the effort. As crime continued within the prison, McManus acknowledged that many of the inmates (such as Keller and Schillinger) had not changed at all. He considered giving up trying to help, but then said, "If I give up on even one of these guys, I might as well open a diner somewhere." He believed that he should try to rehabilitate all inmates. In a later episode, McManus said to Gloria, "We can't save them all, Gloria, but if we can save just one, that's enough." Here he reinforced the notion that his job was to find the good in the inmates because the lives of the inmates mattered. He, like many people in a service role in society, was shown to be motivated by the desire to help others reach their potential, but he suffered personally for his idealism, as did the police officers in *NYPD Blue*, which I will discuss in the next chapter. He attributed his divorce to the fact that his wife did not agree with his desire "to save the world." She resented that he spent so much of his time at work trying to rehabilitate criminals whom she believed to be unable to be rehabilitated.

Oz, a series set in a prison, clearly depicted people who were deviant; no characters were portrayed as wrongly convicted. The characters' actions were not moral, taken as a whole, but the characters exhibited traits while in prison that were redeeming. I see this series as progressive in its representation of criminals because it claimed that it may be possible for them to change their ways. This change was possible because of their families. The message is: If criminals can show they care about their own family members and are able to form relationships, then there is the potential for them to repent for their crimes and eventually become law-abiding citizens. This was not shown to be the case with all characters, but the series does raise the possibility that it could occur. The concept of redemption was exhibited in *Oz* in an episode during the third season, when the name Oswald State Penitentiary was formally changed to Oswald State Correctional Facility. This showed, in theory, that the state was not emphasizing punishment and confinement as much as rehabilitation. (However, as I will show in chapter 8, this philosophy is presented in *Oz* as being in name only. The name change was for public relations purposes and did not signify any change in philosophy of how to best rehabilitate inmates.) By being able to repent for the crime, there is the potential for rehabilitation. This follows Foucault's (1975/1995) account of the process of rehabilitation for criminals.

> [T]he rehabilitation of the criminal is expected not of the application of a common law, but of the relation of the individual to his own conscience and to what may enlighten him from within. Alone in his cell, the convict is handed over to himself; in the silence of his passions and of the world that surrounds him, he descends into his conscience, he questions it and feels awakening within him the moral feeling that never entirely perishes in the heart of man. (p. 238)

In the fictional prison of Oz, however, being confined to "solitary," which the inmates referred to as solitary confinement, was the worst form of punishment for the inmates. The process of examining their consciences was shown to be difficult and painful. In solitary confinement, also referred to as "the hole" by some prisoners, the inmates were naked, living in a dirty and dark cell with no windows or light. Inmates said that an extension to their prison sentence would be preferable to solitary. While these criminals rejected society and its laws, they were also shown at the same time to need interaction with others. Those who interacted with family members, friends, and noncriminals in *Oz* were often shown to be redeemable. Not all the characters were redeemable, and I propose that this was part of the appeal of the series for the audience—watching to see who *would* change. In *Oz*, Schillinger and Keller showed that they were not able to be rehabilitated, while Ryan and Beecher showed they were able to be rehabilitated.

A central theme in *Oz* was that family could be used as a weapon by the inmates, but only because it was something people—even criminals—cared about. This new representation of criminals—not seen in the genre prior to *Oz*—reinforced the importance of family relationships (an American value), which may have accounted for the appeal of the series to audiences. Most viewers would not recognize their own family members in these characters who were murderers—but they might recognize the sanctity of the family relationships. While characters in *Oz* did show contempt for some—or even most—of society's laws, they held their own nuclear family as sacred, and that made it possible for the audience to perceive them as redeemable, and possibly even relatable. For example, at the end of the series, Ryan physically attacked inmates who threatened to hurt his mother once she became an inmate. He also struggled to save his brother's life once he was sentenced to death, seeking the assistance of prison staff.

A MOB FAMILY

Beck (2000) noted: "Through the dissemination of American ideas in movies and popular culture, Italians have come to stand for organized criminality all over the world" (p. 24). Beck pointed out that the images of Italian Americans in popular culture are both rejected and embraced by them. He noted that the images of Italians Americans' involvement in organized crime are "felt by them and by others to be admirable as well as deplorable, fascinating as well as terrifying, endearing as well as off-putting" (p. 25). He continued:

> Those characteristics include some that Italians are happy to identify with, such as warmth, family closeness, loyalty, courage, eloquence, humor, and concern for personal honor. In fact, as the most recent vehicles show, the movie images of Italian Americans in organized crime are used by Italian Americans as sources of amusement and models of personal style. (p. 25)

Beck suggested that it has been Italian Americans—including directors Francis Ford Coppola and Martin Scorsese, actors Marlon Brando and Robert DeNiro, and television producer David Chase—who have continued to depict Italians as gangsters in popular culture, but that in the process the narrative has expanded from earlier depictions.

> Violence, legality, and respectability remain central issues, but they are found side by side with questions about preserving

traditional loyalties, family bonds, and a distinctive national culture that ranges from cooking to emotional displays. These are not the concerns imposed on this culturally embattled ethnic group by a mainstream culture that is derogatory and repressive. They are the concerns raised from within that community by its most accomplished children. (p. 26)

Just as the HBO series *Oz* referenced a famous movie, characters in another HBO series starring a mob family, *The Sopranos*, referred to *The Godfather* movie trilogy, with characters sometimes even directly reciting lines from the film. The themes in the movie stressed protection of both personal interests (that is, the family), and business interests (that is, the family business). These were also prominent in *The Sopranos*. However, I argue that the setting of *The Sopranos*—in a present-day middle-class New Jersey suburb—conveys a different message than that presented in *The Godfather*, which was originally released in the 1970s but was set in the 1940s.

The motivation for the Corleones, who were immigrants from Italy, to engage in criminal behavior was for them to be able to make a better life for their family in America. The *Godfather* series suggested that in America at the time it was difficult for immigrants to obtain jobs and make enough money to make sure their families were cared for. According to the film, at the time, society did not welcome these immigrants. As a result, they turned to their friends from "the old country" for help, and they engaged in criminal acts out of necessity. By creating their own "family business," the Corleones and their associates were able to thrive in America, but to retain their wealth and power—and to remain loyal to the people who helped them succeed—they had to continue the cycle of crime.

Discussing the book and film *The Godfather*, Fields (2004) pointed to the Corleone family as presenting a "peculiar conflation of brutal mob tactics and strict social values in safeguarding a privileged way of life for a limited group of people" (p. 616). Fields (2004) pointed out that we learn in the opening scene of the novel that Vito Corleone believes that his code of ethics is superior to society's laws when "a petitioner…asks for 'justice' because the American courts have failed him" (p. 618). She noted,

> This sense of Corleone as a man with the vision and power to live by his code—one that exceeds the moral justice of American institutions—is perhaps the most compelling aspect of *The Godfather* and explains its lasting influence in popular culture's revision and development of gangster stories. (p. 618)

She said that while Corleone seems "at times a benevolent patriarch, the Don exacts loyalty, friendship, and respect, but wields these as weapons as well. His code calls for effective brutality even as it masquerades as generosity and good will" (p. 618).

The Sopranos certainly addressed organized crime as cyclical and passed down from generation to generation, but did not address inequities in society as an underlying motivation for crime. Therefore, instead of relationships serving as a way for criminals to see the mistakes they have made on a path to becoming law-abiding citizens, as was evident in *Oz*, in *The Sopranos*, relationships were shown to perpetuate crime. Throughout the series, Tony Soprano referenced his deceased father's involvement in the mob crew that Tony later led, but although Tony continued to engage in organized crime himself, he did not want his teenage son, Anthony Jr. (referred to by his nickname, "A. J.," in the series), to become part of the crew. This theme was also explored in *The Godfather*, although eventually, when Don Corleone was gunned down by a rival family, Michael Corleone not only joined the family in its mob activities, but also took over as leader of the Mafia family.

Tony and his wife, Carmela, frequently agonized over A. J.'s future; they feared that if he did not go to college, he would certainly follow in his father's footsteps. In one episode in season 3, when A. J. was expelled from his high school for cheating, Carmela and Tony sent A. J. to a military academy so he would learn discipline and improve his grades—and eventually be admitted to college. They showed that they wanted something better—or at least different—for A. J. This depiction hinted at a need to break the cycle of organized crime, but at the same time, the series predominantly reinforced the notion that membership in the "family business" required loyalty and proof of loyalty. It would be seen as an act of betrayal for an existing crew member to "leave the family business" or to go against an order given by the leader, Tony Soprano.

Family relationships were portrayed as important in the series. Even those in the Mafia crew who were not blood relatives had familial-type relationships with Tony, but a distinction was made between blood relatives and those who were not, with blood relatives receiving preferential treatment. More responsibility was given to blood relatives in the crew, and more was also expected. For example, in one episode in season 4, Tony asked his cousin, Christopher, who was part of his mob crew, to take a more active role in the business. Other crew members resented this decision, because Christopher was the youngest member of the crew. Tony did not trust the nonrelatives because, he said, they are not "blood." In another episode in season 5, Tony illustrated that true family relationships were most meaningful to him when he stopped a rival family from putting a hit on another cousin in his crew, Tony Blundetto, even though Blundetto was performing hits on members of a rival family, which Tony had not sanctioned, and he put the rest of the Soprano crew in danger of retaliation.

Tony Soprano's strong sense of family and his strong ties to his family could have led viewers to see him as redeemable; however, family-business dealings ultimately proved to be *more* important to Tony, as shown in episodes in the series. Eventually, Tony Soprano shot and killed his cousin himself, but, it was shown, to make sure it was a quick kill and to prevent the rival family from getting the satisfaction of carrying it out first. The killing was depicted as a "humane" alternative to what the rival crew would have done, but again it was portrayed as necessary to preserve business relationships.

This was also evident in an episode in season 4, when Johnny Sacramoni, a crew member of a rival mob family, was upset that a member of Tony's crew, Ralph Cifaretto, made a joke about Johnny's overweight wife, and he wanted Ralph killed. Seeking revenge, Johnny asked his family's boss, Carmine, to sanction the hit, but because Ralph was a high-level member of Tony's crew, Carmine did not approve it because the family had business dealings with Tony that he knew would be jeopardized if the hit was carried out. Still, Carmine knew that Johnny would continue to pursue revenge, and he told Tony that he had to put a hit out on Johnny if he wanted to preserve their business relationship. In the meantime, Johnny had arranged a hit on Ralph himself. Both hits were eventually thwarted. After a few days, when Johnny calmed down, he called off the hit on Ralph, moments before it was about to take place, and then he met with Tony to accept Ralph's apology. Tony then called off the hit on Johnny. However, had Johnny not had a change of heart, he would have been killed to preserve the business relationship between the two families.

The Sopranos presented a similar depiction of criminals to that seen in *Oz*. Characters were shown to be neither all good nor all bad, and they had a strong connection to families and other members of their "group." However, the motivations for the crimes in *The Sopranos* were different than in *Oz*. The Soprano family and the other crew members lived in present-day upper-middle-class suburbia, and their crimes, particularly the violent ones, were motivated by a need to retain business dealings, and in turn, their ability to retain power and pay for their upper-middle-class lifestyle. Tony Soprano was an "Everyman," who committed crimes as part of his "job."

The characters in *Oz* committed crimes for revenge, and in some cases to attain or retain power, but they did not benefit financially for their crimes. They were not maintaining a "lifestyle" in the process, but were *confined* to a lifestyle because of their crimes. Their crimes made them Others. Criminals in *Oz* showed that they were trying to rehabilitate themselves by conforming to society's norms, that is, laws. The Soprano mob crew, on the other hand, maintained its lifestyle by breaking society's laws.

Therefore, "redemption" was not a theme presented in *The Sopranos*, as it was in *Oz*, or even *The Godfather*, where from the very first film in the trilogy, Michael Corleone said he wanted to make the business legitimate. While Michael never achieved that, he started out with that intention, as did characters in *Oz*. *The Godfather* audience watched to see whether the Corleones would decide to engage in criminal behavior, just as the *Oz* audience anticipated whether those characters would stop engaging in criminal behavior. In *The Sopranos*, specific crimes may be averted from time to time, as seen in the episode where hits on both Johnny Sacramoni and Ralph Cifaretto were called off, but the main characters in the mob crew illustrated that crime was a useful tool for them, and they needed to use it to retain their power and wealth.

The HBO programs *Oz* and *The Sopranos* have redefined both what is extreme and what is acceptable on television. As a result, the range of representations presented in the genre as a whole has widened. The appeal of these new representations may be attributed to the fact that "marginalized or disempowered social groups (women, African Americans, gays, and others) may develop strategies for focusing on isolated moments within the textual flow that offer the possibility of disrupting and destabilizing the dominant ideology" (White, 1992, p. 191). White explained that while there is a hierarchy through which the range of ideas are presented, audiences may reframe the hierarchy themselves, creating their own "dominant" ideology. For example, stories about families involved in violence, as seen in *The Sopranos*, can be presented in a way that is considered acceptable. Cawelti (1976) also suggested the Mafia saga may represent a departure from real life. He pointed to audiences responding to the message in *The Godfather* that "America is a society of criminals, or the still more disturbing irony that a 'family' of criminals might be more humanly interesting and morally satisfactory than a society of empty routines, irresponsibly powerful organizations, widespread corruption, and meaningless violence" (p. 79).

However, I see the message in *The Godfather* as quite different from the message in *The Sopranos*. While the television series addressed similar themes as the film, set 50 years later, the idea of a "need" to engage in the criminal behavior because there is no other way to make a better life for the family was absent in the television series. *The Sopranos* made the mob members to blame for their crimes. The motivation for the mob crew to commit crimes was loyalty to the group. This representation of the motivation for crime may account for some of the negative criticism it received from

Italian American groups. In 2000, The Commission for Social Justice—a branch of the Order Sons of Italy in America—UNICO National, The Media Institute, Bella Italia Mia, The Italic Studies Institute, and the Italian American One Voice Committee issued a joint written statement to the media supporting New York Columbus Day organizers who "dis-invited" the cast of *The Sopranos*. To these groups, the actors represented a negative view of Italian Americans presented through their characters.

Still, Cavallero (2004) argued that the stereotypes presented in *The Sopranos* are not damaging to Italians because there is not as much discrimination against them, compared to 60 years ago:

> Tony Soprano appears at a time when anti-Italian prejudice is greatly diminished. This is not to suggest that Italians are not still discriminated against or viewed as somehow different. It is not to suggest that Italians do not continue to suffer the effects of these stereotypes. However, it is to suggest that the "plight" of Italians in the twenty-first century is far removed from the plight of Italians in the 1930s. (p. 60)

As a result of focusing on depictions of Italians as mobsters, Cavallero (2004) suggested that groups opposing the representation in *The Sopranos* are overlooking the diversity of Italian characters presented in the media today:

> Unfortunately, by focusing so intently on *The Sopranos*, Italian American groups have missed an opportunity to applaud the multitude of Italian characters offered by today's media and have reduced the diversity that exists to a single program, which they then remove from its sociocultural context. Italian Americans, as a group, have made a great deal of social and economic progress since the 1930s, but this point has been lost or ignored by today's anti-Sopranos protests, which offer the impression that Italians continue to feel as marginalized as other cultures. (p. 61)

While it is true that a myriad of representations of Italians exists in the media today, I contend that the depiction in *The Sopranos* presented an even harsher view of Italians—and members of the Mafia—than in *The Godfather*. The film included depictions through flashbacks of how the Corleones began in the mob, and presented mob crimes as a response to a society that offered little opportunity for the immigrant Others. Even though that is no longer the case in the film's present-day events, these flashbacks, combined with the main character's continued talk of legitimizing the family business, create a context where the characters in the film could be seen as seeking redemption.

Fields (2004) said *The Godfather* changed the American public's perception of the Italian American Mafia by glamorizing the Mafia:

> [S]ubsequent generations lean heavily on Puzo's characterization of the Italian American Mafia in one way or another because his tale drew the mob's mythology so indelibly in our imagination. The myth's power draws not on its social reality...but on a fantasy about the underworld's figures and laws. (p. 617)

Yet, *The Sopranos* offered a different view of the Italian American Mafia. Fields (2004) noted that in the series "the mob is besieged as much by inner infidelity as it is by the federal government" (p. 619). Further, she noted,

> In The Sopranos, the family values central to Don Corleone's code are revealed to be fraught with tensions. What we see so little of in The Godfather is what has popularized the series—the dysfunctions of family and the raw brutality of mob life create the tension and focus of daily life in this world. (p. 619)

Tony Soprano ruled the mob family in a different culture than Vito Corleone, Fields (2004) stressed: "Unlike his idols, Michael and Vito Corleone, Tony lacks the founding sense of an unassailable value structure and clear rules shared and internalized by both families"(p. 621). For example, she pointed to Tony's right-hand man, his cousin Christopher, as "a drug addict enacting a mobster role he's learned from the movies, not from his Family" (p. 622). Fields concluded,

> Tony's violent acts, even his discourse with others, are raw, visceral, and immediate. It has little to do with a philosophy other than the basic tenants of Darwinian survival. Tony's unresolved

desire for power, to fulfill his many lusts, and to ameliorate his angst while being a good leader all play against his overblown romantic notions of Mafia life, derived in large part from his obsession with Coppola's *Godfather* epic. (p. 622)

Fields (2004) pointed out that the series depicts the Sopranos as "[m]arginalized only by their transparent class climbing ambition" (p. 614). She said that as the mob leader "struggles to reconcile the expectations of agency and power of his mob code with his everyday suburban world, he and the other characters express a direct relevance to contemporary life" (p. 614). Fields (2004) saw Tony as "paralyzed by his conflicting desires to inhabit an imaginary mob past and to be a successful twenty-first-century father and businessman" (p. 615). She continued: "Caught in the web of responsibilities he has to his two families, he struggles with irreconcilable upper-middle-class family values and mob family values, an ongoing friction expressed in his anxious dysfunctions as a Don" (p. 615).

The Sopranos, like *Oz*, stars criminals, and the events in the series were unpredictable, with many plot twists and turns that often ended with a crime being committed or averted, specifically when the family-business dealings would be jeopardized if the crime was carried out. As a result, the series offered a glimpse into the motivation for some crimes. The characters in *The Sopranos* also exhibited redeeming qualities, particularly when Tony and his crew interacted with family members in traditional family settings. They ate dinner together, scouted colleges, and disciplined their children, all in an effort to ensure that they would have a productive life, which, as we saw from these interactions, did not involve joining the Mafia. However, the predominant difference between *The Sopranos* and *Oz* is that the criminals in *The Sopranos* were not trying to rehabilitate themselves so they could become law-abiding citizens. Therefore, the series did not create a context where the criminals were seeking redemption.

Representations of criminals who are not redeeming and exhibit negative qualities are noteworthy because they were previously so rarely seen in television programs. White noted that these representations "may find an outlet on television, but these occasions are rare, and they do not necessarily, or usually, occur in the context of network prime-time programming" (White, 1992, p. 190). It is important to note, then, that programs starring criminal characters originated on cable networks, not commercial broadcast networks. *Oz, The Sopranos,* and *The Shield,* as discussed in chapter 4, present "social and cultural attitudes that lie beyond the multiplicity of dominant ideological expressions" (White, 1992, p. 190). *The Shield* airs on FX, a nonpremium-cable channel paid for in part by subscribers and whose content is not regulated by the FCC. *The Shield* was created after *Oz* and *The Sopranos* were already airing on HBO, a subscriber-paid premium-cable channel. The success of the two HBO series that star criminal main characters were likely an indicator to the creators of *The Shield* that there would also be an audience interested in seeing a program that stars a corrupt police officer as a main character.

HBO is not constrained by the demands of an advertiser-paid program and, therefore, is able to portray these depictions of crime without fear of financial consequence. It is also more likely to take a chance on series that star seemingly unlikable characters because the success of the network is not directly tied to audience size, as it is with broadcast networks. FX, which is advertiser supported, is also a basic cable network that has paid subscribers. As a result, it is less influenced by advertiser approval of content than are broadcast networks. Further, the expectations of viewers are different for broadcast and cable networks. Therefore, the cutting-edge nature of some programs on FX and other cable networks may not garner the same criticisms that result with content of broadcast network programs.

HBO, which began in 1972, has been described as setting "the standard when it comes to taking the medium to bold and daring heights" (Turegano, 2003, n.p.). Today, 38 million subscribe to HBO, according to the NCTA (Turegano, 2003). "With the expansion of cable channels and satellite systems, the networks have lost almost a quarter of their audience in the last decade, with average viewership falling (in 2003) to 49.8 million from 65 million, according to Nielsen Media Research"

(Carter, 2004, n.p.). Still, cable hits, excluding *The Sopranos*, "achieve ratings no better than those of weak network shows" (Carter, 2004, n.p.). "HBO is seen in only one-fourth to one-third of American homes" (Carman, 2001, ¶12, Retrieved November 18, 2005, from http://www.Sfgate.com). However, unlike broadcast channels, the goal for HBO executives is not high ratings. In a 2001 *San Francisco Chronicle* article, Chris Albrecht, HBO's president of original programming, said, "I never think about popular. Never. People smarter than me have tried that and failed" (Carman, 2001, ¶14, Retrieved November 18, 2005 from http://www.Sfgate.com). As a premium-cable channel with paid subscribers specifically for the channel, HBO is able to focus on content more than ratings because there are no financial consequences for doing so. Sales of DVD sets of *The Sopranos*, and other original HBO series, have been strong, which also increases revenue generated by the programs. Cable companies have also reported an increase in subscriptions, often just prior to the airing of a new season of *The Sopranos*.

Whether depictions of people from various walks of life and in various roles in society will continue to be shown in the genre remains to be seen. Basic-cable channels rely on subscriber fees and commercial advertisements, but advertisers are paying attention to basic cable audiences, even though they are generally smaller than network audiences. In 2004, "Mitsubishi Motor Company pulled every penny of its advertising from prime-time network shows, $120 million worth, because, as Ian Beavis, its senior vice president for marketing, put it, 'There's nothing compelling in the new network programming'," according to a September 19, 2004, article in *The New York Times*. Further, Beavis said, "Mitsubishi would place more ads on cable and local television shows, as well as spend more on magazines and Internet sites, (and) said he was just one of many advertisers expressing frustration with the networks" (Carter, 2004, n.p.). That may account for the plans by FX executives to air another series depicting a criminal; in the *New York Times* article (Carter, 2004, n.p.), John Landgraf, FX president, said the new program, *Thief*, would be shown from the perspective of the criminal. HBO also aired *Deadwood*, depicting a group of outlaws in the Wild West. *Deadwood* does not present the sanitized view seen in *Bonanza*, but a grittier side to life during that time. For the themes presented in these series to be appealing to viewers, viewers must be able to identify with them, and they evidently are. Network executives have shown that they expect crime shows, including those starring criminals, to remain popular.

CHAPTER 6

SOCIETY

The depictions of criminals' motivations to commit crime and legal authorities' role in identifying, apprehending, prosecuting, and defending them exist not as single acts, but within the context of a society and its structures. Hayakawa (1950) defined the "fully-functioning personality," presumably the law-abiding citizen, "as an (individual)...in and of society of which he is a member, but he is not a prisoner of that society" (p. 55). "The fully-functioning personality is not an outright rebel against the social norms of a society either, given a halfway tolerable society to live in." (Hayakawa, 1950, p. 65). He proposed that if the society is not "tolerable," then rebelling against the norms of that society is not necessarily abnormal or illogical.

Duff (2001), a criminologist, also pointed to the "rhetoric of inclusion" (p. 40) as serving a purpose for law enforcers, primarily that of maintaining a power structure in society where the authority of the law is clearly established. However, this rhetoric, Duff acknowledged, can also serve unintended purposes, particularly that of preventing criminals from ever rehabilitating themselves or becoming fully functioning members of society. Duff noted,

> The...rhetoric of inclusion can cut both ways in the context of crime and punishment. It can, on one hand, be used to include offenders—to emphasize that they are still members of the community whose laws they have broken and to encourage penal policies that seek to keep them in or restore them to the community. (p. 40)

Duff acknowledged that because society creates "structures that will protect 'us', the law-abiding, from 'them', the criminals who would prey on us" (Duff, 2001, p. 40), criminals are often permanently excluded from society. Society at large ("Us") is protected from people who do not abide by society's laws ("Them").

According to Mauer (1999), at the same time that the concept of "the criminal" has been constructed in the mass media, a punitive approach, rather than a preventive one, has dominated crime policy. Mauer noted that "by identifying certain persons or groups of people as 'criminals,' a punitive model of responding to social problems is made to appear almost inevitable. However, this model of problem-solving is hardly preordained" (Mauer, 1999, p. 6). In the process of reinforcing the dominant philosophy, media images also serve to reinforce the status quo in society. In the case of crime policy, this ensures that the dominant philosophy is one of using punitive measures rather than preventive ones. Surette (1998) suggested "that media images locate the causes of crime in individuals and support society's approach to dealing with criminals: 'These messages translate into support for law-and-order policies and existing criminal justice agencies'" (p. 82, as cited in Lipschultz and Hilt, 2002, p. 30). Referring to programs like *Lou Grant* and *Kaz*, Parenti (1980) suggested:

> [W]hile sometimes directing our attention to questions of injustice and oppression, these shows fall short of any kind of systemic critique. Having little to say about economic power, capitalism, class structure and other such issues that would horrify sponsors and

networks, "quality programs" are mostly engaged in packaging "modishness and the cosmetics of rebellion." (p. 178)

This chapter examines how the series I analyzed use depictions of social norms, stereotypes, and structures, specifically those addressing economic and social class, to construct American society and its criminal justice system as equitable, fair, and safe. I will also point to series that acknowledge social inequities in society, including the kinds of social processes, particularly economic structures, that contribute to an inequitable justice system.

CONTEMPORARY AMERICAN SOCIETY

Most series in the crime genre offer a commentary on contemporary American society. I examine how the setting of each series depicts where crime takes place and provides a context for cultural norms in society. I also explore the depiction of a prison society in *Oz*, which is not set in any particular city, but serves as a metaphor for all societies.

While *COPS* is set in some rural locations, and *America's Most Wanted* and *The Sopranos* depict crime in suburban areas, urban areas are the most common settings for fictional series in the crime genre. To examine social norms in the genre, I analyze depictions of society in three major urban cities in America—New York, Boston, and Los Angeles—as seen in *Law & Order, The Jury, The Practice*, and *The Shield*. I selected these series because they specifically address either how the crimes portrayed are specific to the city or how "average citizens," that is, jurors and other people in society, perceive crime, criminals, and legal authorities in society.

The city is essentially a "character" in these series. For example, in an episode of *Law & Order* in season 14, when a Japanese couple was involved in a shooting after visiting Ground Zero, after seemingly getting lost on their way back to their hotel, the wife was killed in a "random" shooting. The husband fingered a black man as the suspect, and denounced the violent city. The Japanese Ministry issued a travel advisory, warning Japanese citizens not to visit New York. The husband claimed, "New York is a jungle," and the "inhabitants are animals." He called the city a "crazy gun culture." The crime and his subsequent response turned out to be an act: He planned the crime against his wife in order to collect the life insurance money and pay off a gang-related debt in Japan. The episode shows that portraying urban areas as dangerous "jungles" has a lasting impact. However, the police in the episode use this tactic anyway. During the trial, the hired gun said the husband wanted the crime committed in New York City because "black people commit so much crime in New York, police can not keep up." The district attorney and the assistant district attorneys contributed to this representation in the episode. Aware that the husband had given a fictional account of the crime and suspect, the DA used a sketch of the black man the husband "described" in an effort to lure the husband back to the United States after he had returned to Japan. By releasing the sketch, the DA hoped the husband would believe he was no longer a suspect.

The district attorney and his assistants reinforced stereotypes in the public discourse about who commits crimes and where crime is likely to occur. The DA did not see this as causing any damage, claiming that he would eventually reveal that the sketch was a fake, but ADA McCoy lamented that the damage was already done by creating the sketch and releasing it to the public. The black man was already suspected as the criminal, and that is what people would remember, McCoy said. Still, he did nothing to block the DA from using this tactic.

BLOCKED OPPORTUNITIES: ECONOMIC MOTIVATORS FOR CRIME

In *The Shield*, the city also serves as an additional "character"—like New York City, a dangerous character. Set in an economically depressed and drug-infested area of Los Angeles, the series addresses whether society is equitable and fair for all citizens. In an episode in season 1, several police officers who responded to a 911 call were shot in their squad cars when they arrived on the scene. Detective Claudette Wyms, an African American woman in her 40s investigating the case, determined that the 911 call was a fake, meant to lure police to the scene so they could be shot as retaliation for police not responding quickly enough to a previous emergency call for help. The delayed response in the previous case led to the injured person's death; therefore, the perception of the people in the impoverished neighborhood was that police did not care about them because they were poor. The fake call was made by an African American man in his early 20s whose father was a heroin addict and whose mother left him when he was 9. When Wyms interrogated the man, she said she understood his frustration, but that crime was not the answer, regardless of how difficult his life had been.

Residents in the lower-class neighborhood believed that police disregarded them because of their lower economic and social status. One of those residents fought back, making the police the target of his crime, to protest the way people in his neighborhood were being treated by police. The crime is the man's attempt to retaliate against police for the inequities in society that enable the police to treat people in his neighborhood differently than people in wealthier neighborhoods. The recurring police character Wyms is not a rogue cop, as the character Mack is. She follows proper police procedure, so in this interaction with the man, when she acknowledges inequities in society, she confirms that he has a right to be frustrated, because society is not fair. However, she also represents the department that the man perceived as inequitable, and because she is not corrupt, she serves to reinforce that not *all* police officers are corrupt or disregard the lives of people in lower social and economic classes. Therefore, when she counsels the man not to continue to act on his frustrations over the societal inequities, she suggests he must change his thinking—not that inequities in society need to be addressed. This is reinforced throughout the series. Police officers such as Mack who do not follow proper police procedure are portrayed in *The Shield* as operating outside the norm of the department, and therefore, the problem is not widespread.

Poverty and Social Status
A problem associated culturally with urban cities, and particularly New York, is homelessness. This societal issue was addressed in one episode

of *Law & Order* in season 14 that I viewed. It specifically addressed economic inequities in society while depicting a homeless man suspected of killing another homeless man.

The episode began with police suspecting a "successful" member of society in the death of the homeless man. A wealthy white woman in her 30s, owner of a public-relations firm, had run over the man with her car. However, police determined that he did not die from the accident. He already had a brain hematoma from a beating he received from another homeless man before she hit him. She was sentenced to probation and community service for obstruction and tampering with evidence because she lied to police about the accident and had repainted the car to hide any evidence that could tie her to the crime. At this point in the episode, the focus turns to the two homeless men involved in the crime. Detectives Lennie Briscoe and Ed Green learned that the two men had quarreled when one would not share his orange with the other, and that led to a fistfight. When two other police officers responded to the scene, they broke up the fight, but would not take either man to a hospital, saying they smelled bad and they would never be able to get the smell out of their car if they transported him. The homeless man was left in the street by police, which led to the businesswoman running over him.

The episode examines norms in interacting with people who are homeless, particularly by people in higher social and economic classes, such as the police officers and the businesswoman. The actions of the first-responding police officers on the scene and the businesswoman—none of whom assisted the man after he had been injured in the fight or the car accident—served a few different purposes in the episode. Narratively, they eliminated the possibility that the homeless man was innocent. There was little discussion about whether the lack of assistance by those who first discovered the injured man contributed to his death; their actions were quickly dismissed by the recurring characters, Briscoe and Green, as peripheral events.

However, at the same time that these nonrecurring characters are shown to treat the homeless men differently, with blatant disregard for their well-being, the recurring characters, Briscoe and Green, question these actions and imply that these three people acted against a social norm—which is that all people should be treated equally in society, regardless of economic and social class. The detectives inquired as to why the first-responding police officers did not take the homeless men to a hospital, so it is clear that normal police procedure was to do so. By not following that procedure because the men were homeless, the police violated the norm. The recurring characters acknowledge here that the police officers' actions were wrong and inappropriate, affirming the social norm and indicating that not all people—and not all police officers—view people who are homeless in the way these two officers viewed them.

While explicitly the actions by the police officers and the businesswoman are presented as "wrong," implicitly these actions are being dismissed as harmless by the recurring characters. For example, the woman was not charged with leaving the scene of an accident, or any other crime directly related to the homeless man. She was charged with lying to police. It was her actions in blocking police that are emphasized as inappropriate—not the fact that she did not help the dying homeless man. She was potentially interfering with the justice system, and that was the problem that police needed to rectify. Leaving the man in street was not portrayed as a serious crime because the man had already suffered the fatal injury; in the episode, the businesswoman caused the man no harm by treating him with such disregard. Further, the community sentence she received was just a slap on the wrist, so even her interference with police procedure can be seen as inconsequential.

In addition, while Briscoe and Green acknowledge impropriety in the police officers' actions by not taking the homeless men to the hospital, no further discussion of action to be taken by the department against them occurs. There are no consequences, beyond the minimal verbal chastising received from Briscoe and Green, who dismiss the actions as a problem with these two individual police officers, not of a culture that dismisses people who are homeless. By having nonrecurring characters, not recurring characters, treat the homeless men disrespectfully, the portrayal suggests that these actions are rare, and when they do occur, they are exposed—and punished—by upstanding citizens (i.e., recurring characters). Therefore, when people in lower social and economic classes in society are treated unfairly, confining and unfair social structures are not to blame—individuals are.

The episode also addresses whether societal factors are to blame for homelessness, and therefore whether social agencies, that is, the government, has a responsibility to assist people who are homeless, or if individuals are to blame for homelessness, and therefore must help themselves overcome their situation. This issue is explored during the trial portion of the episode. In court, the public defender claimed a necessity defense during the trial; she said the need of the individual outweighed the law. She said, "We've evicted the homeless from society. We've made them outcasts. We look at them as less than human. We shun them from society and then turn around and hold them accountable to society's laws. [These are] not the laws they have to live by."

In another scene, when the prosecutors in the case, ADA McCoy and ADA Serena Southerlyn, were having lunch with DA Arthur Branch (played by former Republican Senator Fred Thompson, of Tennessee), Southerlyn said she agreed with the statement by the public defender that homeless people are outcasts, and said, "We see them as scary, subhuman." However, McCoy disagreed with her, and objected to the defense attorney, saying that the homeless men were "animals" and that they did not have to follow society's laws. He saw it as excusing the criminal behavior. Branch attacked Southerlyn for being a "limousine liberal" who served at a soup kitchen on Thanksgiving, saying the work she did that one day of the year did not make a difference. He said there were soup kitchens and shelters for the homeless, so society had not turned its back on them, as the public defender suggested. He claimed it was impossible to end homelessness regardless of how much money was "thrown" at the problem. "It's like sweeping sand off the beach," he said. Branch suggested that trying to help people who are homeless was a lost cause, and that society was not responsible for helping them. The public defender, however, presented a contrasting depiction in court, saying, "We're all two steps away from becoming Max Edgars," meaning that it was not completely his doing that he was homeless. Her statement suggests that homelessness is a result of circumstances out of people's control, in some cases, not a choice. In this discussion, Southerlyn, siding with the public defender, suggests that Max did not "cause" his homelessness and therefore could not change his situation himself. She suggests homelessness happens *to* people, presumably because of circumstances outside of people's control, and therefore cannot be avoided individually. The circumstances in society that lead to homelessness need to be changed, she suggests. As a result, she further promotes compassion for people who are homeless, too, since it is not a position of their choosing. McCoy and Branch, on the other hand, promote individual responsibility to avoid homelessness and overcome it.

The four characters seemingly are evenly split in their opinions: two believe that society contributes to the problem, two believe that society does assist people who are homeless, so they must be held accountable for their individual actions, including crimes they commit. However, the depiction is not of an "equal" and balanced debate, with merits on both sides. The two male characters who do not acknowledge inequities in society as contributing to homelessness are recurring characters, but of the two female characters that sympathize with the homeless, only one is a recurring character. The men's characters are stronger, more dominant characters. They appear in the series certainly more often than the public defender but also more than Southerlyn, who is a newer character. As a result, the audience is more likely to identify with the long-standing characters, McCoy and Branch. I believe that, for the audience, the men's argument is stronger. The context of the lunch scene also makes the men's argument the dominant one. Southerlyn is responding to something the public defender said earlier; she alone is making the argument to the two male prosecutors. When they jointly dismiss her, the message is clear that she is "wrong." This is further reinforced when she is called a "limousine liberal," suggesting she is a hypocrite for saying she cares about the plight of homeless people when she cannot understand what their lives are like because she is financially secure. The women are portrayed by the men as foolishly trying to fix a problem that cannot be fixed. Southerlyn's argument is presented as subordinate, as she is McCoy and Branch's subordinate in the series, and her point of view is dismissed by the more knowledgeable and experienced characters.

The episode also addresses how the suspect became homeless, further assessing where blame for Max's homelessness should be situated. During the trial, the public defender revealed to the jury that Max was injured while working on a construction job and could not work, so he used up his savings until he ultimately lost his house, and his family. He lived in his car for a while, but then sold it so he could eat, and lived in doorways, ATM vestibules, and subway tunnels, until the mayor cracked down on the homeless and started moving them from the streets into shelters. He said he feared the shelters because they were filled with "crazies and junkies" and he said they were not safe. People stole from one another and beat one another up, which he said happened in every shelter he went to. The public defender makes the argument that Max's feeling of failure prevented him from being able to pick himself up and get another job. Dejected, he continued to live on the streets.

Because he lost his job due to an injury, viewers can see his homelessness as not his fault, but because of unfortunate, unlucky circumstances. However, it could also be seen implicitly as a commentary on the high cost of health care in America, as it is implied that in addition to being out of work, he had to pay for his recovery, which exacerbated his financial difficulties. The fact that his family left him is portrayed as the final straw that caused him to give up hope that he could regain what he had lost: There were too many obstacles in society that prevented a homeless person from finding a job and building back the life he once had. Life on the street was his new life, and he was powerless to change that. As a result, the code of the street became the code he adopted, and he said if word got out on the street that he backed down from the fight with Alan, he would be vulnerable to further attacks, and would become a target. Yet, all of these arguments are presented by the nonrecurring public defender, who has already been dismissed in the episode by the long-standing characters, and her argument is dismissed as well when, at the end of the episode, Max is found guilty of manslaughter and sentenced to 12 years in prison.

A final commentary on homelessness—and criminals—is offered at the end of the episode, as ADAs Southerlyn and McCoy walked out of the courtroom following the verdict. McCoy said to Southerlyn, "We just moved him from one jungle to another," but "at least he'll have food and shelter." They acknowledge that prison is the lesser of two evils, but do not discuss society's role in both creating a situation where Max first became homeless, and in creating a prison system that will likely make him less able to function in society once he is released. How the "jungles" came to exist is not discussed, or how society might work to see that they cease to exist. Prison and life on the street are presented as the *only* options for Max. They acknowledge no possibility for him to ever return to his previous way of life, as an employed family man. They imply that it is impossible for him to change his circumstances. He is an "other" in society, and as they see it, there is no hope for him to become part of "us."

An Equitable Justice System

In addition to whether economic societal structures are fair and equitable, series in the crime genre also address whether the justice system is fair and equitable. This is evident in an episode of *Law & Order* in season 11, when Mitch, a teenager, was charged and convicted of murdering a Chinese-food-delivery man. Mitch and his friends ordered the food, and then beat up the man when he delivered it. It is shown to be essentially a thrill killing. The boys were not poor; they were suburban kids who seemingly wanted to pull a prank on the Asian delivery man. They did not plan to kill him. When the case went to trial, Executive Assistant DA McCoy requested that it be a death-penalty case, but the district attorney, Nora Lewin (played by Diane Weist), disagreed primarily because the boy was under 18. McCoy said the prosecutor's office often charged black teens with crack possession, and did not think twice about whether it was appropriate to do so because of their ages.

He questioned whether Lewin was giving this white, suburban teen preferential treatment because of his race and economic class. In her own defense, Lewin said other districts were requesting a moratorium on the death penalty (which did actually happen in 2002 following Illinois Governor George Ryan's commutation of 167 death row sentences in Illinois, which will be discussed further in chapter 10), so it would be too extreme for them to ask for the death penalty in this circumstance. Still, even though she personally disagreed with the charge, she allowed it to be used against the teen. Ultimately, Mitch was convicted and the jury voted for the death penalty.

Throughout the trial portion of the episode, the teen's turbulent home life is depicted as contributing to his troubles. His parents were divorced and both had remarried. His father, who had a drinking problem, had two younger children from his second marriage, which made Mitch feel abandoned. Mitch's mother also said her husband, Mitch's stepfather, had been too strict in disciplining Mitch. This serves to reinforce that society was not to blame for the teen's disregard for the Asian man's life; it was an individual problem, and the blame should lie with the parents for creating circumstances that allowed Mitch to become a criminal. By divulging the boy's family problems, the episode suggests that he was not "evil," but other circumstances led him to become a criminal. However, the reason black teens charged with crack possession engage in crime is never explored—even though that is the example raised by McCoy when he argues that this white, suburban teen should be treated the same way other teens of other races are treated.

Still, while exposing the family history suggests that sympathy for the white teen may be appropriate because of his unfortunate circumstances, the episode stresses that in order to ensure that the justice system is fair, a "tough-on-crime" position—which includes applying the death penalty—must be held, as it is with other types of crimes committed by people of other economic classes, social classes, and races. Therefore, as the question of whether the system treats all people fairly is raised, the system is "confirmed" as fair. The episode does not address whether the system has been overly harsh toward black teens

Society 161

and people of nonwhite, urban backgrounds; whether the death penalty should be used at all; or whether the death penalty has previously been administered unfairly against people who are innocent (regardless of race). Instead, in this episode, the dominant position, depicted through McCoy, is that the death penalty will only *become* unfair if it is *not* used against this white, suburban teen, who will then be receiving special treatment because of his race and economic class. The episode starts from the assumption that the death penalty, when used, is appropriate, and that the system is fair.

The DA, who is sympathetic toward the suspect and is reluctant to charge the boy, is presented as potentially creating inequalities in the justice system; if she had not allowed the death penalty to be requested for the white, suburban teen, then she would have been giving him preferential treatment. People such as McCoy, who apply the death penalty to all, and therefore support a "tough-on-crime" policy, ensure that the system *is* fair for all. McCoy's position is presented as appropriate—and necessary—to ensure an equitable justice system.

In another episode of *Law & Order* in season 11, depicting the trial of a teen charged with killing fellow students in a school shooting, the judge threw out evidence (email messages) police detectives obtained without a warrant. While arguing that the evidence should be allowed, ADA McCoy said putting away a mass murderer should outweigh a technical violation. He said the law had to give people a "sense it will protect them, or they would start protecting themselves." Here, he is arguing that the end justifies the means, and that protecting society and maintaining law and order should outweigh the suspect's rights. The police bent the rules to assure a conviction. The police officers believe they are right in convicting, even though the law is preventing them from carrying out a conviction. In part, rules governing the justice system are meant to protect against police corruption, but here the police excuse the police corruption and the prosecutors defend the use of illegal means as the only way to assure the conviction. The judge sided with the defense and dismissed the case—reinforcing the notion that the system will not permit corruption. However, the state was still able to prove its case, as the boy's father believed his son was dangerous because he had hurt their other children, too. The father told police that the son confessed the shooting to him, which provided new evidence. The boy was ultimately found guilty and received a sentence of life in prison. According to the episode, the unethical and illegal behavior of the police officers has no effect on the justice system.

SOCIAL POWER: ASSUMPTIONS BASED ON CLASS

The Practice, set in Boston, reveals how expectations based on social class and economic class are used—sometimes incorrectly—by juries to determine guilt or reasonable doubt. In one episode in season 6, a man who was on trial for rape was discovered to be covering for the real criminal—his identical twin brother, a successful and wealthy oncologist who was respected in the community. The successful brother admitted his crime on the stand, knowing that the jurors—and even his brother's own attorney, Eugene of the Donnell firm—would not believe him. He expected the jury to believe he was covering for his unsuccessful brother, and trying to create reasonable doubt in the jurors' minds—not that his brother was covering for him. Because they were identical twins, they had the same DNA, and the physical evidence used during the trial could have belonged to either brother. The wrong brother was ultimately found guilty by the jury, but even after his conviction, he showed no animosity toward his brother, saying he did not want to ruin his brother's career as an oncologist; the brother was a success and had a career, while he felt his own life was not as valuable because he was not a "success" by society's standards. The wrongly accused brother was convinced his life was less important than his brother's because of their different social statuses. The use of identical twins in the episode served as a dramatic tool to show that whether someone is perceived to be a criminal is often based on social standing—as that was the only difference between the two brothers. The jury—and even the suspect's lawyer—did not believe that the doctor committed the crime. Based on cultural norms, the unemployed brother was the only "believable" suspect, particularly for the crime of rape.

Society 163

Social norms are further emphasized as a factor jurors rely on in *The Jury*, a series that aired in the summer of 2004. Viewers of *The Jury* were encouraged to cast their own vote online. That "verdict" was revealed just prior to the verdict being read in the episode, enabling the audience to become an active part of the episode. In one episode (which included actors who previously appeared as prisoners in *Oz* cast in this episode as jurors or witnesses), prison inmate Ken Dwyer, a white man in his 30s, was accused of killing a prison priest, a white man in his 60s, during a prison riot. A report named corrections officers as instigators of the fight (a theme also explored, limitedly, in *Oz*) but a guard testified that this was not true. A flashback scene showed that a CO did instigate the fight, so their suspicions are proven to be correct.

It was shown during deliberations that the jury relied heavily on a surveillance tape that showed part of the fight to reach a verdict. The jurors replayed the tape repeatedly to look for more information, beyond what had been presented at trial. At one point, jurors realized that the defendant was not near the priest during the riot, so they questioned whether he could have killed him. The tape ended before the fatal blow was delivered to the priest, so there was no "absolute" proof. Ultimately, jurors found Dwyer guilty because they saw the priest raise his hand in the direction of Dwyer, which they said showed the priest was granting Dwyer forgiveness. For all the information that was presented in the trial, witness after witness, the jurors were convinced of the man's guilt. In the final flashback scene, it is shown that other inmates beat the priest, but Dwyer did, in fact, deliver the fatal blow. This implies that even though the juror used this vague information, they were correct. It also shows that they were right to rely on their own instinct rather than the testimonial evidence, which was not as convincing to them as what they saw with their own eyes on the tape. (An audience poll showed that 62% felt Dwyer was not guilty, and 38% thought he was.)

This pattern continued in another episode of *The Jury*, in a case where two black male defendants in their early 20s were on trial for killing a black female in her 40s in her apartment foyer. In the episode, two black male jurors both in their late 30s argued about what it was like to be from "the street." One said he grew up in Harlem, where the defendants are from, and the other said he still lives there. The juror who grew up in Harlem said he knew cops who would browbeat information out of people, and therefore, he questioned information from police witnesses in the trial. The other juror, who still lived in Harlem, said he saw how prison offered street credibility for people when they got back on the street, so he did not see the defendants as trying to avoid prison. They both questioned witnesses' credibility because a gang member was sitting in the courtroom "staring them down." They wondered if the witnesses feared retaliation by the gang if they testified against the defendants, and therefore they wondered whether anything witnesses testified to was true. All of this speculation stems from the two jurors' own experiences, and ultimately it is the social and cultural norms they "know" from their own lives that guide their decisions as jurors.

Motives were a common discussion point for jurors in *The Jury*, and they, too, were based on jurors' existing beliefs about social norms, including relationships and particularly marriage, as seen in an episode where a white man in his 60s with a military background, Boyd, was accused of killing his 25-year-old Filipino wife, whom he met over the Internet in what was referred to as a mail-order-bride business. After the husband found out that the wife had cheated on him and had a boyfriend, the prosecution claimed, he killed her. The jurors discussed their own marriages to analyze the defendant's marriage and the evidence the attorneys on both sides presented. Female jurors said they had been abused by spouses; male jurors said they perceived the marriage as a business deal. A 30-year-old black, female juror said she believed this was a crime of passion, because the victim's hands were cut off by the killer, and because she was a mail-order bride, she suggested Boyd did not love his wife passionately, and therefore, he would not have killed her in this way. The juror believed Boyd was seeking only companionship, not love, through the marriage, which she determined because he had a Siberian Husky. This seemingly irrational assumption was based on the fact that the juror had the same dog, which provided her with companionship, so she felt she understood Boyd and his motives.

None of this information about the marriage discussed by jurors during deliberations was presented as evidence during the trial, but the jurors read into what was presented as evidence. Evidence that was presented at trial was challenged by jurors as ambiguous, not absolute truth. They ultimately reached a verdict by determining whether Boyd was the "type of person" who would have committed the crime.

- One juror suggested that testimony that Boyd was an Alcoholics Anonymous sponsor to one of the witnesses in the case showed that he was not a sociopath, and therefore, he would not have killed his wife for the thrill of it.
- Another juror suspected that the wife's boyfriend, a black man in his early 30s, was the killer. She contended he was a "playboy" type who would have cut off her fingers after he killed her to steal her jewelry; he had already pawned some of it, witnesses testified. The boyfriend testified that the wife gave him the jewelry, but the juror was not convinced.
- Still another juror interpreted testimony from a witness who said Boyd's wife was not as affectionate with Boyd as she had once been as motive for him to kill her, because he realized she only married him to get her citizenship, and now that the required 3-year period was up, she did not need him anymore.

Ultimately, the first two arguments by jurors were determined to be most convincing to all of them, and the jury found Boyd not guilty. (The audience poll showed 54% believed he was not guilty.) However, in the flashback scene at the end of the episode revealing "the truth," Boyd was shown to have killed his wife because she planned to leave him for the boyfriend. When Boyd found out, he killed her, and cut off her fingers after he she had died. In the final scene of the episode, as Boyd is about to leave the court a free man, he said, "I really did love her." The jury based its decision on the belief that Boyd could not have loved his mail-order wife; he could not have been the killer because this was a crime of passion. The jurors' beliefs that the Boyds had a passionless marriage were not based on evidence but on their own preconceived notions about marriage, and particularly mail-order brides. A witness did provide testimony that suggested Boyd was upset that his wife was going to leave him. However, the idea that a man in his 60s could be passionately in love with his 25-year-old mail-order bride was not plausible to jurors. It did not follow their cultural "norm."

During deliberations, inevitably, jurors relied on cultural norms to interpret "factual" information. Motive was a key factor during deliberations; jurors tried to discern why a defendant would commit a crime. If they could not determine a motive, they were less likely to convict, which was evident in this episode of *The Jury*. In the process of interpreting the evidence, jurors had to rely on their own expectations about human behavior, and those expectations were often formed by cultural norms. *The Jury* illustrated that it was not a foolproof system for evaluation. Often, jurors in the series did not find "the truth" by relying on cultural norms. If jurors recognized this, they would be less likely to rely on those norms during deliberations.

While in the episode of the murdered prison priest the jurors were shown to have relied on information beyond the evidence presented at trial, and were revealed to have decided correctly, in the mail-order bride episode they were revealed to have been wrong to rely on their assumptions. These examples showed how the decision-making process of jurors was not a science, and often was not based on scientific evidence presented at trial, but rather on past personal experiences. Still, jurors showed in the series that they believed that their own past experiences were the most credible evidence they had to rely on during deliberations.

The Jury offered a few new elements not seen in other series in the genre, including the audience verdict. Yet, it was the final scene of each episode revealing "the truth" about whether the jury decided "correctly" that was the most unique depiction in the genre. In addition to viewers being able to determine whether they agreed with the fictional jury's verdict, the "truth" element of each episode specifically created a context through which viewers could judge whether the justice system was fair.

The unpredictable outcomes of the jury verdict and the audience verdict, combined with the revelation of the "truth," underscored that it is difficult to know anything for sure, and that a justice system that relies on this process will not always be fair and equitable. The jury deliberation process was presented in the series as flawed, and therefore, the system was presented as flawed as well.

Oz: A Microcosm of Society

Set in a prison, *Oz* offered a departure from the typical setting of programs in the television crime genre and depicted societal problems more clearly than in other series I analyzed. Rather than depicting life in an urban area, Oswald State Correctional Facility (Oz) was not set in any one particular city; it was essentially Everywhere. I will show, however, that Em City represented not every prison, but every urban society.

Oswald State Correctional Facility was multilayered. Within Oz was the general inmate population ("gen pop"), residing in traditional cells. The seemingly "ideal" place in Oz—to the inmate and administrators—was "Em City," the experimental living area developed by administrator Tim McManus where inmates lived in glass-enclosed "pods" that resembled cells, but had no bars, and few barriers to other inmates. In a discussion panel held at the Museum of Television & Radio in 1998, series creator Tom Fontana said the idea for Em City is based on a similar program in a Southern New Jersey prison. I found several programs in New Jersey prisons on the state's Web site, state.nj.us, that mirror what was depicted in *Oz*—many of which included treatment programs for drug offenders—but the one most resembling the setting in *Oz* is Southern State Correctional Facility in Delmont, where prisoners live in dormitory-like settings, rather than cells. (There is also a weekly program at Riverfront State Prison in Camden, New Jersey, where Shakespeare is taught by a local high-school teacher—reminiscent of the series finale of *Oz*, where the prisoners performed *Macbeth*.) In *Oz*, at first, in season 1, this experimental city was in chaos, a riot ensued, and Em City was closed. In season 2, Em City was reopened, but this time a council was formed with group representatives who were expected to keep order. While there were no additional riots, crime did continue in Em City throughout the six seasons of the series.

For the duration of the series, prisoners were rarely shown to leave prison; those who were released eventually returned, having committed another crime. This could be seen as proposing that criminals are unable to be rehabilitated. However, I suggest, based on the context of the entire series, this pattern of release and return was more a commentary on society than on the criminals. The series showed that circumstances in society made it difficult for criminals to rehabilitate themselves because the situations that led to incarceration initially had not changed in society. This was portrayed in a segment in season 6, featuring the character Augustus Hill, an inmate who also served as the series' narrator; he spoke directly to the camera to comment on the meaning of the actions in the episodes and offered a context for the actions. Here, Hill acknowledged that prisoners did not want to be incarcerated, but they chose not to expect more. They had few opportunities for success before incarceration, and they did not expect life to be different after incarceration. Hill said inmates believe that most people—even those not incarcerated—never realize their dreams, so they did not feel they were missing out on any opportunities by being in prison. However, in some cases, the inmates' lives were *better* in Oz than prior to their incarceration. Many of the inmates of Em City, viewed as "others" in society, were leaders within the experimental city in Oz, and enjoyed their status as members of their respective groups. Outside of prison, the people in these groups were not participants in society but had been rejected by society on some level, while in Em City, they led or belonged to a group, which was a strong motivator for their behavior—sometimes criminal and sometimes law abiding. I explore next how they became leaders, and how their "power" over other people in the prison is exhibited in the series.

The Structure of Power
The characteristics used by McManus to select and classify the four members of each group from the general prison population to live in

Em City—ethnicity, belief system, and sexual orientation—further reinforced the inmates' identity there. In some cases, though, the identification created intergroup animosity. While most were proud to represent their group and feel powerful for that group membership, they often used that power to take advantage of other groups they perceived as less powerful. The least powerful group in Oz were the Others, referring to the classification McManus gave to those in Em City whom he did not see as belonging to any other group. However, the Others were most representative of who *all* the inmates were before their incarceration. The depiction of the Others revealed what life was like for all of the inmates outside of prison. They did not belong anywhere. They were not welcome in the existing groups, so they had to form their own group, by default.

An example of the power structure in *Oz* was evident in season 5, when Adam Guenzel, the son of a friend of Beecher's outside of prison, was incarcerated for rape; Beecher tried to protect him from the other inmates, particularly the Aryans, who, because of Aryan leader Vern Schillinger's rivalry with Beecher, targeted Adam because he was Beecher's friend. In order to protect Adam, Beecher asked his friend, Muslim leader Kareem Said, for protection, but Said refused because he said it could make all the Muslims a target of the Aryans; furthermore, he refused because of the type of sexual crime the man committed. Beecher approached Said because he was powerful in Em City, but Said used his power to prioritize the protection of the other Muslims over the new inmate's safety. Said did not view the new inmate, a rapist, as worthy of his protection. A similar depiction was evident in the last episode of season 4, when inmate Padriac Connelly, an Irish refugee, tried to recruit Ryan to help him bomb Em City. Connelly's intentions, he explained to Ryan, were to fight an unjust system. "Injustice must be met head on…If you live like that you may not win, but you never ever lose." At first Ryan agreed to help him; later he backed out and confessed the plan to the corrections officers to thwart Connelly's efforts. Before he confessed, he said to Connelly: "I've got a brother and even a woman inside these walls who believe in me. They believed in me even when I've given them nothing to believe in...I've always walked tall...For once I'm gong to earn the right to walk that way." He feared for their safety, and the thought of them dying, essentially at his hands, was unthinkable. Connelly thought that Ryan, a fellow Irishman, would be supportive of his efforts, especially because Ryan tried to buck the prison authorities in the past. However, Ryan, like Said, chose to use the power he had as a leader to ensure the safety of the people he loved.

Drugs were also a tool inmates used to gain power—and control—over others. For example, when a new leader of the African Americans, Burr Redding, arrived in Oz in season 4, he sought to get fellow inmate Augustus Hill—whom he knew prior to his incarceration—hooked on drugs because he wanted Hill to be dependent on him in Oz. He knew that if Hill needed him, he would follow his orders. Burr also tried to recruit inmate Omar White to sell drugs for him. Initially Omar resisted because, with McManus' help, he had been able to get off drugs himself recently and in the process, he had earned McManus' respect. Omar told Burr: "I can't risk that now." Burr did not let up, and threatened him, saying he would make trouble for Omar if he did not cooperate, and Omar finally agreed. Omar understood that he had no power in Oz, and he needed Burr's help. He also understood that Burr had more power in Oz than McManus, because McManus could not protect Omar, but Burr could.

The government was clearly a source of power in Oz. It also served as a motivating factor for the inmates to rebel against this authority because it was often presented as corrupt. An example could be seen in one episode in season 5, as inmate Alvarez prepared for a parole hearing. Alvarez was an inmate who had shown the potential for rehabilitation throughout the series. In one episode in season 5, he confessed to the prison priest, Fr. Mukada, that he caused someone's death by convincing another person to commit a crime. The priest told Alvarez he had a "good soul" and that he could right this wrong. In another episode in season 5, Alvarez volunteered to train guide dogs because he blinded a correctional officer in a fight in season 2; he saw this work as a way to make up for the crime. As he prepared for the parole-board meeting, Alvarez said he wanted to get out of prison so he could return to his girlfriend, who had recently been released from prison herself. He talked about having another child with her. He added that he wanted to be a better person than he was before he was incarcerated. In his cell, he even practiced talking to the board while dressed in a suit. Even with all of these preparations, and the intention to make a good impression, he turned violent at the parole hearing after he was taunted by one member. The man said he did not think Alvarez had changed, and Alvarez punched the board member, ending any chance for parole.

In a later episode in season 6—the series finale—McManus counseled Alvarez to make amends with the parole-board member he hit during the hearing. Alvarez apologized to the man, also a Hispanic, who revealed that he intentionally provoked him as a test. He said Alvarez gave "every Latino a bad name."

Alvarez's violent response at the parole hearing may indicate that he should not have been paroled because he was not rehabilitated and that he would have been violent in society at the first provocation. However, it can also be read as society—represented by the parole-board member—being doubtful that criminals can be rehabilitated. The parole-board member was in a position of power and he could have used that position to help Alvarez, or at least not to try to block his parole. When Alvarez returned to his cell after realizing the parole board member wanted him to fail, feeling hopeless, he accepted drugs from his cellmate, and said: "I'm so tired. Tired of trying. The walls. The lies. The fear. The death. I'm so tired." With tears in his eyes, he took the drugs. Alvarez gave up trying to change, implying that he believed that someone in a position of power would always try to block his chances for a better life.

Us Versus Them
While an Us versus Them—society versus criminals—depiction is evident in *Oz*, the depiction also exposed an opposition between society and the criminals before they even committed a crime. While on the surface, the focus of *Oz* was outside of society at large, the criminal behavior of characters in *Oz* was often shown to be a response to society

placing them on the outside, not a position of their choosing. Unlike in programs such as *NYPD Blue* and *Law & Order*, where the acts of criminals were shown to be a detriment to the rest of society, in *Oz* the focus was on understanding the lives and motivations of the criminals and their behavior.

In some instances, the series demonstrated that society created a motivation for their criminal behavior, because the criminals had been outcasts in society—even before they committed the criminal acts—so they did not view the laws of society as their own. They had created their own code of conduct—one where crime was necessary to establish power. Ultimately, the depictions in *Oz* illustrated that for the inmates, life in prison is no different than their previous life in society. A feeling of despair existed prior to their incarceration, not *because of* their incarceration.

Because we see how Em City was "created" with certain groups selected to live there and lead there, the structures of the society were more clearly evident in *Oz* than they are in series such as *Law & Order, The Shield*, and *The Practice*, which emphasize the work of legal authorities. It was clear from the depictions in *Oz* that the structures in the prison society mirror the structures of American society outside of prison. As a result, the audience was able to see how "others" are created in society. The series also used this Us. versus Them depiction to illustrate how power is attained and exerted over people in society. The "creation" of the Em City society was deliberate and explicit—unlike the external American society—so the inequities in the societal structures were more evident as well. These inequities in the prison society exist seemingly in a society of criminals, not a society that viewers exist in, as is the case in *Law & Order, The Shield*, and *The Practice*, all set in nonprison settings.

The audience of a series such as *Law & Order* is more likely to identify with the main characters who are legal authorities—representing "Us," or society—and therefore the actions of these characters are more likely to be perceived as correct and appropriate. Any improprieties or corruption exhibited by legal authorities in this series is either portrayed as necessary or rare, as I discussed in chapter 4. However, in

Oz, the delineation of "Us" and "Them" is less clear. There are prison staff members in the series, but they, too, are operating in a "different" society than the one most Americans live in. This is further reinforced throughout the series as several characters are portrayed as both "Us" and "Them" at different times, as I discussed in chapter 5.

While viewers of *Oz* were encouraged to identify some characters, such as Ryan O'Reily and Tobias Beecher, as redeemable and even rehabilitated as I previously cited, viewers may not have completely identified *with* these characters. As a result, viewers may not have perceived these characters to be part of "Us." On the other hand, viewers who feel oppressed in their lives or have been victims of crime might have identified with the "villains" in *Oz*, who represented a way for these viewers to resolve their frustrations cathartically, as Marchetti (1989) suggested. These viewers may identify more with characters portrayed as unable to be rehabilitated, such as Chris Keller and Vern Schillinger, even though they can still recognize them as evil "others."

The effect of this blurred definition of "Us" and "Them" is that what is depicted as "right" and "appropriate" behavior is also less clear in *Oz* than in series such as *Law & Order* and *The Shield*. The *Oz* audience is not automatically identifying with the law-abiding characters—that is, legal authorities—because there are so few of them in the series and they play a peripheral role to the starring criminal characters. Therefore, the audience is able to consider the structure of Em City to be inequitable and unfair without outwardly condemning its own society in the process. Because the prison society is seemingly a completely different society from the American society, it provides a tool for the series creators to explore issues of race, economic class, and power in all societies.

Series such as *Law & Order, The Practice*, and *The Shield*, set in contemporary American society, do not address inequities in societal structures in the same way as *Oz* because if they did expose these inequities, they would be conveying to their audience that the society it belongs to is unjust. Rather, when *Law & Order, The Shield*, and *The Practice* address inequities in societal structures, they mitigate them by presenting them as rare and harmless, as I also showed. By showing corruption among police officers, lawyers, and judges as harmless, the justice system is also shown to be fair. *Law & Order*, *The Shield*, and *The Practice* assure the audience that society is fair and safe for law-abiding citizens. *The Jury*'s ambiguous depiction suggests that society, and its justice system, is not always unfair, but also not always fair either.

Oz, however, clearly offers a society that is neither fair nor safe. The viewing audience is still assured that its own society is fair and safe because the society in *Oz* exists in a prison, but because of this setting, the series also presents these issues in a context that enables and encourages viewers to see inequities in the prison society, which serves as a metaphor for American society. In the process, *Oz* illustrates how inequitable societal structures, primarily based on economic and social status, can provide a motivation, at least in part, and the conditions for crime to occur, and suggests that those conditions need to change. Preventing crime is not presented as being solely within the power of individuals because the motivation for crime is not solely within the individuals either. Inequitable economic and social structures are shown to be contributing factors that cause frustration, and ultimately create motivation for some crimes. Viewers of *Oz* may be more willing to acknowledge these inequities because they are in the role of an "observer" and not a "participant" of the society depicted, as is the case with *Law & Order*, *The Shield*, *The Practice*, and *The Jury*.

Chapter 7

Reality Series

From 1998 through 2004, several reality shows emerged, including *America's Most Wanted* and *COPS*, both airing on Fox. MTV's *The Real World*, which debuted in 1992 (Deery, 2004) and *Survivor*, which aired in 2000, are considered the first reality shows (Quinby, 2002) The genre has been described as a combination of several existing genres.

> What we can say is that the reality of Reality TV is usually translated as the experience of real or ordinary people (i.e., unknown non-actors) in an actual and unscripted environment. It does not require that the situation be ordinary, but that there be a particular kind of viewer access: in fact, Reality TV is selling access as much as any particular subject matter. (Deery, 2004, p. 5)

Reality TV "departs from classic voyeurism in that the participants know they are being watched" (Deery, 2004, p. 6). Nabi, Biely, Morgan, and Stitt (2003) specified that reality television includes the following characteristics:

a. people portraying themselves (i.e., not actors or public figures performing roles),

b. filmed at least in part in their living or working environment rather than on a set,
   c. without a script,
   d. with events placed in a narrative context,
   e. for the primary purpose of viewer entertainment. (p. 304)

Bratich (2006) pointed out,

> RTV's [reality television's] integration of audiences into its programming design turns seemingly passive viewers into laboring subjects, whose participation alters both programming outcomes as well as their own place in the televisual medium (audiences are not considered coprogrammers and coproducers). RTV has altered audience power, the mediated capacities to affect and be affected, by harnessing those powers as the shows' lifeblood. (p. 68)

As "potential" candidates, "audiences now partially constituted the texts" and "ordinary people are transformed into players and/or participations whose actions can alter future arrangements" (p. 68). As a result, "[r]eality itself becomes articulated as that which is transformable—a malleable domain, a set of variables and phyla to be continuously modified" (Bratich, 2006, p. 68). Bratich further noted that reality programs that have a game or competition component take "the game into a separate virtual sphere" and "seek to immanentize game dynamics into everyday life" (p. 70).

In this research, I focus on the crime-based reality programs, specifically *COPS* and *America's Most Wanted*.

Combating crime in *COPS* and *America's Most Wanted*

Fishman (1999) compared *America's Most Wanted*'s focus on individual action with *COPS*'s emphasis on the role of police officers in combating crime:

> *AMW* endorses civic agency and the individual's efficacy, minimizing the difference between the crime-fighting responsibilities of state institutions and the general public. Alternatively, *COPS*

emphasizes the subordination of the public's power to those who have been invested with the power of the state and thus deemed responsible for maintaining law and order. (p. 270)

As a result of the public's involvement in *America's Most Wanted*, Fishman (1999) stressed, catching criminals is presented as the public's responsibility. "In reality-based crime television's populist myths, everyday people are the heroes; civilian surroundings constitute their arena; and the narrative is one in which order unravels and justice depends upon the public's collective anti-crime efforts" (Fishman, 1999, p. 270).

Yet, *COPS* conversely stresses police power. As a result, Fishman noted, the two series

> represent competing (though not mutually exclusive) beliefs on how to best control crime. In part, the fact that *COPS* and *AMW* do not portray a common means of establishing order and maintaining justice is a consequence of systematic selection differences since these programs focus on two distinct stages in crime investigation...[I]n *AMW* the focus is on locating criminals while in *COPS* the location of the criminal is typically known and the focus is on their immediate arrest. (p. 271)

Fishman (1999) further pointed out that the focus of *America's Most Wanted* is often on the victims, not the criminals, since "*AMW* gets well acquainted with the victim in every episode, setting a tone of deep sorrow, outrage, and anguish" (p. 282). Yet, both *America's Most Wanted* and *COPS*, Fishman suggested, support a punitive crime policy. "Even though *AMW* explicitly criticizes the police, courts, and other legal institutions, it functions to put deviants behind bars and, like *COPS*, demonstrates the need for a punitive legal system" (Fishman, 1999, p. 283). She said the series accomplish this by presenting criminals as deviant. "Both programs share a crucial moral component, for both programs link notions of 'deviance' with a deeply ingrained cultural sense of a 'right' and 'natural' social order" (Fishman, 1999, p. 283).

The reality programs *COPS* and *America's Most Wanted* adopt filmic techniques of both the documentary and fictional genres. The cameras do follow officers out in the field, unscripted, but some scenes are reshot to get better lighting and angles, so they are not documentaries. In this chapter, I will explore depictions in the reality series *COPS* and *America's Most Wanted*, adding to others' previous research on the programs. I will specifically examine whether the portrayals of crime, criminals, and legal authorities can be situated in these two "reality-based shows" as either reinforcing what is presented in the "wholly" fictional series, or offering new representations.

Cops

The reality program *COPS* began airing on Fox in 1989, and the half-hour program is still airing original episodes. Each week the work of a different police officer is profiled in a documentary-style format. Cameramen "ride along" with police officers as they patrol the streets on their beat. Most episodes include three segments, each profiling three different municipal or county-police or sheriff departments. Some episodes, such as "Jersey Cop," "Armed and Dangerous," and "Bad Girls," profile one type of crime or one department for the entire half-hour episode. In a documentary style, the program follows the officer as he or she patrols the beat.

Many of the calls the officers respond to are either traffic violations, which often lead to drug arrests, or domestic disputes. Unlike the content in the fictional programs, which portray violent crimes such as murder or attempted murder, the crimes in *COPS* are much less severe. Creator John Langley, in a 2003 article by the Scripps Howard News Service, said, "My favorite episodes are not so high crime oriented as they are funny or just weird" (Morrow, 2003, n.p.). The tone of the show is evident from the beginning of each episode, as the theme music of "Bad Boys" plays. Viewers are also reminded of the serious nature of the program as the following disclaimer airs: "All suspects are presumed innocent until proven guilty in a court of law." As I will argue, however, the police officers' actions do not always reinforce this notion. Many suspects are portrayed as guilty, and follow-up episodes of previous arrests in *COPS* are never shown, which also adds to the perception of guilt.

COPS is produced by a crew experienced in television and news, but has no police officers on staff. It has no recurring characters, although some officers appear in more than one episode. Still, the focus is not on the individual stories of officers, as much as it is on the process of apprehending criminals. While the series has a documentary-type look, it employs some filming techniques that are typically used with fictional programs. A behind-the-scenes look was offered by an article in *The Fresno Bee*, on December 19, 2004. According to the article, officers in Fresno were profiled in an episode of *COPS* and said some scenes were reenacted. "For example, they asked police to search a shed after the officers had already looked there for a suspect. Or they would ask officers to search a suspect's car from an angle that had better lighting." (Eberly, 2004, n.p.). Even though the series is presented in documentary style, according to the article, elements are staged, and this is likely not apparent to viewers. Still, the series remains popular with viewers. During the week of December 11, 2004, *COPS* was ranked first in the ratings for the night in households and in the 18–49 age range, a desired audience for advertisers, with 4.8 million people watching (Berman, 2004). The show is often ranked first or second for the night.

In the episodes of *COPS* I analyzed, all airing on FOX in the summer of 2004, a "lighter" side of police work is depicted than what is presented in any of the fictional series. *COPS*, which first aired in 1989, seems constructed primarily to show police officers in a favorable light. The police are the "stars" of the series, even though there are rarely "recurring characters." In each 10-minute segment profiling an arrest, the officers become the main characters, not the suspects who are arrested. The officers are given the opportunity by the *COPS* crew to explain their motivations for becoming a police officer; as they apprehend and arrest the suspects, they speak directly to the camera to explain how and why they make specific decisions, which can include whether someone is arrested, how they obtain evidence, and what the ultimate charge will be. As such, the series offers insight into police procedures and constructs "your neighborhood police officer" as someone who enjoys his work, which involves steering criminals in the right direction.

Each segment of *COPS* opens with an officer speaking directly to the camera as he or she is patrolling the streets. Officers often talk about the area or why they became police officers. In one episode, a white male officer in his 30s from Palm Beach County, Florida, said that he joined the force at 18 because he liked guiding people in the right direction, which he also did as a Little League coach. This depicts the officer, who is seemingly representative of "everyone's" neighborhood officer, as endearing and dedicated to the greater good of society.

COPS depicts crime as occurring in many places throughout the country—not just in one place, as in the fictional series, which are set only in one location, primarily urban areas. Each segment of an episode takes place in a different location. The episodes I viewed took place in Florida, New Jersey, Washington state, Kansas, New Mexico, and Pennsylvania. Most of the arrests police make are either drug-related or domestic disputes. These appear to be the most common types of arrests by patrol officers throughout the country, based on the depictions in the series. While the fictional series focus primarily on murders, *COPS* offers a depiction of the daily routine of officers, which, according to the series, involves lesser crimes, not the sensational and violent crimes committed weekly in *Law & Order, NYPD Blue, Cold Case, The Shield*, Oz, and *The Sopranos*.

In *COPS*, crime is committed in urban and rural areas—but not in middle-class, suburban areas. *COPS* suggests that most crimes—or at least drug-related and domestic disputes—occur outside of suburbia. As a result, the series also constructs criminals as existing outside of suburbia. The criminals in *COPS* are not depicted as "dangerous." They are essentially harmless. They rarely get violent with the officers, and even the domestic disputes never rise to the level of physical violence, at least not in the segment. The disputes are generally only verbal in nature.

Making Decisions
Officers in *COPS* are shown to routinely make decisions about the extent of force that will be used on suspects and the charges that will be

filed against the suspects. As a result, the audience is ostensibly provided some insight into how officers make these decisions. Rather than harassing suspects until they offer incriminating information, as seen particularly in *NYPD Blue*, a tactic commonly used by police in the episodes of *COPS* I analyzed was for the officers to establish a rapport with the suspects in order to coax them into admitting to their crimes and turning over evidence. For example, when an officer from Jacksonville, Florida, a white female in her 30s, responded to a "suspicious person" call, she asked the suspect, a white female in her late 20s, if she could search her car. Her compliance apparently eliminated the need to get a search warrant. The suspect was willing to cooperate with the officer, who was very relaxed and nonthreatening toward the suspect, saying things such as "do me a favor and open the glove compartment." After the officer found crack cocaine in the woman's car, there was little discussion between the officers and the suspects. The officer clearly used a friendly demeanor to coerce the woman to comply with the search. Once the woman gave the officer permission to search the car, the officer's demeanor became harsher.

Humor is often used by officers to establish a rapport with suspects. In "Jersey Cop," profiling the Passaic County Sheriff's Department in Paterson, New Jersey, an officer watched a car pull out of a parking lot where he believed a drug deal occurred, and he stopped the driver. The driver asked the officer to let him go without arrest, because he said he did not buy drugs. The driver said he was in the area because he had a court date coming up on other drug chargers, and he returned to scout the area so he could tell the judge about the previous arrest. The officer did not believe him, but he continued to banter with the man. The driver said, "I'm upset," to which the officer responded, "I'm upset, too." The officer also made a light-hearted comment to the passenger in the car about how he must really like crack, which put the passenger at ease, and the passenger handed the officer his crack pipe. The officer continued to search the car and found crack. He arrested the driver and his passenger, charging them both with loitering and crack possession. He even charged the driver additionally for not using his directional when turning. When he handed them the summonses to appear in court, he said, "See how easy it is to get you." In another episode profiling the same department and following the same officer, a driver stopped on suspicion of drug possession asked the officer if he could make a call, to which the officer responded, "Who you gonna call, Ghostbusters? 911, to come help you?" The driver laughed. In another episode, an officer from Albuquerque, New Mexico, was called to a home for a domestic dispute and found a drug dealer hiding under a mattress. The officer jokingly said, "When you were playing hide-and-go-seek as a kid, you were caught first all the time, right?"

In some cases, the rapport an officer develops with a suspect and cooperation from a suspect can lead officers to choose a lighter punishment. In one episode, a Spokane, Washington, officer arrested a teen for marijuana possession; instead of impounding the car, however, he allowed him to call his mother to pick it up. The officer, speaking directly to the camera, acknowledged that he was giving the driver a break because the teen admitted that he had marijuana in the car and was cooperative. The three white suspects in the car were also released with summonses; the officer did not bring them in to the jail, which he said he could have. This shows, first, that the police have leeway in how they handle these types of cases, and second, that this officer chose to exercise leniency in this case.

Evidently, police can also go harder on some suspects when they want to. For example, in another segment of the "Jersey Cop" episode, the officer followed a young suspect, who looked to be about 14, into the entrance of an apartment building. He opened the door, and with his gun drawn, screamed at the boy to stop what he was doing. The boy, clearly afraid the officer was going to shoot him, kept calling the officer "poppy," and asked that he let him go home. In this case, the officer refused, saying he had already arrested him once for having drugs. In another episode from Palm Beach County, Florida, a driver was pulled over, suspected of having drugs and being in a car his father reported as stolen. He claimed to be working with an undercover officer. The cop seemed to believe him. He did not verify his status with the department. Yet, he was not lenient with the driver, saying, "You're out here trying to do the right thing helping us, but you did the wrong thing, which jammed you. That's why you're going to jail."

An officer's personal belief about the role of police—and the law—emerges as a factor in how the officers decide the charges that will be filed. For example, when the officers in the Jersey and Palm Beach County episodes did not show the suspects leniency, they suggest it is for the suspects' own good—to teach them a lesson and to try to steer them in the right direction. The officers suggest that charging the suspects with a crime might deter them from engaging in further crimes, but they do not discuss whether this is an effective approach. The Jersey officer acknowledges that he had arrested the boy before, but does not acknowledge that it does not seem to be deterring the boy from taking drugs.

Using Force

Even though the crimes depicted in *COPS* are primarily nonviolent, officers do sometimes use force at times when apprehending the suspects. An episode involving a white, male officer in his 30s from Spokane, Washington, showed him responding to a domestic dispute between an Asian son and his father from a lower-middle-class home. The officer used a type of gun that shoots pins into the suspect to apprehend the son. The son was difficult to understand, in part because of a language barrier, as it seemed English was his second language, and also because he appeared to have a diminished mental capacity. The son cursed often at the father and the officers, who pushed his face into the gravelly rocks after they subdued him. They later put a towel under his face, when the backup officers arrived, to protect his face from the gravel. The officer who used the pin gun spoke directly to the camera to explain that the shot would not do permanent damage, and that the pins would be removed later. As the suspect was led away to the patrol car, police explained, again speaking directly to the camera, that the gun was a new device and they were waiting to have a chance to use it.

In the series, the officers' actions are depicted as appropriate, even though, upon closer analysis, questions emerge. For example, in the Spokane episode, many details remain sketchy about the incident, primarily whether using the pin gun was necessary. The audience never learns the cause of the fight; the events that transpired to warrant the son being taken into custody; the charges that were filed against him, if any; and the threat he posed to police to warrant the use of the pin gun, as he did not have any weapons on him and police never indicated that they suspected he posed a physical threat to them or the father. However, the segment does not encourage viewers to question whether the pin gun was needed. Police officers—in this segment and throughout the series—are allowed to explain their actions, so it is their interpretation of events that the audience is encouraged to accept. If the officers do not question whether using the gun was necessary, the audience is not encouraged to either. On the other hand, viewers reading against the grain could interpret many of the police officers' actions as excessive and unnecessary.

COPS constructs crime fighting as a role for legal authorities, as does *Law & Order*, *NYPD Blue*, *The Practice*, and *The Shield*. As a result, it continues to portray the role of police officers as it has traditionally been depicted in the genre. However, I would argue that because these traditional depictions are now being offered along with other depictions—particularly in *The Shield*, which portrays blatant police corruption, and *Cold Case*, which demonstrates that police can recognize redeeming qualities in criminals—they have a new connotation. *Law & Order*, *NYPD Blue*, *The Practice*, and *COPS* are not offering the only depictions in the genre, so they represent one version of police officers, while *The Shield* and *Cold Case* represent another version of police officers. As a result, the fairness of the justice system can be called into question. Whether the police officers are part of an equitable system is questioned in series such as *The Shield* and *COPS*, and may impact how citizens view the justice system as a whole.

AMERICA'S MOST WANTED

America's Most Wanted, a 1-hour reality program that began airing on Fox in 1988, continues to air original episodes. Based on the FBI's Most Wanted list, created in 1950, the goal of the program is to report on crime suspects in the United States or neighboring countries (Canada and Mexico) who are still at-large. The audience is encouraged to call in to a toll-free telephone number if they think they have seen any of the suspects.

Creator and host John Walsh, father of a boy who was abducted in 1981 at age 6 from a Florida mall and later killed, narrates the program profiling suspects. His beliefs about crime policies drive the program, but he is also very sensitive to parents of victims. "It's actually part of my deal with Fox, that I'll never do a story a victim doesn't want me to do," Walsh said in a November 15, 2004, article in the *Daily News*/Knight Ridder/Tribune News Service. "We'll never show the face of a molested or abused child. That criteria has been my standard for 17 years. And if they don't want to say something, or are uncomfortable—this is not '60 Minutes,' this is my show. If they don't want to talk abut it, it's okay" (Bianculli, 2004, n.p.).

The program profiles five cases in each episode, and goes beyond the focus on fugitives that its title suggests. Some crimes are presented in a news-report style that include interviews with the victims, their families, and law enforcement involved in the case; others are reenactments of a crime, but are not labeled as such, and include narration similar to the news-style reports; and still others are even more dramatic in style, strictly presenting the crime as a drama, without narration. In some cases depicted, the suspect is already apprehended. Like the original federal Most Wanted list, most suspects on *America's Most Wanted* are male.

In all, more than 1,000 criminals who have been profiled on *America's Most Wanted* have been apprehended, according to the series' Web site. The most well-known case involved Elizabeth Smart of Salt Lake City, who had been missing for nearly 9 months; she was found after two separate viewers called police after a photo of Brian D. Mitchell, suspected abductor, was broadcast.

The series still draws a large audience. In the first week of March 2004, *America's Most Wanted* topped the list of total viewers for the night, with 8.1 million, and also among 18–49-year-olds, tied with *COPS*, at 3.1 million. Ratings for the week of December 11, 2004, had *America's*

Most Wanted ranked second, behind *COPS*, in total households and among viewers 18–49, with 4.8 million people watching (Berman, 2004).

The work of police officers evident in fictional depictions was also present in the reality series *America's Most Wanted* in the episodes I analyzed (which originally aired in the summer of 2004). These episodes included "news" reports, with reporters "covering" the story from the scene of the crime and interviewing victims and law enforcement involved; dramatic recreations, which are not labeled as such; and a mixture of dramatization and news-reporting style.

Suspects in *America's Most Wanted* have not been convicted of anything, but they are often presented as if they are escaped convicts, already found guilty of a crime. The photos used of the suspects often make them look psychotic or possessed. Excessive zooms are used on the suspect's eyes to make him or her (although most suspects are men) look even more distorted and deranged. All of this serves to create a sense that these suspects are dangerous, as is also presented in *The Practice*.

The suspects' guilt and the danger they pose are further conveyed through language used in the narration, especially by host John Walsh. Using sensationalized portrayals to show how society is victimized by the "low lifes" and "thugs" that commit crimes against society, the program depicts traditional family life as being jeopardized by criminals, as Williams (1993) also asserted in her analysis of the series. The voice-over narration in each segment creates a context of guilt. In one episode, Walsh narrated a story of a suspected predator of a 14-year-old girl, calling him a "low-life." He often refers to suspects as "criminals," "bandits," and "creeps." An example in *America's Most Wanted* can be seen in a segment about a police hunt for two white men in their 30s, suspected in the disappearance of a couple who lived near them in the Ozark Mountains of Arkansas. Walsh called the two suspects "creeps," and said when these people who "didn't belong" came to town, the Van Buren County Sheriff's Department moved in on them. Of the shootout that ensued between the suspects and police, Walsh said the police "escaped with their lives" and the criminals "escaped into the wild."

Still, it is rare that people other than Walsh use such sensational language. Because Walsh has been impacted by crime, it is likely the audience does not question whether the language he uses to describe criminals is "fair." The audience is encouraged to give his account more credibility because he has had personal experience with crime. The audience knows Walsh's 6-year-old son was abducted from a Sears store in Florida and killed. Walsh serves as a reminder to viewers that he has been a victim of crime, which is often portrayed in the series as random. The notion that crime can happen to anyone is reinforced not only by Walsh in *America's Most Wanted* but by others reporting stories in the series as well. In one report of a missing 20-year-old woman, a police detective on the case says, "What if it was my child who was missing?" Walsh symbolically represents this notion in every report, as it *was* his child who was a victim of a horrific crime. The audience is encouraged to identify with Walsh.

A Call to Action
In addition to creating a context of guilt, the language used by Walsh promotes a mob mentality. For example, following one report, speaking directly into the camera to the viewing audience, Walsh says: "Let's get him." In another segment, just before Walsh went to commercial, he said: "We need your help to take down some more criminals, when we get back." It may not be a coincidence that the logo used when these programs aired were of the letters AMU in a formation that looked like the "bat signal" in Batman comic books. *America's Most Wanted* offers the same message as the Batman series. Batman was depicted as a "regular guy" fighting crime, and Walsh is encouraging viewers—regular guys—to do the same.

While the show can be read as encouraging people to work with authorities by calling in a tip to the show, it can also read by the audience as a call to action in their own lives, specifically to fear crime and to combat it. Rather than leaving crime solving to the police—society's "official" authorities—Walsh and *America's Most Wanted* are encouraging people to get involved in the process. In this way, by seeking the involvement of the public, it can alleviate the sense of victimization the audience may feel. However, I see the program itself as creating that fear in the audience, even where it would not have existed otherwise. For example, after profiling a counterfeiter, Walsh said, "If you lock your doors at night, you do not want to be a victim of crime." Another segment profiled a scam artist who would place a classified ad in a newspaper for truck drivers, and when people applied for the job, he would conduct a "credit check," and used the information they gave him to steal from their checking and savings accounts. He would also steal IRS refund checks out of people's mailboxes. The program suggests that if the audience was not worried about these types of crime before they watched the program, they should be. I see this as an example of the program seeking to create fear in viewers.

Evidence
In the segments I analyzed, "evidence" presented about both victims and suspects is sketchy. For example, one episode involved a fan-club member of musician Duff from the heavy metal group Guns 'N Roses, who was killed while she was working on the computer in her apartment. Duff said, "If it can happen to Lori, it can happen to anybody." He described her as "innocent," "nice," and "genuine," even though, based on the vague details presented in the program, there are a lot of things about her he could not have known. The audience is told she was a groupie who had moved to the United States from Italy. There is no further explanation of what her life was like, and no proof that Duff even knew her, except for a few brief encounters at concerts. Was she really like everybody else? Do many people move to another country to follow an obsession with a rock group? Was the crime related to her obsession with the band? She is depicted solely in her role as a groupie of the band, but a motivation for the crime is never presented. Based on the information presented in the segment, it is impossible to say whether she is the "Everywoman" victim the show presents.

Another example of sketchy details can be seen in an episode where a jewelry-store owner, who was robbed 10 years before, beat a man who recently came into her store because she believed it was the same person. Again, there is no evidence presented to support the assertion that he was the same person, but the program presents it as fact. "She remembered him for 10 years," the narrator stated. The possibility that the woman beat an innocent person is never presented. Instead, we are encouraged to see her as a random, innocent victim who decided to fight back 10 years later. The vague information presented, combined with an authoritative-sounding narrator and a fast-paced recounting of the events, work to make the segment appear complete, absolute, and plausible—even though very little is known about the event.

The American Dream
Often, *America's Most Wanted* depicts well-known cases, including the 2004 disappearance of Lori Hacking in Utah. Lori, a married and reportedly pregnant woman in her late 20s, was described in the *America's Most Wanted* segment as "living a dream." At the time of her disappearance, she was preparing for a move to North Carolina with Mark, her husband of 5 years, as Mark was to attend medical school there. Mark was presented by the program as a suspect because he reportedly had never been admitted to medical school, which his wife was not aware of until a few days before her disappearance. Mark reportedly confessed to his two brothers that he had killed Lori and put her body in a garbage dumpster, and the report on *America's Most Wanted* showed police searching a landfill based on this information.

At first glance, it is surprising that this crime would be part of *America's Most Wanted*, as there is no need for audience involvement. It is unlike other famous cases, such as the disappearance of Elizabeth Smart, also in Utah, where a tip from an *America's Most Wanted* viewer led police to find her several months after she had been abducted. In Lori's case, Mark Hacking was the only known suspect, and he was already in police custody. The suspect was not "wanted," but instead fits the "profile" of an *America's Most Wanted* case: Someone living the "American Dream," who becomes an innocent victim of a deranged criminal. Another *America's Most Wanted* report by Maureen O'Boyle explained how a wife who lived in Long Island was waiting for her husband to return home from work one night when she heard a popping noise outside their home. She went outside, and found that her husband had been shot. The narrator said, "With every last breath he tried to get to his family." In addition, one report of a nightclub bouncer in Toronto, who was shot during a shootout at the club, cited that he worked extra shifts "so he could earn the cash he needed to buy a home for his family."

It is clear that the cases that appear on *America's Most Wanted* are not selected based solely on whether audience involvement is actually necessary, but whether they reinforce the notion that criminals are inhuman, "low-life" thugs victimizing families who are living the American Dream. While middle-class, suburban families are depicted as primary victims of crime, the show also seeks to empower them to fight back against crime.

While the show acknowledges the work police officers do, ultimately it suggests that fighting crime is not just the role of police officers, but of individuals as well. Therefore, it implies that crime can be averted by individuals, which is also suggested in *Oz, The Sopranos*, and *Cold Case*. These three fictional series depict the power to prevent crime as lying within the criminals to choose not to commit crimes; the battle that must be waged is within the individuals to overcome criminal urges. In these series, apprehending and incarcerating criminals does not indicate that the battle has been won; crime must continue to be averted by removing the motivations for criminal acts. However, *America's Most Wanted* situates the power to prevent crime as lying within noncriminal individuals; the battle that must be waged is between society and criminals. *America's Most Wanted* indicates that by apprehending criminals, the battle has been won.

CHAPTER 8

FOUR CRIME DOCUMENTARIES

In this chapter, I analyze four documentaries that address crime and the criminal justice system in America: *America Undercover: Gladiator Days: Anatomy of a Prison Murder*, *Capturing the Friedmans*, *In the Jury Room*, and *Deadline*. *Gladiator Days* focuses on what motivated two inmates to murder another inmate, and particularly the influence of group membership. The other three documentaries point to flaws in the justice system, including in how police collect evidence to charge someone with a crime, how juries deliberate, and how strict sentencing laws, including the death penalty, are applied.

Tracing the history of documentary filmmaking, Barnouw (1993) described the different roles documentary filmmakers have assumed: prophet, explorer, reporter, painter, advocate, bugler, prosecutor, poet, chronicler, promoter, observer, catalyst, and guerrilla. Barnouw also noted that documentary filmmakers often take on more than one role at a time. Barnouw saw the industry as one that has evolved, sometimes out of desire, and at other times out of necessity. "The redefining has necessarily been an ongoing process as each decade brought social upheavals that cried for documentation, and media technology innovations to meet the challenges. The medium grew in resources as history offered proliferating agendas" (p. 297). Barnouw also pointed out how documentaries are produced outside the "big-studio" system in films and television.

> [Documentarists] remained a minority voice in the industries—cinema and television—in which they had won footholds. And the industries—on every continent—continued to be ambivalent about these intruders. Industry leadership leaned toward recycling social mythologies. Documentarists seemed out of step. They were the ones most likely to say: "Look, the emperor has no clothes!" A disturbing presence, their work tended to be unprofitable, financially and politically. (p. 297)

In contemporary American society, documentaries are quite accessible to the public, particularly through cable programming. HBO's *America Undercover* series airs weekly, and The Independent Film Channel, The History Channel, A&E, and The Discovery Channel are among the channels primarily offering documentary films and programs. In addition, documentaries are regularly offered on public television and on broadcast networks.

In addition to analyzing the four documentaries, I discuss mainstream news reports that mirrored events presented in the documentaries. Allan (1998) suggested,

> [The] televisual news account, far from simply "reflecting" the reality of an event, is actually working to construct a codified definition of what should count as the reality of the event...The complex conditions under which the text is both produced and consumed or 'read' will need to be accounted for in a cultural studies approach to news as a form of hegemonic discourse. (p. 113)

REALITY OR DOCUMENTARY?

The criteria used by Nabi, Biely, Morgan, and Stitt (2003) to define reality television, described in chapter 7, also describes the nature of many documentaries, including the four I analyzed. Nabi and colleagues defined reality television as people portraying themselves, not filmed on a set or with a script, where events are placed in a narrative context. These are all also usually the case with documentary films. Where the forms may differ, however, is in what is perceived to be the primary purpose of the documentary. Nabi and colleagues defined the primary purpose of reality television as viewer entertainment, but following Barnouw's description of the last century of documentaries, the primary purpose of documentaries has been to inform and to advocate for social change.

In addition, documentaries are generally not produced to garner a profit, but to educate people about a social issue that the filmmaker believes is undercovered by society, while reality programming has become so prevalent on television because it is profitable for networks. The Center for Independent Documentary, founded in 1981, has described documentary filmmakers as having "the creative passion and courage to achieve that vision, often against all odds. They take on unpopular and eccentric subjects, offer views that are often underrepresented, and usually have to struggle to raise funds" (documentaries.org).

Further blurring the definition between reality and documentary is the fact that many texts previously referred to as documentaries are now considered reality programs. For example, before the term "reality television" existed, in 1973, PBS aired *An American Family*, profiling the life of the Loud family in California. At the time it first aired, the text was referred to as a documentary, but it mirrored popular reality programs that followed, including *The Real World* on MTV, among others. Today the documentary is considered reality programming, rather than a documentary, by the television industry and even by the filmmakers, suggesting that the two terms are seen as interchangeable to some. In retrospect, *An American Family* was referred to as the first reality program by *TV Guide*, as well as in a Q&A interview posted on pbs.org with the filmmakers. In it, they described the piece as culturally significant, and a reality program. They said,

> Lance Loud was an incredibly important cultural signifier, the first real gay person to appear on television as an integral member of

American family life. He impressed himself on a nation's generation of young people as not only openly gay but also as a free spirit seeking to live his life on his own terms. According to *TV Guide*, ten million viewers weekly watched *An American Family*, thereby making Lance the first reality TV star as well. (Retrieved August 11, 2008, from http://www.pbs.org/lanceloud/about/qanda.html)

As Barnouw suggested, documentaries do not always fit into a specific definition; they can serve to advocate, report, and prosecute, at the same time, as was the case with the four documentaries I analyzed. Each of the four documentaries I analyzed mirrors depictions in the fictional and reality programs, and serves as a catalyst for society to acknowledge that the criminal justice system is flawed. While Barnouw identified documentarians as traditionally responding to social change that "cried for documentation," the documentaries I viewed advocate for change by seeking to expose inequities in the justice system. They serve a different purpose than the fictional and reality programs, which primarily seek to entertain, but they address similar issues and add to the discourse that is presented in these genres.

While the documentaries I analyzed all aired on television between 1998 and 2004, only two were originally produced for television, *In the Jury Room* and *Gladiator Days: Deadline* and *Capturing the Friedmans* were originally produced as cinematic films. The popularity of reality programs, however, may have made the documentaries more appealing to network executives, who likely believe there is an audience for them. While traditionally documentaries have not been seen as profitable, as the nature of television continues to change, documentarians are finding more outlets for their work. Kilborn (2004) described how the documentary format is changing in response to new programming on television, specifically reality programs:

> The popularizing tendencies so clearly discernible in today's docudramas provide still further evidence of a more general trend in contemporary documentary, at least as far as work commissioned for television is concerned. The fear on the part of those committed to serious documentary is that, as public service values are further

eroded, the space once reserved in TV schedules for the more deserving or challenging forms of documentary will gradually be usurped by popular, entertainment-oriented factual programming. (p. 31)

Kilborn suggested the purpose of documentaries is to "raise awareness about socially important matters" (p. 27). For Kilborn, the subject matter largely defines whether a film is a documentary (vs. reality program) and whether it is serious. He acknowledged, however, that more and more documentary filmmakers "feel justified in combining within a single documentary-like presentation techniques and modes of address as disparate as home-movie material, archive footage and various forms of dramatic reconstruction and enactment" (p. 30). This is evident in *Capturing the Friedmans*, which I discuss below, as a combination of home movies and interviews are used.

Yet, even though documentarians have adopted elements found in reality programming, Kilborn (2004) still distinguished the documentary from reality programming, by citing the "seriousness" with which it presents socially significant subject matters, and said, even with the commodification of "the real through the apparently endless stream of performance-oriented reality shows—there remains a tangible public appetite for the type of cutting-edge documentary which attempts a serious engagement with real-life events and concerns" (p. 31). Kilborn (2004) concluded that even with "the increasing commercialization of broadcasting it seems likely, however, that much of this more thought-provoking work will originate in the world beyond television where documentarists are not as subject to the exigencies of ratings-obsessed TV executives" (p. 31).

AMERICA UNDERCOVER: GLADIATOR DAYS: ANATOMY OF A PRISON MURDER

The documentary *Gladiator Days: Anatomy of a Prison Murder*, part of the HBO *America Undercover* series, depicts a stabbing that led to the murder of a Utah State Prison inmate by another inmate. To produce the documentary, filmmakers spent three years visiting prisons and spoke to inmates, guards, and officials about violence in prisons. *Gladiator* focuses on the 1994 death of a black inmate in his 30s who was stabbed 67 times by two white inmates of the same age.

During the murder, which was recorded on the prison security camera, inmate Lonnie Blackmon was stabbed by fellow inmates Troy Kell and Eric Daniels. Kell identified himself with the white-supremacist group, just as the character of Vern Schillinger did in *Oz*. As he carried out the killing, he repeated "white power." The members of Kell's group also referred to themselves as "soldiers," a reference also often made in *The Sopranos* by members of the mob crew, who show that they view their roles, even in carrying out murders, as a duty. This reference suggests that they commit crimes because they are ordered to; they see it is a way to show they belong to the mob crew and support its leadership.

At the time of the killing, Kell had been in prison for 15 years, since the age of 18; he told interviewers of the documentary that he formed his philosophy in prison, where he learned not to respect anyone. Through this act, other prisoners identified Kell as a member of the "white-power" group. Yet, Kell said he did not see his actions as racist, but as an act of standing up for his group. Kell used race, he said, to justify the "power trip." He said: "I did not weigh the fact that (Blackmon) was a father or brother or son to anyone. I did not see him as a human being." Characters in *Oz* echo Kell's statements about why crimes are committed even within the prison walls. Many inmates in the fictional series show that they feel superior to other inmates based on race and power associated with the status of the group they belong to within the prison community. The way the hierarchy of power is established in the fictional series mirrors the way power is established in society, based on race, as well as economic and social status.

While in prison, Kell met fellow inmate Eric Daniels, who became his accomplice in the prison stabbing. Daniels, sent to a maximum-security prison for forgery, said he, too, was changed by prison. He lashed out against authority and saw the corrections officers in the prison as evil, and he became violent toward them. Following his involvement in a riot shortly after arriving at the prison, Daniels was placed in solitary confinement; he said it was there that he developed psychological problems. He plotted against a female guard, telling interviewers it made him feel "on top of the world" to see her run out of his cell with feces on her hair and face. He clearly felt powerless in prison, and tried to regain some measure of power over others, particularly over people in positions of authority over him. Daniels said the white-supremacist group gave him a much needed sense of belonging. Similar instances often occurred in *Oz*; the need to belong to a group can sometimes lead to the perpetuation of violence, while the inmates clearly do not view others outside their own group as human beings. In an attempt to avoid "other" status, they joined a group, and then adopted the code of that group. In the process, they stop thinking for themselves, and follow the group leaders, ultimately perpetuating the cycle.

After Kell's conviction in the prison murder, Daniels was moved to a New Jersey prison and sentenced to life in prison without the possibility of parole. He then became a born-again Christian and said he no longer saw people "in terms of skin color." Yet, during the interview, the permanent tattoo of a swastika and "HH" are clearly evident on his body. He said he now regards white supremacist beliefs as "nonsense," but before, he had "bought into it." Daniels showed remorse for his behavior, including his part in the murder and his participation in the white supremacist group. He connected his participation in the group, and the power he felt being part of it, to his participation in the crime. On his own, he said, he would not have killed Blackmon, but he felt empowered by the group to do so.

Events in this documentary mirrored events shown in *Oz*, particularly related to group members. The documentary shows that while belonging to a group can, in some instances, lead to rehabilitation, it can also lead to additional criminal acts. Membership in the white-power group led to Daniels committing a crime, but later, after he regretted his behavior, he joined different groups, including the prison band, and formed relationships with other inmates—not based on power and control, but shared interests in music.

In the Jury Room

In the summer of 2004, ABC aired *In the Jury Room*, a documentary of a real jury deliberation in a double-murder case (which is considered a mass murder) in Ohio. ABC asked all parties—the judge, defendant, and jury—for permission for the deliberations to be filmed for the first time in a capital murder case, and all agreed. The 12 "ordinary citizens," as the opening narration suggests, decided whether Mark Ducic was guilty of murdering both his common-law wife, Barbara, and the owner of the house they lived in, Don. Barbara died of what originally was ruled accidental drug overdoses by medical authorities. When Don died 16 months after Barbara under similar circumstances, his death led authorities to suspect that both deaths were homicides.

Once the case was brought to trial, the process of selecting the jurors involved questioning 48 potential witnesses in front of the judge, attorneys, and defendant about whether they could impose the death penalty if the defendant was found guilty. Testimony included that of a prison inmate who served time with Ducic and who assisted police in recording Ducic. In one conversation, Ducic asked the inmate to hire someone to kill someone using the same method that killed Barbara and Don. In these recordings, Ducic admitted he killed both Barbara and Don; he was heard saying their deaths were not accidental.

The defense strategy focused on Ducic's pattern of telling grandiose stories. His court-appointed attorney depicted him as a compulsive liar and bragger, not a killer. The prosecution's key evidence focused on the fact that the day before Barbara died, Ducic bought Oxycontin, found in her bloodstream after her death. The day before Don died, Ducic's ex-wife brought over cough medicine at his request, which he returned to her empty. The prosecution said these medications were the murder weapons. Still, the defense pointed out, some evidence was not considered reliable. Upon finding out about the audiotapes from the wired informant, the coroner officially changed her ruling from accidental death to homicide. She admitted it was not based on any change in the medical information, only the additional evidence police found. Without the change in her ruling, the prosecution could not bring the murder charges against Ducic.

When the jury began its deliberations, only two jurors believed that Ducic was not guilty of killing Barbara. Ten others believed he was guilty.

Soon, only Carmela, a white woman in her 40s, remained as the lone holdout who believed that he was not guilty. The others forcefully explained to Carmela why they believed that he was guilty. She broke down under the pressure and asked the judge to excuse her from serving on the jury. After a discussion with the judge, where Carmela was asked to formally say she would not continue, she agreed to return to deliberations, where she quickly changed her mind to guilty. She said she believed that the killings were premeditated. The jury ultimately found Ducic guilty of the second count of murdering Don, so it became a capital case, and was considered mass murder. The jury deliberated further on other charges, primarily drug charges, and Ducic was found guilty of 30 of the 32 counts.

Following the verdict, the jury was required to deliberate a second time to determine Ducic's sentence. As guilt was already established by the jury, the sentencing options were: death, life without the possibility of parole, life with the possibility of parole in 30 years, or life with the possibility of parole in 25 years. Initially, the jurors were split: seven voted for death, three for life with no parole, and two for life with parole in 25. One who voted for parole in 25 said she now did not believe he killed Barbara, so she did not feel it was mass murder and she would not agree to the death penalty. Carmela, who also voted for parole in 25, said she felt this phase was an opportunity for a "second chance" and that she was "bullied" into her original verdict. Another juror, a white male in his 30s, said he would like to "push the plunger," but he was not an "animal" so he would not go for the death penalty. All jurors ultimately agreed to life without parole, except Carmela, who held out for parole in 30 years. She refused to change her mind or to deliberate further. Because a verdict was not reached, the judge could not impose the death penalty herself, under state law; instead, she issued two consecutive sentences of life in prison without the possibility for parole.

As in the fictional series *The Jury*, this documentary reveals flaws in the criminal justice system. In the documentary, during deliberations, jurors who did not believe that the evidence was credible were pressured into compliance by the need for the verdict to be unanimous. It was only through the process of deliberating a second time for the sentencing phase that it was revealed, after the fact, that some jurors did not believe that Ducic was guilty of one or both of the murders. The credibility of the jury process is presented as questionable, and even arbitrary, as is also shown in the depictions of the fictional series *The Jury*. The verdict in the documentary does not reflect the beliefs of all those who served on the jury.

The criminal justice system is also seen as complex in *In the Jury Room*, because the justice system relies on people to interpret information and motivations for behavior for it to be carried out. The documentary illustrates how 12 people on a jury can see the same piece of evidence differently, and how sometimes one small piece of evidence can override all other evidence to create a context of guilt.

The documentary shows that jury deliberation becomes a process of conflict resolution among a group, rather than a deciphering of the evidence. In the documentary, Carmela was the only person who believed that Ducic was not guilty, and the process was difficult for her. She seemed to take the others' votes of guilty as an attack on her, evident by her wanting to be removed from the jury. In order to resolve the conflict among the people in the group, she conformed to the beliefs of the group, but then in the sentencing phase, showed that she still believed that he was not guilty, and decided she would not be swayed again. When she stood her ground in the sentencing deliberations, another juror, who had not previously stated any doubts about the initial verdict, also voiced concerns and sided with Carmela.

This glimpse into the process of jury deliberations is reminiscent of the 1954 fictional work *Twelve Angry Men*, whose contentious jury process has been performed for film, television, and stage. In this fictional version, the majority of jurors believe the suspect is guilty, while one believes he is innocent. After much deliberation and arguing, the 12 ultimately use the evidence presented to prove that the suspect could not have committed the crime, and vote to acquit. In the movie version, the contentious process did not stifle the juror in the minority from voicing his concerns about the guilt of the suspect. Yet in the documentary *In the Jury Room*, one female juror was overwhelmed by the contentious process and was unable to convince the other jurors to see the evidence the way she did. With a mix of men and women on the jury in the Ducic case, Carmela did not feel free to continue to argue her point, but rather sought to create a harmonious group, which may indicate that gender plays a role in how the process is carried out.

It is interesting to note that in August 2005, following the acquittal of Michael Jackson on molestation charges, three jurors told of similar circumstances in the jury deliberation process of that trial. They told journalists they regretted the verdict and believed Jackson was guilty, but because of the contentious nature of deliberations, they went along with the group after the foreman threatened to have them removed from the jury. In an August 8, 2005, interview with anchor Rita Cosby on MSNBC (during the premiere of her new program on the network, *Live & Direct*), jurors Ray Hultman, 62, and Eleanor Cook, 79, both white, said they believed that Jackson was a pedophile and that he had molested the boy accusing him in the trial. In the interview, Hultman said: "I think, prior to deliberations, I think that there was some camaraderie. It wasn't really until we got into the deliberation room and found out what was in people's minds that we realized that, we're not all in the same key here" (*Live & Direct*, August 8, 2005).

Hultman said that initially, two-thirds of the jurors believed that Jackson was not guilty, but along with Cook, he believed that Jackson was guilty. Cook said: "They came after me with a vengeance. I really got attacked." Ultimately, their desire to stay on the jury—not the evidence—made them change their verdict, they explain. Hultman said,

> You wind up thinking, OK, if I stay with my convictions that I believe that Michael Jackson is a child molester and that he did, in fact, molest this accuser, then what's the next thing that could happen? OK, you will probably wind up with a hung jury. You wind up with a mistrial. Whatever. With this kind of cloud hanging over your head and you're thinking, I have spent five months of my life in this trial, and nobody is going to kick me off of this trial until it's over. (*Live & Direct*, August 8, 2005)

According to Cook, during deliberations, jury foreman Paul Rodriguez said if Cook did not change his mind "or go with the group or be more understanding," Rodriguez would notify the bailiff and "the bailiff would notify the judge, and the judge would have me removed."

This *Live & Direct* August 8, 2005, news report about the Jackson jurors speaks to the same issues raised in the fictional series *The Jury*, and the documentary *In the Jury Room*. Peer pressure is shown to dominate the deliberation process, and being removed from the jury is viewed by the jurors as an indication that they did something wrong. Therefore, they want to avoid being removed, more than convicting, or acquitting, when they do not believe that the verdict is correct.

Deadline

In the summer of 2004, the NBC news program *Dateline* presented a 2-hour segment of the documentary *Deadline*, produced by filmmakers Katy Chevigny and Kirsten Johnson, depicting the decision by then-Illinois Governor George Ryan to commute the sentences of 167 inmates on death row in that state. The film, first shown at the 2004 Sundance Film Festival, presents Ryan as having a change of heart about the death penalty. In the film, Ryan said he did not think much about the death penalty for most of his life, and even supported it at times, voting for its reinstatement in Illinois when he was a legislator in 1977. However, while he was governor, following a series in *The Chicago Tribune* on the death penalty, pointing to many injustices and problems with the administration of it, he decided to take a closer look at it and ultimately decided to take a bold stance just prior to the end of his term. In the documentary, Ryan said he was concerned when he learned that 33% of the people on death row had an attorney who was later disbarred. He questioned whether they had received proper representation. Clemency hearings began in Illinois in October of 2002 for the 167 death-row inmates.

The film included interviews with *Chicago Tribune* journalists who wrote the newspaper articles, people working to exonerate wrongly convicted inmates on death row, prison guards, people on death row, and people who had been freed on DNA evidence that revealed they were innocent. It may be surprising to some that the news program *Dateline*—which presents objective reports—presented this documentary, which as Stone Philips acknowledged in the introduction of it, was not objective but had a point of view, clearly against the death penalty and in support of Ryan's decision. No explanation was presented by Philips about why the film, which was not objective, was being presented as part of the *Dateline* program.

The film depicts the death penalty in political terms. Illinois House Rep. Leader Tom Cross said, "All legislators want to be able to in their next election say, 'I'm tough on crime.'" An example of this used in the documentary is that while governor of Arkansas in 1992, the year he ran for and won the presidency, Bill Clinton allowed the execution of a mentally challenged man, so he would not look weak on crime, according to the film. The man asked to have his dessert saved for him until after the execution, which the filmmakers present as proof that he did not understand what was happening to him.

Two days before Ryan left office as governor, he commuted the 167 sentences of people on death row, saying he had "frustrations and deep concerns about both the administration and the penalty of death." During the press conference where he made the announcement, he said he wanted to provide "something to victims' families other than revenge," and quoted Abraham Lincoln, saying: "I have always found that mercy bears richer fruits than strict justice." He said the criminal justice system is racist, although not by intent. Poor defendants do not have the resources to challenge the federal or state government's resources. He said, "Power is abused, all in the name of good government and (being) tough on crime."

Ryan was nominated for the Nobel Peace Prize and, according to the *Dateline* report, many applauded him for his decision. There is a caveat, however. The *Dateline* report also cited people who were critical of Ryan, charging that he commuted the sentences to divert attention away from himself. In 2003, after he left office, he was charged with racketeering, fraud, and conspiracy, and was accused of taking payoffs while governor. He was found guilty of all charges in April 2006.

In addition to profiling Ryan's decision and the political ramifications of supporting or opposing the death penalty, the film also profiles inmates in prison, and those recently released. Some maintain they are innocent, and others explain the motivation for their crimes. The interviews with these inmates and exonerated men serve to reinforce that the criminal justice system is highly imperfect. Innocent people are sometimes convicted, particularly in the era prior to DNA evidence.

- Inmate Gabriel Solache, a man in his 30s born in Mexico, said he confessed to the murder of two parents and two children "to stop the beatings" he was receiving from the police. He said he could not hear out of one ear; since the police only spoke English, and he only spoke Spanish, the process was brutal. He said one detective in the case served as the interrogator, translator, and transcriber for Solache, which was not proper procedure.
- David Keaton, a black man in his 40s convicted of murder in 1971 and exonerated and released in 1979, said that before he went to prison he was optimistic and interested in life, but not any more. Now an alcoholic, Keaton said he still believes he will overcome his addiction.
- Lawrence Hayes, a black man in his 50s, was convicted of murder in 1972. He explained that he questioned a lot of things during his childhood and was impacted by the Black Panther Party. Party members were talking about poverty and helping the poor, but he said the media did not cover that aspect of them, just that they were a "paramilitary group." He saw a future, a promise with them, but heroin took hold of the community in 1969. He joined a group to infiltrate the cities and destroy the drugs. During one confrontation, while he did not pull the trigger, two people died. "That's a burden I carry," he said. After serving 19 years in prison, he was released in 1991. He now works for a law firm that focuses on clearing wrongly convicted people.

Echoing the depictions in *In the Jury Room* that suggest that the process of jury deliberations is often arbitrary and not always as focused on the evidence as the "system" suggests it should be, *Deadline* raises a further consideration, which is that the system is so flawed that the death penalty is an unfair punishment. While the fictional series *Law & Order* addressed this issue and suggested that the death penalty is applied fairly, series such as *Oz* show the process of carrying out executions, which were shown to be applied unfairly, particularly when the character of Cyril O'Reily, a mentally disabled man, was put to death by electric chair. This mirrored the real-life event in Arkansas in 1992, when then-Governor Bill Clinton was running for president and returned to the state from the campaign trail to witness the execution of a mentally disabled man.

The purpose of *Deadline*, and its dominant argument, was to show that a pro-death-penalty politician changed his position once he realized it was unfairly being applied. Ryan said he was pro-death penalty in the abstract, but when he examined the application of it on an individual case-by-case basis, he could no longer support the death penalty.

I see the fictional programs that star criminals, particularly *Oz*, and others that star legal authorities, including *Cold Case*, as presenting crime in a similar way. They attempt to point to tough-on-crime policies as easy to support in the abstract, but much harder when criminals are seen as people who have families, and they show that sociological and sometimes psychological circumstances led to them committing a crime. The fictional series and the documentary *Deadline* do not advocate for the criminals to be set free because of the circumstances that led to the crime, but they do advocate for a more humane way of dealing with criminals. More specifically, they call for abolition of the death penalty. They suggest that crime policy, particularly the application of the death penalty, be seen in the context of a justice system that is flawed.

A criminologist, in discussing the death-penalty reform in Illinois that followed Ryan's decision, stressed the wrongful convictions in the state system (Warden, 2005):

> Stunningly, for each defendant executed in Illinois, 9.5 death sentences had been overturned. Furthermore, because that accounting reflected only mistakes that had been documented—caught,

in other words—the actual magnitude of mistakes in the Illinois capital punishment system no doubt was somewhat greater than it ever would be possible to prove. (p. 382)

Further, he discussed the factors that led to the wrongful conviction, with the "leading factor being snitch testimony...who might be motivated to lie in order to protect friends or relatives. Prosecutors used testimony of that sort to win the convictions of fourteen of the eighteen Illinois capital case exonerees" (p. 382). He also cited false confessions, "inaccurate eyewitness identification testimony, forensic fraud or quackery, police perjury, ineffective assistance of counsel, and prosecutorial misconduct" (p. 383). As mentioned in earlier chapters, the fictional television series analyzed included examples of each of these in plots in the fictional series, specifically in *The Practice* and *Law & Order*, which focused on court proceedings.

The reforms in Illinois, Warden said, include the acknowledgement that it was "a movement that, for the first time in American history, spawned an effective constituency for the wrongfully convicted" (p. 383). Warden sees this movement as significant because of the infrequency with which the "fairness and accuracy of the criminal justice system" has been called into question by mainstream journalists. He said this was "best evidenced by the fact that not a single national news organization contemporaneously reported one of the most far-reaching criminal justice developments of the Twentieth Century—the dawning of the DNA-exoneration age" (p. 396). He cited early examples of DNA exoneration in 1989 in Virginia and Chicago receiving little attention in the news media. Still, he acknowledged that reforms of the Illinois justice system were likely due to legislators' desire to resume executions. However, he predicted that the death penalty will be abolished in the near future, by "the least democratic of democratic institutions—the courts—on proportionality grounds" (p. 410).

This documentary reflects the opinions expressed by those polled between 1998 and 2004, with 37% saying they support life sentences in 2000, compared to 32% in 1994. As a result, politicians are having a harder time supporting it in specific cases, rather than in the abstract. Further, the documentary points to social issues as contributing to inequities in the justice system, specifically low-income defendants receiving inadequate counsel.

CAPTURING THE FRIEDMANS

Capturing the Friedmans is a documentary by Andrew Jarecki that profiles a 1987 a sexual-molestation court case and conviction of Great Neck, Long Island, high-school and computer teacher Arnold Friedman, 57, and his youngest son, Jesse, 19. The molestation was believed to have occurred in 1984 by Arnold Friedman while he gave computer and piano lessons out of his home. The documentary, which aired on HBO in 2004, comprises home movies taken by the Friedman's eldest son, David, and news-style interviews conducted by the filmmaker with the Friedman family, detectives in the case, and alleged victims. The film shows the impact of the accusations on the Friedman family—Elaine and Arnold Friedman and their three sons, David, Seth, and Jesse. The film, which won the top prize at Sundance Film Festival in 2003, has received critical acclaim, and has been profiled in mainstream publications, including *The New York Times* (Cohen, 2003). In *The Washington Post*, Jarecki was described as taking "viewers into the heart of an anything-but typical suburban family as it is propelled along a strange, often horrifying journey through a well-meaning but Kafkaesque legal system" (Hornaday, 2003, n.p.).

The focus of the film is how preconceived notions and sketchy evidence lead police and others to assume a person is either guilty or innocent of a crime. Arnold and Jesse are not clearly presented as guilty or innocent; the film emphasizes that the evidence used to convict them was ambiguous. Some circumstances in the film suggest they are guilty, but the film also presents opposing evidence that suggests that the evidence is inaccurate. For example, both Jesse and Arnold confessed to the crimes, but later said they were forced into it in order to secure a shorter sentence for Jesse. Further, one student, who did not want to be identified during the interview and was shown only in silhouette in the film, said he just wanted to end the questioning by police when he was being interrogated, so he told police that he saw molestation occur, even though that was not true.

The main detectives on the case, two middle-aged white men, each used a different approach to collecting information from people during the investigation. When asked by the documentarian about his style, one said he did not lead the witnesses, but asked, "And then what happened?" The other, however, said he told the people being interrogated that police knew the molestation occurred, and asked them to corroborate that it happened, essentially leading the parents and students to respond as the police expected, or to eventually give up and concede to what the officers were charging after being exhausted from hours of interrogation. According to the documentary, their interrogation style influenced the witnesses.

The documentary shows several of the students being interviewed for the documentary. Many said nothing happened, while others said it happened right out on the floor of the classroom, where everyone witnessed it. No definitive physical evidence proved the case either way, according to the documentary; the testimony evidence that did not fit with what police believed happened was dismissed by the officers. Police said they believed that those who said that nothing happened were lying, and those who said molestation did occur were telling the truth. The detectives said they were sure that Arnold and Jesse committed the crimes, even though one detective admitted that the parents in the community were so competitive, during the investigation they would try to "one-up" one another about how many times their kids were molested. The detective acknowledged that if one parent said it occurred five times, the next would say it happened six times, yet the detective dismissed this as a normal reaction, even while acknowledging there was little or no physical evidence to support the charges. Police assumed that the Friedmans were guilty based on very little evidence. The documentary quoted no legal authorities raising concerns about the accuracy of the evidence.

The way evidence is collected in the case, at least as shown in the documentary, is similar to how it is presented and judged in the fictional programs *NYPD Blue*, *Law & Order*, *The Practice*, and *The Shield*, starring legal authorities. For example, the coerced confession by the student echoes events in the episode of *The Practice* in which the waitress accused of kidnapping admits to the crime after hours of interrogation in order to end the process. In the documentary, as in the fictional series, police are quick to assume guilt and do not analyze the evidence further. They seek the evidence that confirms their assumptions of guilt. However, unlike in the fictional programs, in the documentary, unreliability—or potential unreliability—of evidence used by police to bring charges against Arnold and Jesse is also shown. For example, in interviews with the filmmaker, a journalist who covered the case for a local newspaper at the time the alleged crimes occurred said she believed the charges were unwarranted. She cited the fact that if the crimes occurred the way the boys described, they would have been bleeding and their clothes would have been soiled, so their parents would have been aware of it and would have seen their children visibly upset when they picked them up from class. Further, she said that after the children completed one course, the parents continued to register for additional advanced courses with Friedman, which she said they would not have done had they thought the children were being abused by Arnold. She said she did not believe that the police were framing Arnold and Jesse Friedman, but said that nobody questioned the police, so their imaginations were "allowed to run wild."

While the documentary never specifically proves or disproves the charges against Arnold or Jesse, the film does imply that if the sexual molestation did occur, it may have emerged from the fact that Arnold Friedman, a married high-school teacher and father of three, had "homosexual feelings" from the time he was a teenager. However, he felt he could not act on them because it was considered "abnormal" by society at the time, according to statements made in the film by his brother and wife. Repressing those feelings, the film implies, may have led Arnold to molest the children.

However, this, too, is presented in the film ambiguously, through interviews with Arnold's brother, who is gay. The brother revealed a troubled childhood, and the audience is left to fill in whether Arnold's experiences as a child could have resulted in his molesting the students. The brother said that when he and Arnold were young, their baby sister died of blood poisoning; their father, who was distraught, left the family. As a result, their mother was left with little income and they lived in a very small house, so they all slept in one bedroom. As children, they watched their mother having sex with men. He said that from watching this, they learned that sex was with men. Arnold said he started having sex with his brother at age 8, although in an interview depicted in the film, the brother said he did not remember it. In his late teens, Arnold admitted that he was still attracted to boys that were the age his brother was when they first had sex, but he suppressed these homosexual feelings as an adult, and married Elaine.

Elaine said Arnold told her of his sexual past, but that he dismissed it as normal experimentation. After Arnold's children were born, he said he worried he would molest them, so he went to a therapist, who told him he had everything under control. After Arnold's arrest, Elaine learned that he had been buying child pornography from Europe, and police had traced a shipment of magazines from the Netherlands. After Arnold pled guilty to the charges, Elaine divorced him.

According to police in the documentary, parents enrolled their children in Arnold's computer classes because they wanted their children to have more opportunities and an advantage over non-computer-literate students. The documentary shows that the parents did not consider the possibility that he could be a child molester because he did not fit the perception of a pedophile. A white female detective in her 40s who worked on the case said in an interview for the documentary: "[I]t was hard for people to accept him as a pedophile. All over the home there were plaques and articles written about him. He was an award-winning teacher." The cultural connotation of a pedophile is not of a professional, middle-class man. People in that community did not expect that a pedophile would be living among them in Great Neck. One parent of a victim, who concealed his identity for the documentary, addressed this issue, saying, "Things that were being said upset the community. You do not expect that here."

This speaks to the perception that crime occurs in large, urban cities, not in the suburbs. Pedophiles and child molesters look like everyone else, according to a behavioral analysis of child molesters written by Kenneth V. Lanning, a former supervisor of special agents in the FBI, posted on the National Center for Missing and Exploited Children's Web site (missingkids.com). Lanning said that it is a misconception—perpetuated by the FBI with educational posters in the 1950s and 1960s—that pedophiles are old men in trenchcoats handing out candy to young children, particularly girls. Boys and girls can be victims of child molesters and pedophiles, he notes. He also identifies several psychological profiles, reinforcing that there is not one accurate physical or psychological profile.

In the documentary, Arnold Friedman is not shown as clearly evil, because it is not even clear whether he committed the crimes. The film presents him as a complex person, with sociological and psychological problems that may account for his behavior, criminal or otherwise. As in the depictions of jury deliberations in the fictional series *The Jury* and the documentary *In the Jury Room*, *Capturing the Friedmans* shows that perceptions based on social norms can often be erroneous, and possibly even damaging, especially when they are used to "identify" criminals. *Capturing the Friedmans* presents conflicting approaches: Evidence collected by police point to Arnold Friedman as a child molester, but the film also suggests that the evidence is unreliable. In the documentary, we see that police trust only the evidence that supports their theory that he is guilty, and they dismiss all other evidence that discounts their theory. The "truth" about his innocence or guilt is never clear. The documentary shows that once police started investigating Arnold, because he had child pornography in his home, he was automatically perceived by them to have molested the children, even though there was conflicting physical evidence and testimony that cast doubt about his and Jesse's guilt.

Like the other three documentaries I examined, *Capturing the Friedmans* explores similar situations to those depicted in fictional series I analyzed. While the depictions in this documentary did not mirror specific depictions in *Law & Order* and *NYPD Blue*, they did explore procedures similar to those portrayed in these two fictional series. *Gladiator* explored the reasons people engage in criminal activity, and also examined how one prison inmate was rehabilitated, mirroring depictions in *Oz* and *The Sopranos*. *In the Jury Room* depicted the jury deliberation process, and revealed flaws in the process, particularly how peer pressure contributed to a jury decision that not all jurors agreed with, echoing portrayals in the fictional series *The Jury*. *Deadline* also examined flaws in the justice system, particularly in the application of the death penalty, an issue explored in *Law & Order*.

These four documentaries support Kilborn's (2004) assertion that documentaries differ from reality programming primarily in addressing "serious" issues. Each documentary addressed a different aspect of crime, and mirrored depictions in the fictional programs I viewed, particularly regarding rehabilitation, crime causes, and the types of crime policies that should be supported. This indicates that the fictional depictions are realistic.

CHAPTER 9

AUDIENCE IMPACT

In a study of television audiences, Morley (1992) noted, "[T]here is, in television, no such thing as 'an innocent text'—no programme which is not worthy of serious attention, no programme which can claim to provide only 'entertainment' rather than messages about society" (p. 82). Yet, research has shown that audience response to these television texts can be difficult to predict. In a classic study of audiences of *All in the Family*, Vidmar and Rokeach (1974) found that "some viewers applaud Archie for his racist viewpoint, while others applaud the show for making fun of bigotry" (p. 37). While the intent of producer Norman Lear was to expose Archie Bunker as a bigot, "many viewers saw nothing wrong with Archie's use of racial and ethnic slurs" (Vidmar and Rokeach, 1974, p. 42).

Kubey (1996) pointed to popularity of programs as an indication that television programs elicit similar responses in audience members. "The active audience approach...neglects to recognize that relative to print, certain cognitive and affective responses to television and film are much more likely to be uniform as a result of the pacing and pictorial nature of these media" (p. 198). However, Kubey (1996) also noted that researchers who follow an active audience approach, and do not view television viewing as negative, tend to dismiss audiences who find this to be the case. He suggested that audiences can independently come to similar conclusions about media messages having a negative effect, which would be an active response.

Bratich (2005) noted that in early audience studies, using propaganda analysis, "media subjects were defined as passive and often unknowing recipients of persuasive messages" (p. 251). He continued,

> However, this passivity was not simply a description of a numb or paralyzed audience. It must be remembered that propaganda researchers had two main objectives regarding the homefront: to defend the citizenry against pernicious foreign communication and to mobilize the same citizenry via domestic state communication. This dual goal of propaganda—to protect from foreign effects and to provoke domestic effects—acknowledged audience power as an increasing component of warfare. (p. 251)

Bratich explained that "in the limited-effects tradition...[r]ather than finding audiences passive (as lack of activity), they were characterized by the capacity to be affected, the *power* to be activated" (p. 253). Bratich pointed out that, "[b]y problematizing the audience as vulnerable and reactive, rather than active, the discourses of protection were able to empower themselves as active agents of intervention into media subjectivity" (p. 257).

Researchers have examined how television is incorporated in people's everyday lives, and sought to determine the reasons people watch television. Gantz and Zohoori (1982) studied viewers in Indiana, and specifically looked at whether television scheduling changes that occur during standard time and daylight-savings time in the state would have an effect on viewing habits. They found that viewers were "willing and/or able to structure their lives around their television preferences" (p. 271). They attributed these changes to the fact that prime-time programs were entertaining and often new episodes, not reruns. They also noted that the 1-hour time change that occurred in scheduling likely did not overlap with their bedtime. However, little change in the frequency with which viewers watched news programs was found, even when the news aired at a more "accessible" time. Respondents did indicate changes in viewing habits of late-night programs, such as *The Tonight Show* (with Johnny Carson at the time). They were more likely to forgo viewing late-night programs when the schedule shifted to a later hour, which Gantz and Zohoori attributed, in part, to the fact that these late-night programs did not air new episodes each evening.

Kubey and Csikszentmihalyi (1990) studied habits of television viewers and found that among subjects in the study, "a heavy night of television viewing is preceded by significantly lower affect than a light viewing night" (p. 98). "Subjects were...somewhat more likely to be alone both before and during a heavy night of viewing than before and during a light night, suggesting that a parasocial motive may also underlie subjects' viewing" (p. 96). They concluded that "subjects appear to engage in heavy viewing, in part, to escape solitude and negative experiences. The strategy may be partly successful insofar as people do feel relaxed while they view" (p. 98). Heavy viewing, they noted, appeared to indicate that "the viewer has chosen to indulge him or herself and avoid reality demands" (p. 99).

In an early survey of cable subscribers, Metzger (1983) found the most frequent response as to why people subscribed to cable services was "to obtain greater variety or more and better programs" (p. 43). This was at a time when HBO and other premium channels did not produce original series, such as *Oz*, *The Sopranos*, and *Sex and the City*, but aired mostly movies that had previously been released only in theaters. In the study, Metzger concluded that cable television would have little or no effect on television usage, and specifically no effect in prime time. However, Metzger did not account for the influence that original series produced by HBO would later have on the content of broadcast programming, specifically in prime time, as I have discussed in this research.

In this chapter, I will discuss the potential impact of media messages about crime on the audience. I specifically look at a "CSI effect" that has been identified by prosecutors and defense attorneys who notice a difference in expectations among jurors who are familiar with *CSI* and similar programs in the fictional television crime genre.

I also discuss Web site message boards, which may provide a forum for less powerful or subordinate groups in society to discuss their status and powerlessness. Haas and Steiner (2001) pointed to public journalism as historically providing a forum for this type of discussion, and noted that "[s]ubordinate social groups need to be able to deliberate about their particular interests to a degree equivalent to what dominant social groups already enjoy and to be able to challenge the public/private dichotomy" (p. 140). They continued: "By facilitating the development of a public sphere composed of multiple discursive domains, with potential participatory parity for dominant and subordinate social groups, public journalism will indeed invigorate public life" (p. 140). I point to examples from the message board for the television series *Oz* on the HBO Web site as evidence that Web site forums now serve this function as well.

The CSI Effect

Depictions of crime in the television crime genre have had an impact on society by establishing expectations in jurors about how cases should be presented. Popular culture has influenced real-life decision making, even in court cases. Christopher Stone, the director of the nonprofit Vera Institute of Justice, said in a 2004 *Time* magazine article,

> When Perry Mason first aired, lawyers were not allowed to approach witnesses to question them...But you couldn't fit Mason and the witness in the same frame, so the directors had Mason walk over and lean on the witness rail. Then juries expected lawyers to do that, and if they didn't, jurors thought something was wrong. (Lennard, Goehner, Lofaro, Novack, 2004, p. 69)

Since it aired in 2001 on CBS, the television program *CSI* has depicted a new focus in the justice system that relies much more heavily on physical evidence. Coscarelli (2005) explained,

> Shows such as "CSI," its two spinoffs, plus the *"Law & Order"* franchise, and others like *"Cold Case"* focus on splashy police investigations where crime scenes can be mapped using lasers, virtual autopsies can be performed, and hair, fingerprint and DNA evidence are not only always attainable, but also always definitive. Fingerprints are easily smudged and hard to recover from most surfaces. DNA results take weeks or months, not hours. And fabric and thread analysis can be impossible if the material is too common, like from a white cotton T-shirt. (n.p.)

In recent years, however, the impact of *CSI* has extended beyond the television industry, as jurors have come to expect forensic evidence before they will return a guilty verdict, known as "the CSI effect" in legal circles. Its impact was seen as a result of its "popularity and fecundity," and *Time* magazine reporters called it "the most dramatic new influence on a justice system that has always been affected by books, movies and TV" (Lennard et al., 2004, p. 69).

Some, specifically prosecutors and judges, see "the CSI effect" as having a negative effect on the deliberation process of jurors, because the result has been often longer and more expensive trials (Coscarelli, 2005). Frederick DeVesa, a New Brunswick, New Jersey, Superior Court criminal judge, said: "Television...creates the impression that this type of full-fledged investigation and crime scene investigation can be done in every case" (Coscarelli, 2005, n.p.). In addition, even when these detailed investigations and forensic-evidence collections are done, the results are not always as definitive as presented in the television series. Coscarelli continued:

> Schooled in the easy solutions and the over-the-top science of these new shows, jurors are coming to the courtroom with unrealistic ideas about how a trial should unfold. There is even concern in the legal community that the CSI effect may make jurors more

prone to return verdicts that aren't based on details presented in court, but on what television has taught them about casework and justice. (n.p.)

The result, they believe, is that in real court cases, when forensic evidence is not presented, jurors are more likely to acquit. In a Texas trial in 2004, jurors found a defendant not guilty, specifically citing the lack of forensic evidence. Lennard and colleagues (2004) noted,

> Last November [2004] prosecutors in Galveston, Texas, despite a plethora of nonforensic evidence, couldn't convince a jury that Robert Durst had murdered Morris Black, even though Durst admitted inadvertently killing him, because Black's head couldn't be found. The head, the defense argued, contained key evidence that Durst had acted in self-defense. "The CSI effect is real, and it's profound," says jury consultant Robert Hirschorn, who also says he purposely selected jurors familiar with CSI and forensics-type shows for the Durst trial. (p. 69)

In some cases, the depictions on crime shows may even be affecting the way criminals carry out a crime. Barry Fisher, the crime-lab director for LA County, told *Time* that recently a rapist forced his victim to shower after the attack to wash off any evidence. "I'm sure he's reacting to the stuff on TV where they have an understanding that there is trace evidence available," Fisher said (Lennard et al., 2004, p. 69). The same article quoted Fisher saying: "[A] woman who allegedly robbed a Bantam, Conn., bank used a diaper bag to store the money, an idea she said she picked up from CSI" (p. 69).

"The CSI effect" has been widely reported in the mainstream media, appearing in *Time* and *USA Today* in 2004, and *US News and World Report, The Washington Post*, MSNBC.com, BBC News, the *CBS Evening News* in 2005. The Poynter Institute, a journalism school, also included an article on its Web site. The reports indicate that "the CSI effect" favors defense attorneys. Lennard and colleagues (2004) explained,

> Defense lawyers love...*CSI* shows because they have caused juries to demand DNA analysis in nearly every two-bit 7-Eleven

Audience Impact 219

holdup. Prosecutors, meanwhile, feel hampered by the fact that 10 eyewitnesses are not enough to satisfy *CSI*-watching jurors who crave the supposedly conclusive proof of hair follicles on a knife. (p. 69)

One prosecutor, in Maricopa County, Arizona, responded to "the CSI effect" by issuing a press release in 2005 asking network executives to

> provide a disclaimer at the beginning of forensic crime programs informing viewers that the stores are not real, the techniques used in the story are not always available to law enforcement, and that the absence of physical or scientific evidence does not mean defendants are automatically innocent of the charges. (maricopa-countyattorney.org)

This raises the question of whether it is better for the justice system to include jurors who have no knowledge of forensics or jurors with some knowledge, but possibly one that is distorted by fictional media messages. The Arizona prosecutor's request for a disclaimer can be seen as a response to his job being made harder by jurors who ask a lot more questions and need a lot more evidence to convict a suspect. While that may be a problem for prosecutors, it might, in the long run, ensure a more equitable criminal justice system. With a lot more attention seemingly being focused on physical concrete evidence, less attention is being paid to behavioral evidence, which is apparently less convincing to jurors because it can be interpreted in various ways, as stressed in fictional programs, such as *The Jury*, and in the documentaries *In the Jury Room* and *Capturing the Friedmans*. The Maricopa County prosecutor said the lack of physical evidence does not mean the defendants are innocent. Yet, jurors, essentially, are not deciding whether the defendants are innocent, only if the prosecution has proven its case.

Programs such as *CSI* that focus on forensics are reflecting changes in the technology used to collect evidence against suspects, particularly with the emergence of DNA evidence. It has been widely reported in the mainstream news media that DNA evidence has been used in recent years to determine the guilt or innocence of suspects/defendants, as well as to reveal the innocence of convicted criminals. As a result, jurors today expect more concrete evidence before convicting, because forensic science has shown that the types of evidence previously relied on may be inaccurate and misleading. The burden of proof does seem to have been raised, with jurors expecting more scientific evidence and more rigorous proof of guilt. However, if the goal in society is an equitable justice system, higher standards and a higher burden of proof are needed. Jurors may not understand the science involved in forensics evidence from the knowledge gained on *CSI* and other similar programs, but they do know the technology exists. In an ideal and equitable criminal justice system, convicting someone of a crime should require irrefutable evidence. When that evidence is not available, or is not irrefutable, through forensic evidence, and jurors acquit a defendant, they are not weakening the process because they watch crime shows on television. They are seeking the strongest evidence available, and are responding accordingly when the evidence presented is weak.

Web-Site Forums

In recent years, another way that viewers have responded to messages in the media is by discussing them in Web-site forums on the Internet. Virtually every show has a forum available. Entries offer a glimpse into the different ways media messages can be interpreted by viewers. An example can be seen in the message board for fans of *Oz* on HBO.com. Web-site messages enable viewers to discuss their expectations of the program, offer analysis of the programs, provide information about where additional articles can be found about the show and the actors, and comment on the way the programs are produced. In some instances, as in the entries below (where spelling, punctuation, and capitalization are left as in the original), writers discussed how realistic the events are. For example, one writer said,

> Gosh, I hope New York prisons are A LOT different than OZ. Though I watched and enjoyed the series, it is far from

realistic...except for the "games" that the inmates played with each other and staff, OZ was not representative of true prison life. At least not from the stand point of security issues and public safety. But I guess you gotta give up something to make the show entertaining—and entertaining it was—I will miss it! (dtsb 1097, February 27, 2003)

Another writer cited her own experiences working in the legal system in California:

> As a public defender in California for 19 years I have a wing in each California prison with inmates who have been represented by me. I've heard from a few of them over the years and have seen some following their incarceration. While some did change, it was not because of the experience in prison—rather it was a decision not to go back. (MsLadyPD, February 24, 2003)

In a separate entry on the same day, MsLadyPD posted a message about segregation in California jails, which mirrors depictions of group formation in *Oz*. She wrote,

> The most disturbing trend over the last 10 years has been the institutional segregation inside the jails. Asians and Blacks and Whites are housed together. Hispanics and Whites are housed together. Declared homosexuals are housed together. In the California jails there is a constant feud between the Black and Hispanic inmates and the local jails reinforce the conflict by segregating them. (MsLadyPD, February 24, 2003)

Frat-In-Oz said he had spoken to his "prison connection," who said,

> getting a prison employee fired is extremely hard to do....... most prisons are "working for the state" jobs......he said if he wanted to fire someone, he almost never gets to....it's just too much red tape.......you hear of prison employees staying for many, many years......firing sumone on the spot, outside of killing sumone, would just NOT happen......not in Nevada State prisons at least .... . (August 1, 2000)

Viewers also use the Web-site forum to discuss crime policies. One discussion focused on the death penalty:

> I think personally that the death penalty should be implemented more often then they use it, people go free, when in fact they should be executed. It isn't right that they can take a life or hurt someone severely and nothing and i do mean NOTHING gets done about it, they just sit and rot, waist our money when the truth is that we should give them what they deserve. (beacherschild, June 20, 2003)

Another writer agreed that the death penalty is appropriate, even though it may not deter others from committing crimes. Fan O Reily wrote: "I believe in the death penalty when used properly, yet I do not feel it is either a crime deterrent or social detriment" (May 30, 2003). However, kipp648 disagreed, and said, "the death penalty is not a deterrent at all in my opinion" (May 19, 2003).

The writers also showed sympathy for characters, even when they commit horrible crimes. For example, phdzulu wrote: "My heart really went out to Keller because he was as bad as the rest of the crew in Oz but his aspirations were so much greater because he wanted love to heal him" (May 30, 2003). Tieme wrote: "If Beecher dies, the show is over. He is the common man, good at heart, in with the scum. He is the appeal to everyone cause deep down, that could be me" (August 1, 2000).

Some writers analyzed the motivations for the crimes committed. Mindchild64 wrote,

> Hands down the best is Ryan O'Reily!!! There's no one smarter or slicker. He can have just about anything done. Most times he has someone else do his bidding, but he dosen't mind gettin' is hands dirty either. Said was a good too, but he seemed to be fighting a war within himself. (May 30, 2003)

The administrators of the prison are also discussed. For example, Wizard of Oz said,

> McManus is OZ's anti-hero, a fascinating, hot-headed man who one minute you want [to] commend and the next you want to slap. All the

ideals and good intentions in the world, but with a temper as nasty as any of the prisoners, and an occasional hypocritical tendency. (July 7, 2000)

The character of Augustus Hill, who serves as narrator and a character, is a common topic for discussion. Jfc wrote,

> It is ironic that in his opening S3 monologue, Hill as narrator says that in Oz no one is sorry. Yet, Hill as inmate comes close at times to seeming to experience some sort of remorse for shooting a cop. Actually, much of S3 turns out to study how various OZ characters learn what being truly sorry entails, so that opening mono may be one of TF's backhanded, ironic ways of getting us to think about ethical/moral/spiritual issues. (July 9, 2000)

Some writers specifically identified themselves as having resisted the "addictive" nature of television in the past, but stressed the compelling nature of the series. For example, ozowl wrote,

> Amazing how so many of us are consumed by Oz, tho many of us have never been so enthralled by a TV show before. I'm beginning to wonder if there are subliminal messages flashing on the screen to cause such addiction. ;) (November 28, 2000)

The attraction of the show for these self-described atypical television viewers may be due to the nature of the series, which is not typical of its genre, as I discussed in previous chapters. While the Web-site respondents do not consider themselves to be regularly addicted to television, they are self-described fanatics about the show, and willingly and unapologetically discuss their viewing habits. Dorothy wrote: "I have been addicted for 4+ years. I chat about it, I post about it, I think about it AND it is the only show worth watching......I am just one of the happiest women in the world!!!!! :) :) :) :)" (November 28, 2000). Another wrote,

> ...I need to take frequent breaks from work so I can look at the boards and the Oz related sites...I will not go out on Wed nights so I can view Oz (even if it is a rerun). I have also contacted strangers

all over the internet that share my Oz enthusiasm. I knew about this show from the beginning but have only recently subscribed to cable. I would like to thank all of the Oz characters because it was the first time I have been interested in anything besides breaking up with my boyfriend—on the outside, I look like a normal professional single working girl—no one knows about my addiction except my sister and she is slowly becoming an addict as well. (kbc, November 28, 2000)

At times, posters incorporate terms from the show in their correspondence. For example, ktstarn3 wrote,

> Hi, I'm STAR, and I am finally admitting that I have a serious addiction......OZ. But, I don't want to stop, I love it, its a good addiction! Sorry, I have to go now, I am about to put my kids in their pods and yell "Lights Out." (November 28, 2000)

Through their responses, these viewers show that they have taken on the role of "listener" (Hayakawa, 1950, p. 32), where "listening means trying to see the problem the way the speaker sees it—which means not sympathy, which is *feeling for* him, but empathy, which is *experiencing with* him. Listening requires entering actively and imaginatively into the other fellow's situation and trying to understand a frame of reference different from your own" (Hayakawa, 1950, pp. 32–33). The *Oz* Web-site respondents show that they are trying to understand what the characters experienced, which often lead to the writers sympathizing with, empathizing with, and sometimes rooting for the prisoners to rehabilitate themselves.

Oz creator Tom Fontana has stressed that he intended to show the characters' potential for redemption. Peden (2001) quoted Fontana:

> There are lessons and there are morals to the stories in "Oz"...It's like, look at what we do to each other. I mean, it's really about the world: it just happens to take place in a prison...There are genuine moments of redemption, several of them involving major characters. (n.p.)

Posters on the Web-site forum clearly show that participating in discussions on the site has added to their appreciation of the show by enabling them to process the information they receive from the show by sharing their reactions with others who have a strong interest in the program. This form of "power viewing," as Hartley (1996) suggested, "is not confined to academics, but is already being reworked into a new generations' cultural politics." (p. 229). Web-site message boards provide a forum where this process can take place. The posts from the *Oz* Web-site forum suggest that viewers find the series compelling, even if they are not regular television viewers, and that they compare what they see in the series to real-life events, either from personal experience or news reports. The writers use the Web-site forum to discuss crime-policy issues, and the posts confirm that not all viewers perceive the "message" of the series in the same way.

Hartley (1996) pointed out that "[i]n a cultural theory of television, power is pervasion—the power of the species to do what the species is capable of doing, the power of Veblen's 'matter-of-fact knowledge of mankind and of everyday life' (1953: 252)" (Hartley, 1996, p. 231). The audience of *Oz* is an example of viewers exercising their power by sharing everyday knowledge of life with other members of the audience. Through these posts, writers show that they are actively analyzing the fictional depictions, and comparing them to real-life situations involving crime, criminals, and the justice system.

"The CSI effect" is another example that viewers' real-world perceptions about the justice system are influenced by fictional media representations. "The CSI effect" suggests that the representations in the genre, specifically of the reliability and usefulness of forensic evidence in criminal investigations, have influenced procedures in the justice system. Primarily, "the CSI effect" has changed jurors' expectations, which has forced prosecutors to change the type of evidence presented, even in routine cases that are not strengthened by this type of evidence, attorneys acknowledge. From *CSI* and similar programs, jurors perceive forensic evidence to be more trustworthy than eyewitness or other types of testimony. Therefore, jurors feel more confident deciding guilt or innocence of a suspect based on forensics. Prosecutors point out that forensics is not the foolproof science portrayed in *CSI*; it can be unreliable or inconclusive. Yet, that message is not conveyed in *CSI*, and jurors, according to prosecutors, rely heavily on depictions in *CSI* to determine the reliability of forensic evidence. As Watt and van den Berg (1981) suggested, this may be attributed to the fact that when viewers have little direct experience with a situation, media representations, including fictional representations, can have a strong effect. Without any direct experience to disprove the fictional representations, the fictional representations seem entirely plausible to viewers.

CHAPTER 10

PROGRESSIVE DEPICTIONS

Between 1998 and 2004, the television genre presented a multiperspective discourse about crime and why it occurs. As we continue to see characters who are complex and flawed, both as law enforcement and criminals, the notion that people are not all good or all bad is reinforced. In this chapter, I discuss how the crime genre continues to present more stories than just the police and the prosecutors' roles, and the implications of these portrayals. I also offer suggestions for future studies, particularly in the area of victim representation. In addition, I discuss my interpretive framework while conducting this research.

THE CRIME GENRE: AN UPDATE

Since I began conducting this research, additional shows have emerged in the genre with different depictions than what I found in the series I analyzed. NBC's *Medium* aired in 2004, and explores the work of a medium who assists police with investigations, focusing on the supernatural. The show received strong ratings and continues to air new episodes. In 2005

ABC aired *Blind Justice*, profiling a blind police officer who returns to his job as a detective, to the dismay of his coworkers, who fear that his disability will impede their investigations and possibly put their lives in danger because he will not be able to provide the proper backup in confrontations with suspects. Due to low ratings, the series was cancelled after one season. *Night Stalker* on ABC, a 2005 update of the 1970s series by the same name, follows the format that made *Medium* popular, by profiling a newspaper reporter who, after a car accident that killed his wife, investigates crimes that may be the result of supernatural events. The series was cancelled after six episodes. The CBS series *Numb3rs* also aired in 2005, and features an FBI agent and his brother, a math whiz, who together solve crimes in Los Angeles. It will begin its 5th season in fall 2008.

COPS and *America's Most Wanted* remain popular, proven reality-show successes. On the other hand, a crime-related reality show on NBC that had a competitive element failed in 2005. Likely seeking to capitalize on the success of the reality show *The Apprentice*, where two teams compete and one person is eliminated weekly until Donald Trump chooses his next business apprentice in the finale, NBC aired *The Law Firm* in the summer of 2005. In the series, lawyers were involved in actual cases. As with other courtroom reality series, such as *The People's Court*, the series included real cases with binding verdicts. Trial attorney Roy Black served in the "Trump" role, and as managing partner in the law firm, eliminated one attorney from the competition each week. According to NBC.com, the cases included First Amendment issues, neighbor disputes, and wrongful death. After two episodes, NBC pulled the series due to low ratings and aired the remaining episodes on its sister cable network Bravo, which is less reliant on ratings.

New series that aired in 2005–2006 offer both new depictions and those that have already been successful for other networks:

- CBS' *Criminal Minds* depicts a group of FBI agents in the Behavioral Analysis Unit, who construct profiles of killers and other criminals. On the CBS Web site, the characters are described as "determined to get inside the criminal mind and get the criminals off the streets." The focus of the show appears to be to assure viewers that society is safe, similar to the depictions I described in *NYPD Blue* and *Law & Order*, but it also appears to offer insights about the reasons crimes are committed.

- The NBC comedy *My Name is Earl*—about a man who decides to make amends for his past crimes after winning the lottery—marks the first time a criminal stars in a sitcom. As a sitcom, it could be culturally significant in the way it addresses issues about crime and criminals, much in the way that *All in the Family* addressed important social issues of the time through comedy. The main character, Earl, does not continue to commit crimes in the series, but seeks to provide restitution, in some form or another, to his victims and the people he has wronged, mostly through low-level crimes.
- A Fox series, *Prison Break*, also began airing in fall 2005. It is set in a maximum-security prison in Illinois. Its two main characters—brothers—are inmates, but are not "guilty." Lincoln Burrows was framed by the secret service, and seemingly the Vice President of the United States, for killing the Vice President's brother. Burrows was sentenced to death and was on death row when his brother, Michael Scofield, staged a bank robbery so he could be imprisoned with his brother and devise an escape plan. Scofield, a structural engineer, helped renovate the prison years earlier, so he is familiar with the infrastructure, and seemingly has the knowledge to carry out the escape plan. Scofield seeks the help of other inmates. This series is similar in many ways to HBO's *Oz*, in setting and in theme. The equity of the justice system and rehabilitation are addressed. However, its overall premise departs from the premise of *Oz* because the two main characters are "innocent."
- The ABC series *In Justice* debuted in January 2006. It depicted an attorney—identified by producers as having "questionable ethics"—who worked to free prisoners who have been wrongfully

convicted of crimes. It mirrored depictions in *The Jury*, of a flawed justice system. It was cancelled after its first season aired.
– *Thief*, a mini-series that debuted in March 2006 on FX, depicted a group that was planning a heist. It was similar to the depictions in *Heist*, first airing on NBC, also in March 2006. Following *Oz* and *The Sopranos*, these series' main characters were criminals. *Heist* was cancelled in its first season.

It is similar to the depictions in *Heist*, first airing on NBC, also in March 2006. Following *Oz* and *The Sopranos*, these series' main characters are criminals.

Future Studies

The genre continues to change and progress, offering more depictions of rehabilitation and an inequitable justice system, now on network television, not just on cable. Many episodes in the crime genre continue to focus on the reasons criminals commit crimes, yet, even with the dominance of the crime genre providing many hours of representation, there is still the potential to offer additional depictions. While a more complete narrative about criminals exists in the genre, one aspect of crime that appears to be nearly nonexistent is the impact of crime on victims. I suggest that future studies of the crime genre should seek to identify existing representations of victims, specifically, whether the impact of crime on victims is minimized, as I found in most series. In the series I examined, victims were only peripherally addressed or presented as not credible. To confirm these initial perceptions and to further explore representations of victims in the genre, I would propose the following research questions be explored in programs in the television crime genre:

a. why particular victims are targeted by criminals;
b. how victims deal with the trauma following a crime;
c. whether victims support punitive or preventive crime policies; and
d. whether they support rehabilitation efforts.

I would also suggest that additional studies focus on audiences who watch programs in the crime genre in an effort to confirm "the CSI effect" and potentially identify additional effects. I propose that researchers seek to determine the following:

a. Whether viewers of the television crime genre view forensics evidence as more credible than other types of evidence. In addition, do they view forensics evidence differently than nonviewers?
b. Whether viewers of the television crime genre consider economic inequalities in society as providing motivation for crime. If they do, does that influence whether they support specific crime policies? Does it influence how they deliberate as jurors?
c. Whether viewers of the television crime genre support rehabilitation efforts for prison inmates, or if they reject these efforts, on the basis that they are ineffective.
d. Whether prosecutors or defense attorneys perceive viewers of the television crime genre to be more informed or less informed jurors.

I focused on the messages presented in the texts, but further studies seeking to answer these questions could determine how audiences perceive the messages, and whether that influences beliefs about crime, criminals, and the justice system. These studies could identify the impact the genre has on audiences, particularly those who participate in the judicial process, seeking to confirm whether a "CSI effect" exists among viewers who watch programs in the television crime genre. Further, they would confirm whether a dominant message exists about victims.

INTERPRETIVE FRAMEWORK

My interest in conducting this research was to examine how crime and criminals are represented in the fictional crime genre as well as nonfiction representations, to determine whether the depictions encouraged citizens to continue to strive for the ideal justice system, or to adopt a new theory about how best to combat crime. In addressing crime representations in this research, I inevitably incorporated my own beliefs: that confining social structures can provide motivation for crime; that rehabilitation of criminals should be the goal of the justice system; and that the American justice system is not always applied in a fair and equitable way, favoring people in upper economic classes while disadvantaging people in lower economic classes.

My concept of the ideal criminal justice system, as espoused in a democratic society, is one that captures, judges, and punishes criminals for crimes committed. In the process, its function is to ensure that society is safe for all citizens. It also includes the provision that once time has been served, a criminal is returned to society, having paid his or debt to society for the crime. This guided my analysis of representations about rehabilitation, blocked opportunities in society, and crime policies. The criteria I used to determine whether the representations in the television crime genre were either positive/progressive depictions or negative depictions are based on this ideal theory of the purpose and function of the criminal justice system.

Does Rehabilitation Work?

I view an ideal justice system as one that is based on the concept of rehabilitation, even if that includes rehabilitation while serving a life sentence. In the series I analyzed, I found pluralistic representations of criminals and about whether rehabilitation works; I did not find a singular depiction that only viewed rehabilitation as ineffective. I find this encouraging, in that several series portrayed criminals as people who exist in the same culture as law-abiding citizens. Like law-abiding citizens, they, too, are shown to have families, and it is through portrayals of these relationships that criminals are humanized. As a result, they are depicted as able to be rehabilitated, particularly if the motivation for crime, sometimes shown to be confining societal structures, is addressed.

Oz, in particular, told stories of people in society who felt powerless, and who turned to crime as a result. Narratives in *Oz* suggest that these people gain power by "taking" from society and posing a threat or danger to society and its structures, which confine them. *Oz* also identified confining societal structures as potentially playing a role in creating a motivation for criminals. These blocked opportunities are shown to contribute to crime. In examining portrayals of criminals' motivations and causes of crimes, I viewed those that addressed societal factors as a cause of crime as the most progressive because they had not been seen in the genre previously, and they also were the most groundbreaking in that they sought to expose inequities in society, particularly economic inequities, as creating frustrations in people and ultimately motivation for crime.

I found progressive, positive representations in the genre relating to judging guilt or innocence of suspected criminals. *The Jury, In the Jury Room, Deadline,* and *Capturing the Friedmans* directly acknowledged that the justice system was imperfect, and unfair, and needed to be changed. In these series and documentaries, an equitable justice system was the goal. The filmmakers used specific examples of the process of judging a suspect's guilt or innocence to offer a big-picture view of the system. As a result, these depictions suggest that if the process was shown to be flawed in the cases depicted, it may be flawed as applied to other cases as well.

Authority and Power
The genre also shows legal authorities as well as criminals as complex, complicated people who are neither all good nor all bad. I found that a binary depiction of good versus evil no longer dominates in the genre. The concept of good and evil is now presented as a gray area. Acts of killing and murder alone do not mark people as "evil." While some depictions serve to assure audiences that order is being maintained in society, other representations in the genre raise questions about how criminals are perceived in society:

   a. Is the rogue cop in *The Shield* who murders a "criminal" or are his crimes justifiable? If they are justifiable, does that suggest that crimes committed by other "criminals" are also justifiable? How does/should society make a distinction between justifiable and unjustifiable crimes? Is the rogue cop an "Other" like the criminals, or is he still part of "Us," or is he in a separate category?

b. Is the detective in *Cold Case*, who shows compassion for criminals, atypical of officers? If a detective—whose sole responsibility is apprehending criminals–can understand their motivations and sympathize with them, does that suggest that criminals are not "Others"?

By raising these questions, various fictional series could lead viewers to consider issues about crime in more informed ways when they serve on juries, support or vote for politicians, serve as legislators themselves, write about crime as journalists, or work within the justice system as a legal authority. The multiple representations now exhibited in the genre blur the lines between Us and Them—that is, good and evil. As a result, they offer a more realistic depiction of criminals.

Representations that I did not see as progressive, specifically regarding the way criminals are apprehended, were found in *Law & Order, NYPD Blue, The Shield, The Practice*, and *COPS*. These series suggested that the justice system was flawed and that legal authorities could be corrupt, but the corruption resulted because it was the only way legal authorities could ensure criminals are punished for their actions. Any corruption or illegal acts by police were seen as a direct response to an evil in society that threatened the safety of all. The ultimate goal, according to these programs, is to ensure a safe society for noncriminals. The protection of innocent victims in society was shown to outweigh any damage done either to suspected or convicted criminals. This collateral damage is not portrayed in these series as a failure in the system that needs to be addressed, but as a necessary evil that is unavoidable. I see these representations as overlooking, and even condoning, inequities that exist in social structures, specifically economic status. They do not address the fact that these inequities could provide motivation for crime.

Crime Policies

I identified depictions that supported preventive crime policies, specifically rehabilitation and treatment for offenders, as positive and progressive. How criminals should be punished was addressed in *In the Jury Room, The Jury, Deadline, Oz,* and *Law & Order*, which addressed the death penalty. Only *Law & Order* showed strong support for the death penalty as necessary to ensure that the government is tough on crime and that citizens in society are safe. The documentaries *In the Jury Room* and *Deadline*, and the fictional series *The Jury*, however, showed that the death penalty is often supported only in the abstract by politicians and jurors, but not in actual cases when they have to personally decide that someone will be put to death. *Oz* presented the death penalty as unfairly and harshly applied, even to convicted criminals with mental disabilities. Collectively, *Oz* and the documentaries present the death penalty as cruel and inhumane punishment and one that does not deter crime. I applaud these representations, particularly on television, where tough-on-crime depictions dominated in the past.

However, I find the framing of crime policies by criminologists, sociologists, and media-studies researchers alike as strictly *either* preventive or punitive to be misleading. Preventive crime policies can and do, in fact, punish criminals for crimes committed. Framing the policies as either one or the other forces people to express support for only one, rather than acknowledge the dual purpose that preventive policies can have, which includes punishment through prison sentences, but also incorporates rehabilitation and treatment. Punitive policies, which include the death penalty and longer mandatory sentences for less violent crimes, can also theoretically be preventive as well, yet as pointed out specifically in the documentaries *In the Jury Room* and *Deadline*, in the context of the current flawed justice system, the application of punitive policies are unfair. The application of these punitive policies further serves to create frustration in disadvantaged groups in society, primarily those economically disadvantaged, who cannot afford adequate legal representation to expose the inequities. As a result, those feelings of frustration are shown in the genre to be exacerbated by an unfair justice system, and in turn, can perpetuate crime.

Returning to the political frames identified in chapter 3, I see the conservative philosophy, which demonizes offenders and seeks to punish "in the name of deterrence," as one that does not encourage an equitable criminal justice system or a safer society. Rather, I see the liberal philosophy, which is focused on ensuring equal opportunities in society and removing barriers imposed by confining social structures, as a more effective way to ensure a fair justice system and safer society because it strives to eliminate the motivations for crime.

Rapping (2004) cited television as a unifying force, and says television producers in the crime genre, "coincidentally in concert with law enforcement and other government agencies, [have] 'chosen' crime as the issue and 'criminals' as the enemy against whom we as Americans can most readily and passionately unite" (p. 264). However, in this research I have pointed to recent programs in the genre that show criminals not as the enemy of society, but as a group that has been disadvantaged by confining social structures—particularly based on economic class. These confining structures are shown in some series in the crime genre to lead to feelings of frustration in individuals, and that has provided the motivation for some crimes.

Rather than seeking to unite citizens *against* criminals, programs such as *Oz*, starring criminals, and even *Cold Case*, which stars legal authorities, encourage viewers to understand the reasons criminals commit crimes. In the process, inequities in society and the justice system are revealed. The programs do not condone or excuse the crimes, but point to unfair social structures as contributing to crime.

A primary goal of this research is to show that the genre is not presenting crime in a singular way. Rather, with the proliferation of crime series in the genre, new stories are being told, including explanations about the backgrounds and motivations of criminals. As I have shown, between 1998 and 2004, the genre offered new representations of the problem of crime in America. The representations suggest that for crime policy to be effective, an equitable justice system must exist within an equitable and just society.

Appendix

Timeline of the Criminal Genre

The Lone Ranger (ABC)/(CBS)	49–57/53–57
Dragnet (NBC)	52–59/67–70
Perry Mason (CBS)	57–66
Bonanza (ABC)	59–73
The Fugitive (ABC)	63–67
Mission: Impossible (CBS)/(ABC)	66–73/88–90
Mannix (CBS)	67–75
The Mod Squad (ABC)	68–73
Columbo (NBC)	71–77
Kojak (CBS)	73–78
The Rockford Files (NBC)	74–80
Starsky & Hutch (ABC)	75–79
Baretta (ABC)	75–78
Quincy, M.E. (NBC)	76–83
Magnum, p.i. (CBS)	80–88
Hill Street Blues (NBC)	81–87
Cagney & Lacey (CBS)	82–88
Miami Vice (NBC)	84–89
Murder, She Wrote (CBS)	84–96
Moonlighting (ABC)	85–89
Wiseguy (CS)	87–90
America's Most Wanted (Fox)	88–Present
COPS (Fox)	89–Present
Law & Order (NBC)	90–Present
NYPD Blue (ABC)	93–2005
Oz (HBO)	97–2003
The Practice (ABC)	97–2004

The Sopranos (HBO)   99–2007
C.S.I. (CBS)   2001–Present
The Guardian (CBS)   2001–2004
The Shield (FX)   2002–Present
Hack (CBS)   2002–2004
Cold Case (CBS)   2003–Present
The Jury (Fox)   2004 (Summer season)

Source. Dictionary of Teleliteracy.

REFERENCES

Agnew, R. (2001). A revised strain theory of delinquency. *Social Forces, 64*(1), 151–167. (Original work published in 1985)

Allan, S. (1998). News from NowHere: Televisual news discourse and the construction of hegemony. In. A. Bell and P. Garrett (Eds.), *Approaches to media discourse*, (pp. 105–141). Oxford, U.K.: Blackwell.

Altheide, D. L., & De Gruyter, A. (2002). *Creating fear: News and the construction of crisis*. New York: Aldine de Gruyter.

Barbaree, H. E., & Marshall, W. L. (1988). Deviant sexual arousal, offense history, and demographic variables as predictors of reoffense among child molesters. *Behavioral Sciences & the Law, 6*(2), 267–280.

Barnouw, E. (1993). *Documentary: A history of the non-fiction film* (2nd Rev. ed.). New York and Oxford, U.K.: Oxford University Press.

Barson, M. (1985). The TV Western. In B. G. Rose (Ed.), *TV genres: A handbook and reference guide* (pp. 58–71). Westport, CT; London: Greenwood.

Barthes, R. (1977). *Image music text*. (S. Heath, Trans.). New York: Hill and Wang.

Bates, A., Falshaw, L., Patel, V., Corbett, C., & Friendship, C. (2004). A follow-up study of sex offenders treated by Thames Valley Sex Offender Groupwork Programme, 1995–1999. *Journal of Sexual Aggression, 10*(1), 29–38.

Bawarshi, A. (2000, January). The genre function. *College English, 62*(3), 335–360.

Beck, B. (2000). The myth that would not die: The Sopranos, Mafia movies, and Italians in America. *Multicultural Perspectives, 2*(2), 24–27.

Bednar, R. (Senior Executive Producer). (2004). *In the jury room*. [Television documentary]. New York: American Broadcasting Company.

Benson, J., & Romano, A. (2005, May 23). Five secrets of the new fall season revealed: Deciphering prime time in a tough upfront ad market. *Broadcasting & Cable*. Retrieved August 15, 2005, from Lexis-Nexis database.

Berman, M. (2004, December 13). *The programming insider*. Retrieved August 15, 2005, from http//www.MediaWeek.com.

Bianco, R. (2004, June 8). Fox's new "Jury" is in no hurry. *USA Today*. Retrieved August 15, 2005, from Lexis-Nexis database.

Bianculli, D. (2004, November 15). "America's Most Wanted" still captures viewers. *Daily News*. Retrieved August 15, 2005, from Lexis-Nexis database.

Bilandzic, H., & Rossler, P. (2004). Life according to television. Implications of genre-specific cultivation effects: The gratification/cultivation model. *Communications, 29*, 295–326.

Bochco, S. (Executive Producer). (1993–2005). *NYPD Blue*. [Television series]. New York: American Broadcasting Company.

Bratich, J. Z. (2005). Amassing the multitude: Revisiting early audience studies. *Communication Theory, 15*(3), 242–265.

Bratich, J. Z. (2006). "Nothing is left alone for too long": Reality programming and control society subjects. *Journal of Communication Inquiry, 30*(1), 65–83.

Brioux, B. (2005, March 1). Bye, Bye Blue: ABC's gritty cop show left its mark on TV history. *The Toronto Sun*. Retrieved August 15, 2005, from Lexis-Nexis database.

Bruckheimer, J. (Executive Producer). (2003–Present). Cold Case. [Television series]. New York: Columbia Broadcasting Company.

Bryant, C. D. (2000). *Encyclopedia of criminology and deviant behavior*. (Vols. 1–3). Philadelphia, PA: Brunner-Routledge.

Burnett, R., & Maruna, S. (2004). So "Prison Works," does it? The criminal careers of 130 men released from prison under home secretary, Michael Howard. *The Howard Journal, 43*(4), 390–404.

Carman, J. (2001, April 3). Why HBO is king of the box. "Sopranos" network isn't hooked on ratings, seeks challenging shows. *San Francisco Chronicle*. Retrieved November 18, 2005, from http://www.SFGate.com

Carter, B. (2004, September 19). As season begins, networks struggle in cable's shadow. *The New York Times*. Retrieved November 18, 2005, from Lexis-Nexis database.

Casey, B., Casey, N., Calvert, B., French, L., & Lewis, J. (2002). *Television studies: The key concepts*. London, New York: Routledge.

Cavallero, J. J. (2004). Gangsters, fessos, tricksters, and Sopranos: The historical roots of Italian American stereotype anxiety. *Journal of Popular Film and Television, 32*(2), 50–63.

Cawelti, J. G. (1975). *The six-gun mystique*. Bowling Green, OH: Bowling Green University Popular Press.

Cawelti, J. G. (1976). *Adventure, mystery, and romance*. Chicago; London: The University of Chicago Press.

CBS News. (2001, June 25). *Sex offenders could go free*. New York. Transcript retrieved November 14, 2005, from CBSNews.com.

Centerwall, B. (1989). Exposure to television as a risk factor for violence. *American Journal of Epidemiology, 129*, 643–652.

Chase, D. (Executive Producer). (1999–Present). *The Sopranos*. [Television series]. New York: Home Box Office.

Chevigny, K., & Johnson, K. (Directors). (2004). *Deadline*. [Documentary]. New York: Big Mouth Productions.

CNN.com. (1999, July 22). *"Sopranos" beats network shows for most Emmy taps*. Retrieved August 11, 2008 from http://www.cnn.com/SHOWBIZ/TV/9907/22/emmy.noms.02/

Cohen, A. (2003, July 6). What "Capturing the Friedmans" says about getting tough on crime. *The New York Times*. Retrieved November 18, 2005, from Lexis-Nexis database.

Coscarelli, K. (2005, May 1). The "CSI" Effect: TV's false reality fools jurors. *The Star Ledger*. Retrieved November 15, 2005, from Lexis-Nexis database.

Craig, R. (1999).Communication theory as a field. *Communication Theory, 9*, 119–161.

Cullen, F. T. (2005). The twelve people who saved rehabilitation: How the science of criminology made a difference. *Criminology, 43*(1), 1–42.

Curiel, J. (2004, May 16). Decency gets some heavy opposition: FCC urged to start regulating cable TV, but free-speechers say enough, already. *San Francisco Chronicle*. Retrieved November 18, 2005, from http://www.SFGate.com

Deery, J. (2004). Reality TV as advertainment. *Popular Communication, 2*(1), 1–20.

Dixon, T. L., Azocar, C. L., & Casas, M. (2003). The portrayal of race and crime on television network news. *Journal of Broadcasting & Electronic Media, 47*(4), 498–523.

Doyle, J. (2004, July 12). Public's overriding fear: Will they do it again? Anxiety remains despite low recidivism among many offenders. *San Francisco Chronicle*. Retrieved November 14, 2005, from Lexis-Nexis database.

Duff, R. A. (2001). *Punishment, communication, and community*. Oxford, U.K.: Oxford University Press.

Duffett, M. (2004). A "strange blooding in the ways of popular culture"? *Party at the Palace* as hegemonic project. *Popular Music and Society, 27*(4), 489–506.

Eberly, T. (2004, December 19). Fresno police star in "COPS": Fox TV series spent more than five weeks with local officers. *The Fresno Bee*. Retrieved November 18, 2005, from Lexis-Nexis database.

Elber, L. (2004, April 20). Legal drama "The Guardian" makes its case for renewal. *The Associated Press.* Retrieved November 18, 2005, from Lexis-Nexis database.

Falshaw, L., Bates, A., Patel, V., Corbett, C., & Friendship, C. (2003). Assessing reconviction, reoffending and recidivism in a sample of UK sexual offenders. *Legal and Criminological Psychology, 8,* 207–215.

Felson, R. B. (1996). Mass media effects on violent behavior. *Annual Review Sociology, 22,* 103–128.

Fergusson, D., Swain-Campbell, N., & Horwood, J. (2004). How does childhood economic disadvantage lead to crime? *Child Psychology and Psychiatry, 45*(5), 956–966.

Feuer, J. (1992). Genre study and television. In R.C. Allen (Ed.), *Channels of discourse reassembled: Television and contemporary criticism* (pp. 138–159). Chapel Hill, NC: University of North Carolina.

Fields, I. W. (2004). Family Values and feudal codes: The social politics of America's Twenty-First Century gangster. *The Journal of Popular Culture, 37*(4), 611–633.

Fishman, J. M. (1999). The populace and the police: Models of social control in reality-based crime television. *Critical Studies in Mass Communication, 16,* 268–288.

Fiske, J. (1987). *Television Culture.* New York: Routledge.

Fiske, J. (1996). *Media matters: Race and gender in U.S. Politics.* Minneapolis, MN: University of Minnesota Press.

Fiske, J., & Dawson, R. (1996). Audiencing violence: Watching homeless men watch Die Hard. In Hay, J., Grossberg, L., & Wartella, E. (Eds.), *The Audience and its landscape* (pp. 297–316). Boulder, CO: Westview Press.

Foucault, M. (1980). *Power/knowledge: Selected interviews and other writings 1972–1977 by Michel Foucault* (C. Gordon, Trans.). New York: Pantheon.

Foucault, M. (1995). *Discipline & punish. The birth of the prison* (A. Sheridan, Trans.). New York: Vintage Books. (Original work published in 1975)

Furst, R. (2004, May 3). Study: New take on sex offenders: While legislators propose dramatic increases in sentences, researchers suggest that, in fact, sex offenders are less likely to commit new crimes. *Star Tribune*. Retrieved November 14, 2005, from Lexis-Nexis.

Gantz, W., & Zohoori, A. R. (1982). The impact of television schedule changes on audience viewing behaviors. *Journalism Quarterly, 59*, 265–272.

Gerbner, G. (1998). Cultivation analysis: An overview. *Mass Communication & Society, 1*(3/4), 175–194.

Gitlin, T. (1972). Sixteen notes on television and the movement. In. G. White & C. Neuman (Eds.), *Literature in Revolution* (pp. 335–366). New York: Holt, Rinehart, & Winston.

Gitlin, T. (1985). *Inside primetime.* New York: Pantheon.

Glynn, K. (2000). *Tabloid culture.* Durham, NC: Duke University Press.

Goldberg, J. (1997, July 20). Animal farm: Those sexy brutes of HBO's new prison series, *Oz. Slate*. Retrieved November 18, 2005, from http://www.Slate.com

Good, L. (1989). *Power, hegemony, and communication theory.* In I. Angus & S. Jhally (Eds.), Cultural Politics in Contemporary America (pp. 51–64). New York, London: Routledge.

Goodman, T. (2003, Jan. 7). Tension builds in FX's "Shield." *San Francisco Chronicle*. Retrieved November 18, 2005, from http://sfgate.com

Grabe, M. E. (1999). Television news magazine crime stories: a functionalist perspective. *Critical Studies in Mass Communication, 16*, 155–171.

Gramsci, A. (1971). Selections from the prison notebooks. (Q. Hoare and G. Nowell-Smith, Trans.). London: Lawrence and Wishart.

Griffith, J. P. (2005, February 27). Bye bye "Blue": Groundbreaking, controversial series, memorable detective bid farewell Tuesday. *Herald News*. Retrieved November 14, 2005 from Lexis-Nexis database.

Haas, T., & Steiner, L. (2001). Public journalism as a journalism of publics: Implications of the Habermas-Fraser debate for public journalism. *Journalism, 2*(2), 123–147.

Hall, S. (1996). Signification, representation, ideology: Althusser and the post-structuralist debates. In J. Curran, D. Morley, & V. Walkerdine (Eds.), *Cultural studies and communications* (pp. 11–34). London; New York; Sydney, Auckland: Arnold.

Hartley, J. (1996). Power viewing: A glance at pervasion in the postmodern perplex. In J. Hay, L. Grossberg, & E. Wartella (Eds.), *The Audience and its landscape* (pp. 221–234). Boulder, CO: Westview Press.

Hayakawa, S. I. (1950). *Symbol, Status, and Personality*. San Diego, CA; New York: Harcourt Brace Jovanovich, Publishers.

Hiltbrand, D. (2003, August 19). Fresh characters promise to brighten the feel of CBS' "Hack." *Philadelphia Inquirer*. Retrieved August 15, 2005, from Lexis-Nexis database.

Hoffmann, J. P. (2003). A contextual analysis of differential association, social control, and strain theories of delinquency. *Social Forces, 81*(3), 753–785.

Hoffner, C., & Buchanan, M. (2002). Parents' responses to television violence: The third-person perception, parental mediation, and support for censorship. *Media Psychology, 4*, 231–252.

Hornaday, A. (2003, June 13). In "The Friedmans," a family implodes. *The Washington Post*. Retrieved November 18, 2005, from Lexis-Nexis database.

James, C. (1997, July 12). High-tech prison and the face of horror. *The New York Times*. Retrieved November 18, 2005, from http://www.NYTimes.com

Jarecki, A. (Director). (2003). *Capturing the Friedmans*. [Documentary].

Jarolmen, J., & Sisco, H. (2005). Media effects on post-traumatic-stress disorder and the World Trade Center tragedy. *Best Practices in Mental Health, 1*(2), 133–139.

Jasperson, A. E., Shah, D. V., Watts, M. Faber, R. J., & Fan, D. P. (1998). Framing and the public agenda: Media effects on the importance of the federal budget deficit. *Political Communication, 15*, 205–224.

Johnson, C. (2005, April 20). State moves on tougher sex offender sentences: The House passes the Jessica Lunsford Act, which moves to the Senate for debate today. *St. Petersburg Times*. Retrieved November 18, 2005, from http://www.sptimes.com

Johnson, K. E. (2002). AIDS as a US national security threat: Media effects and geographical imaginations. *Feminist Media Studies, 2*(1), 81–96.

Katz, S. (Supervising Producer). (1988–Present). *America's Most Wanted*. [Television series]. New York: Fox Broadcasting Company.

Kelly, D. (Executive Producer). (1997–2004). *The Practice*. [Television series]. New York: American Broadcasting Company.

Keum, H., Devanathan, N., Deshpande, S., Nelson, M. R., & Shah, D. V. (2004). The citizen-consumer: Media effects at the intersection of consumer and civic culture. *Political Communication, 21*, 369–391.

Keveney, B. (2003, April 20). ABC's "Practice" may say goodbye. *USA Today*. Retrieved August 15, 2005, from http://www.USAToday.com

Kilborn, R. (2004). Framing the real: taking stock of developments in documentary. *Journal of Media Practice, 5*(1), 25–32.

Klein, S. R., Bartholomew, G. S., & Bahr, S. (1999). Family education for adults in correctional settings: A conceptual framework. *International Journal of Offender Therapy and Comparative Criminology, 43*, 291–307.

Kleinhans, C., & Morris, R. (2004). Court TV: The evolution of a reality format. In L. Ouellette & S. Murray (Eds.) *Reality TV: Remaking television culture* (pp. 157–175). New York, London: New York University Press.

Klevens, J., Roca, J., Restrepo, O. & Martinez, A. (2001). Risk factors for adult male crimininality in Colombia. *Criminal Behavior and Mental Health, 11*, 73–85.

Kubey, R. (1996). On not finding media effects: Conceptual problems in the notion of an "active" audience (with a reply to Elihu Katz). In J. Hay, L. Grossberg, & E. Wartella (Eds.), *The audience and its landscape* (pp. 187–205). Boulder, CO and Oxford, U.K.: Westview Press:

Kubey, R. W., & Csikszentmihalyi, M. (1990). Television as Escape: Subjective experience before an evening of heavy viewing. *Communication Reports, 3*(2), 92–100.

LaFond, J. Q. (2000). The Future of Involuntary civil commitment in the U.S.A. after Kansas v. Hendricks. *Behavioral Sciences and the Law, 18*, 153–167.

Lang, R. A., Pugh, G. M., & Langevin, R. (1988). Treatment of incest and pedophilic offenders: A pilot study. *Behavioral Sciences & the Law, 6*(2), 239–255.

Langley, J. (Creator). (1989–Present). *Cops.* [Television series]. New York: Fox Broadcasting Company.

Laurence, R. P. (2003, September 28). "Cold Case," they wrote: CBS sexes up Sunday detective series. *The San Diego Union-Tribune.* Retrieved November 14, 2005, from Lexis-Nexis database.

Lee, T. (2005). Media effects on political disengagement revisited: A multiple-media approach. *Journalism & Mass Communication Quarterly, 82*(2), 416–433.

Lennard Goehner, A., Lofaro, L., & Novak, K. (2004, November 8). Where CSI Meets Real Law and Order: Ripple effect. *Time.* p. 69.

Lett, M. D., DiPietro, A. L., & Johnson, D. I. (2004). Examining effects of television news violence on college students through cultivation theory. *Communication Research Reports, 21*(1), 39–46.

Levin, G. (2003, January 2). The inside story on HBO's "Oz." True to form, its final season won't be pretty, either. *USA Today*. Retrieved November 18, 2005, from Lexis-Nexis database.

Levin, M. (Director). (2003). America Undercover: Gladiator Days: Anatomy of a prison murder. [Documentary]. New York: Home Box Office.

Levinson, B. (Executive Producer). (1997–2003). *Oz*. [Television Series]. New York: Home Box Office.

Levinson, B. (Executive Producer). (2004). *The Jury*. [Television Series]. New York: Fox Broadcasting Company.

Lewis, J., & Wahl-Jorgensen, K. (2005). Active citizen or couch potato? In S. Allan (Ed.). *Journalism: Critical issues* (pp. 98–108). Berkshire, U.K.: Open University Press.

Linz, D. G., Donnerstein, E., & Penrod, S. (1988). Effects of long-term exposure to violent and sexually degrading depictions of women. *Journal of Personality and Social Psychology, 55*(5), 758–768.

Lipschultz, J. H., & Hilt, M. L. (2002). *Crime and local television news: Dramatic, breaking, and live from the scene*. Mahwah, NJ; London: Lawrence Erlbaum Associates.

Lowenkamp, C. T., & Latessa, E. J. (2005). Increasing the effectiveness of correctional programming through the risk principle: Identifying offenders for residential placement. *Criminology & Public Policy, 4*(2), 263–289.

Lowry, T., & Grover, R., Brady, D. (2005, May 9). NBC: Now it's Wait-and-See TV: The ex-ratings champ hopes its fall lineup will still be worth a premium to advertisers. *Business Week*. Retrieved November 18, 2005, from Lexis-Nexis database.

Lykken, D. T. (2000). The causes and costs of crime and a controversial cure. *Journal of Personality, 68*(3), 559–605.

Mantle, G., & Moore, S. (2004). On probation: Pickled and nothing to say. *The Howard Journal, 43*(3), 299–316.

Marbley, A. R., & Ferguson, R. (2004). Putting back together our communities of color: A systemic model for rehabilitation. *Journal of African American Studies, 7*(4), 75–85.

Marchetti, G. (1989). Action-adventure as ideology. In I. Argus and S. Jhally (Eds.), *Cultural politics in contemporary America* (pp. 182–197). New York: Routledge.

Martin, J. (2004, July 3). Sex offenders' release could be a tough sell; Nonpartisan study cites low risk of reoffending: Lawmakers see solutions to state prison overcrowding. *The Seattle Times.* Retrieved November 18, 2005, from Lexis-Nexis database.

Mauer, M. (1999). *Race to incarcerate.* New York: The New Press, The Sentencing Project.

McAlinden, A. (2000). Sex offender registration: Implications and difficulties for Ireland. *Irish Journal of Sociology, 10,* 75–102.

Memmott, M. (2005, March 25). Girl's death raises questions about tracking of sex offenders. *USA Today.* Retrieved November 14, 2005, from Lexis-Nexis database.

Metzger, G. D. (1983). Cable television audiences. *Journal of Advertising Research, 23*(4), 41–47.

Miller, T. (1997). *The Avengers.* London: British Film Institute.

Mills, S. (1992, May). Negotiating discourses of femininity. *Journal of Gender Studies, 1*(3), 217–231.

Moore, F. (2005, February 28). "Trial By Jury," the 4th *"Law & Order"* drama series, convenes its audience this week. *The Associated Press.* Retrieved November 18, 2005, from Lexis-Nexis database.

Morley, D. (1992). *Television, audiences and cultural studies.* Routlege: London and New York.

Morrow, T. (2003, November 18). "Cops" producers revels in the quirky episodes. *Scripps Howard News Service.* Retrieved August 15, 2005, from Lexis-Nexis database.

Nabi, R. L., Biely, E. N., Morgan, S. J., & Stitt, C. R. (2003). Reality-based television programming and the psychology of its appeal. *Media Psychology, 5*, 303–330.

Neuendorf, K. A., Atkin, D., & Jeffres, L. W. (2000). Explorations of the Simpson trial "racial divide." *Howard Journal of Communications, 11*(4), 247–266.

Norden, M. (1985). The detective show. In B. G. Rose (Ed.), *TV genres: A handbook and reference guide* (pp. 33–55). Westport, London: Greenwood.

Oliver, M. B. (1994). Portrayals of crime, race, and aggression in "reality-based" police shows: A content analysis. *Journal of Broadcasting & Electronic Media, 38*(2), 179–192.

Ouellette, L. (2004). Take responsibility for yourself: *Judge Judy* and the neoliberal citizen. In L. Ouellette & S. Murray (Eds.), *Reality TV: Remaking television culture* (pp. 231–250). New York, London: New York University Press.

Owen, R. (2003, January 5). In-your-face TV: Gritty drama "The Shield" brings FX Network's niche into focus. *Pittsburgh Post-Gazette*. Retrieved November 18, 2005, from Lexis-Nexis database.

Parenti, M. (1980). *Democracy for the few* (3rd ed.). New York: St. Martin's Press. Peden, L. D. (2001). The inmates of "Oz" move into a new Emerald City. *The New York Times*. Retrieved November 18, 2005, from Lexis-Nexis database.

Pennington, G. (2004, June 8). Fox awaits viewers' verdict on "The Jury." *St. Louis Post-Dispatch*. Retrieved November 18, 2005, from Lexis-Nexis database.

Petersilia, J. (2003). *When prisoners come home: Parole and prisoner reentry*. Oxford, U.K., and New York: Oxford University Press.

Pfau, M., Moy, P., & Szabo, E. A. (2001). Influence of prime-time television programming on perceptions of the federal government. *Mass Communication & Society, 4*, 437–453.

Poniewozik, J. (2004, November 8). Crimetime lineup: How the slick show changed television—in part by dragging it back into the past. *Time*, 63–66.

Potter, W. J., & Smith, S. (2000). The context of graphic portrayals of television violence. *Journal of Broadcasting & Electronic Media, 44*(2), 301–324.

Prosise, T. O., & Johnson, A. (2004). Law enforcement and crime on Cops and World's Wildest Police Videos: Anecdotal form and the justification of racial profiling. *Western Journal of Communication, 68*(1), 72–91.

Quinby, L. (2002). Just Discourse: The limits of truth for the discourse of social justice. *The Review of Education, Pedagogy, & Culture Studies, 24*, 235–249.

Quinn, E. (1999). *A dictionary of literary and thematic terms.* New York: Facts on File, Inc.

Rapping, E. (2003). *Law and justice as seen on TV*. New York: New York University Press.

Rapping, E. (2004). Aliens, nomads, mad dogs, and road warriors: The changing face of criminal violence on TV. In L. Ouellette & S. Murray (Eds.), *Reality TV: Remaking television culture* (pp. 214–230). New York, London: New York University Press.

Reber, B. H., & Chang, Y. (2004). Assessing cultivation theory and public health model for crime reporting. *Newspaper Research Journal, 21*(4), 99–112.

Rhodes, J. (2005). Race, ideology and journalism: Black power and television news. In S. Allan (Ed.), *Journalism: Critical issues* (pp. 30–41.) Berkshire, U.K.: Open University Press.

Robards, B. (1985). The police show. In B. G. Rose (Ed.), *TV genres: A handbook and reference guide* (pp. 11–31). Westport, London: Greenwood.

Rohan, V. (2003, May 26). "Practice" gutted by a new reality. *The Record.* Retrieved August 15, 2005, from Lexis-Nexis database.

Ryan, S. (Creator). (2002–Present). *The Shield.* [Television series]. New York: Fox Broadcasting Company.

Sample, L. L., & Bray, T. M. (2003). Are sex offenders dangerous? *Criminology & Public Policy, 3*(1), 59–82.

Sasson, T. (1995). *Crime talk: How citizens construct a social problem.* New York: Walter de Gruyter.

Seiter, E. (1992). In R. C. Allen (Ed.), *Channels of discourse reassembled: Television and contemporary criticism* (pp. 31–66). Chapel Hill, NC: University of North Carolina.

Shanahan, J., Scheufele, D., Yang, F., & Hizi, S. (2004). Cultivation and spiral of silence effects: The case of smoking. *Mass Communication & Society, 7*(4), 413–428.

Shaw, D. R. (1999). The impact of news media favorability and candidate events in presidential campaigns. *Political Communication, 16,* 183–202.

Shrum, H. (2004). No longer theory: Correctional practices that work. *The Journal of Correctional Education, 55*(3), 225–235.

Sjostedt, G., & Langstrom, N. (2002). Assessment of risk for criminal recidivism among rapists: A comparison of four different measures. *Psychology, Crime and Law, 8,* 25–40.

Skardhamar, T. (2003). Inmates' social background and living conditions. *Journal of Scandinavian Studies in Criminology and Crime Prevention, 4,* 39–56.

Slaton, B. J., Kern, R. M., & Curlette, W. L. (2000). Personality profiles of inmates. *The Journal of Individual Psychology, 56*(1), 88–109.

Sloop, J. (1996). *The cultural prison: Discourse, prisoners, and punishment.* Tuscaloosa, AL; London: University of Alabama Press.

Sotirovic, M. (2001). Affective and cognitive processes as mediators of media influences on crime-policy preferences. *Mass Communication & Society, 4*, 311–329.

Sourcebook of criminal justice statistics 30th edition online. (2002). Bureau of Justice Statistics. Retrieved March 24, 2005, from www.albany.edu/sourcebook

Stanley, A. (2004, June 8). They meet secretly, bicker and try to return a verdict [Television Review]. *The New York Times.* Retrieved November 14, 2005 from Lexis-Nexis database.

Strauss, A., & Corbin, J. (1998). *Basics of qualitative research: Techniques and procedures for developing grounded theory* (2nd ed.). Thousand Oaks, CA: SAGE.

Tamborini, R., Mastro, D. E, Chory-Assad, R. M., & Huang, R.H. (2000). The color of crime and the court: A content analysis of minority representation on television. *Journalism and Mass Communication Quarterly, 77*(3), 639–653. http://ezproxy.wpunj.edu:2393/ids70/p_search form.php?field=au&query=&log=literal&SID=6566bb76468c806673fa6e4806d45669

Tavener, J. (2000). Media, morality, and madness: The case against sleaze TV. *Critical Studies in Media Communication, 17*(1), 63–85.

Thompson, K. D. (2004, June 27). "Cold Case" works by keeping you guessing. *Palm Beach Post.* Retrieved August 15, 2005, from Lexis-Nexis database.

Turegano, P. (2003, August 31). Cable Shootout: HBO, Showtime square off in a battle of best original programming. *The San Diego Union-Tribune.* Retrieved November 18, 2005, from Lexis-Nexis database.

Turner, B. W., Bingham, J. E., & Andrasik, F. (2000). Short-term community-based treatment for sexual offenders: Enhancing effectiveness. *Sexual Addiction & Compulsivity, 7*, 211–223.

Turow, J. (1989). *Playing doctor*. New York; Oxford: Oxford University Press.

Turow, J. (1991). A mass communication perspective on entertainment industries. In. J. Curran & M. Gurevitch (Eds.), *Mass media and society* (pp. 160–177). New York: St. Martin's Press, Inc.

van Dijk, T. (1998). Opinions and ideologies in the press. In. A. Bell & P. Garrett (Eds.), *Approaches to media discourse* (pp. 21–63). Oxford, U.K.: Blackwell.

Vidmar, N., & Rokeach, M. (1974). Archie Bunker's bigotry: A study in selective perception and exposure. *Journal of Communication, 24*(1), 36–47.

Wanta, W. (1988). The effects of dominant photographs: An agenda-setting experiment. *Journalism Quarterly, 65*(1), 107–111.

Warden, R. (2005). Illinois death penalty reform: How it happened, what it promises. *The Journal of Criminal Law and Criminology, 95*(2), 381–426.

Watt, J. H., Jr., & van den Berg, S. (1981). How time dependency influences media effects in a community controversy. *Journalism Quarterly, 58*, 43–50.

White, M. (1992). Ideological analysis and television. In R.C. Allen (Ed.), *Channels of discourse reassembled: Television and contemporary criticism* (pp. 161–202). Chapel Hill, NC: University of North Carolina.

Williams, A. (1993). Domestic violence and the aetiology of crime in *America's Most Wanted*. *Camera Obscura, 31*, 96–119.

Wolf, D. (Executive Producer). (1990–Present). *Law & Order*. [Television series]. New York: National Broadcasting Company.

Wood, W., Wong, F. Y., & Chachere, J. G. (1991). Effects of media violence on viewers' aggression in unconstrained social interaction. *Psychological Bulletin, 109*(3), 371–383.

World News Tonight Saturday. (2005, June 18). [Television series]. A closer look: Serial molester. Transcript retrieved November 14, 2005, from Lexis-Nexis database.

Zgoba, K., Sager, W.R., & Witt, P.H. (2003). Evaluation of New Jersey's sex offender treatment program at the Adult Diagnostic and Treatment Center: Preliminary results. *The Journal of Psychiatry & Law, 31*, 133–164.

INDEX

agenda setting, 16
Allan, Stuart, 25
Altheide, David L., 3
America's Most Wanted, 33, 91, 184
America Undercover: Gladiator Days: Anatomy of a Prison Murder, 91
audiences
    active, 29, 187
    power, 29
Avengers, The, 6, 101

Barnouw, Erik, 191–192
Barson, Michael, 7
Barthes, Roland, 10
Bawarshi, Anis, 7–8
blocked opportunities, 47
Bratich, Jack Z., 176

Capturing the Friedmans, 91
Cawelti, John G., 32
Centerwall, Brandon, 16
civic participation, 21–22
Cold Case, 84–85, 118–121
COPS, 33, 91, 178
court rulings, notification laws, 60
Craig, Robert T., 25
crime genre, 12
crime policies
    conservative, 40
    liberal, 47
    preventive, 47
    punitive, 40
crime representations, 31

crime theories
    control, 44
    individual-psychology based, 38
    labeling, 44
    socially based, 41
    strain, 43
critical-cultural studies, 25
critical discourse analysis, 94
crossownership, 71
CSI effect, 216
Cullen, Francis, 37
cultivation theory, 18
cultural studies, 24

Dawson, Robert, 24, 29
Deadline, 92
death penalty, 51
De Gruyter, A., 3
discourse analysis, 10, 65
documentaries, 88
Duff, R. Antony, 149–150

FCC, 73
Feuer, Jane, 6, 9
Fishman, Jessica, 33
Fiske, John, 8, 24, 29, 35
Foucault, Michel, 7, 11
framing, 16

Guardian, The, 68
genre theory, 5, 7–8
Gerbner, George, 18
Gitlin, Todd, 68, 93
Good, Leslie, 28

Grabe, Maria E., 34
Gramsci, Antonio, 28

Haas, Tanni, 27
Hack, 68
Hall, Stuart, 9
Hayakawa, Samuel I., 149, 224
Hoffmann, John P., 42

ideological analysis, 8
ideological categories, 94–95
ideological square, 94
ideology, 9, 12
In the Jury Room, 92

Jury, The, 79–81, 163

Kubey, Robert, 213–215

Law & Order, 1, 81–83, 105–107
Lykken, David T., 41

Marchetti, Gina, 9, 29
Mauer, Marc, 3
media effects, 15
media representations, 27
Mills, Sara, 10–11
Morley, David, 213

NYPD Blue, 3, 83–84, 107–110

Ouellette, Laurie, 91
Oz, 77–79, 125, 167

Parenti, Michael, 32
Petersilia, Joan, 45
popular culture, 27
power, 27
Practice, The, 87–88, 110–113
public opinion and crime, 49–51

Rapping, Elayne, 32
Rational Emotive Behavior Therapy, 39
reality series, 88
recidivism and sex offenders, 52
rehabilitation, 129, 136

Sasson, Theodore, 95
Seiter, Ellen, 24
Shield, The, 85–87, 114–118
Shrum, Harvey, 39
Sloop, John M., 26
social structures, 153, 162, 172
statistics (crime), 48–49
Steiner, Linda, 27
Sopranos, The, 66–76, 138

Turow, Joseph, 5, 28

Us versus Them, 171–174

van Dijk, Teun A., 94
vertical integration, 71
violence, 22, 30

Web site forums, 220
White, Mimi, 9–10
Williams, Anna, 10, 33, 186
World's Wildest Police Videos, 33

www.ingramcontent.com/pod-product-compliance
Lightning Source LLC
Chambersburg PA
CBHW071833230426
43671CB00012B/1952